KEVIN
BARRY

In memory of Patrick Barry Moloney MA
(1927–1989)

Eunan O'Halpin, Professor Emeritus of Contemporary Irish History at Trinity College Dublin, is a grand-nephew of Volunteer Kevin Barry, Dublin Brigade, executed in November 1920, and of Captain Paddy Moloney, 3rd Tipperary Brigade, killed in combat in May 1921. His major works include *The Decline of the Union: British Government in Ireland, 1892–1920* (Gill & Macmillan, 1987), *Defending Ireland: the Irish State and its Enemies* (Oxford University Press, 1999), *Spying on Ireland: British Intelligence and Irish Neutrality During the Second World War* (Oxford University Press, 2008), and (with Daithí Ó Corráin) *The Dead of the Irish Revolution* (Yale University Press, 2020).

KEVIN BARRY

AN IRISH REBEL IN LIFE AND DEATH

EUNAN O'HALPIN

MERRION
PRESS

First published in 2020 by
Merrion Press
10 George's Street
Newbridge
Co. Kildare
Ireland
www.merrionpress.ie

978-1-78537-349-7 (Paper)
978-1-78537-350-3 (Kindle)
978-1-78537-351-0 (Epub)

A CIP catalogue record for this book is
available from the British Library.

Typeset in Sabon Lt Std 11/15.5 pt

Front cover image courtesy of Canvaz (canvazstreetart.com).

Merrion Press is a member of Publishing Ireland.

Contents

Preface   vii

Acknowledgements   ix

Abbreviations   xii

    Introduction   1

1. The Barrys in Context   7

2. The Education of a Rebel   22

3. Training and Military Service, 1917–20   37

4. Church Street   60

5. Defending Kevin   70

6. Reprieve or Rescue   92

7. Dying a Good Death   105

8. The Immediate Impact of Kevin's Execution   117

9. Not Forgotten   128

10. Writing About Kevin   140

11. A Martyr in the Family   164

    Conclusion   207

Endnotes   212

Bibliography   237

Index   249

Preface

This book was the brainchild of my second cousin Síofra O'Donovan, who developed the idea of a new historical treatment of our shared great-uncle Kevin Barry and suggested to me that I take part.

Both Síofra and I have other family links to the Irish revolution, Síofra through her grandfather Jim O'Donovan, for years the IRA's leading expert on explosives and a significant republican intellectual, although now remembered largely for his disastrous dalliance with Nazi Germany, and I through the Moloneys of Tipperary and the Halpennys and Rices of Down. The interplay between those connections, and Kevin Barry's life and afterlife, is a marked feature of what follows.[1]

One reason why I was initially hesitant about the idea of writing a book on Kevin Barry is that Síofra's late father Donal O'Donovan (1928–2010) produced a good one, *Kevin Barry And His Time*, as long ago as 1989.[2] It was that which first led me to realise that Kevin was something more than a plaster saint with a jammed automatic in one hand, rosary beads in the other, and a rope around his neck. The case for producing a further study, lay in the fact that a lot more material is now available both in official records and in family papers. Also, while we are blood relatives, we are two generations away from Kevin, not that Donal was unduly reverential. Indeed, perhaps the best summation of his balanced analysis of Kevin's life comes in his poem 'A Crowded Year', with its memorable opening 'Are you the nephew of?' This itemises Kevin's serial departures from the straight and narrow in terms of girls and drink.

This study reflects my own interests and perspective, and is less a retelling of Kevin's story than a reflection upon the dynamics of having a 'martyr' in the extended family and an exploration of how and why his name has continued to resonate in Irish republican as well as popular culture.

Covid-19 has had a significant hand in this book: it has meant the closure of libraries and archives and has made travel even within Ireland impossible. I had left it until March to do final research in the Jim O'Donovan, Donal O'Donovan, Piáras Béaslaí and Seán O'Mahony papers in the National Library, in various series in the National Archives, and in the Elgin O'Rahilly, Sighle Humphreys, Katherine Barry Moloney, Patrick Barry Moloney, Moss Twomey and other collections of papers in UCD Archives. I had also planned to do some further research in the Bodleian Library in Oxford and in the British Library in London, to visit the Barry's Carlow homestead, Tombeagh. All other descendants of the Barrys have just as much right as do I to pronounce upon their great-uncle and the impact of his fate upon their families.

Acknowledgements

I am extremely grateful to Síofra, to my Barry and O'Rahilly relatives and to the many selfless archivists in the various libraries and archives in Ireland and Britain whose holdings I have cited, and to Dr Eve Morrison, who has found time in the midst of her own writing to hear me out on how mine was progressing. I must particularly thank Professor Ruth Barton, Damien Burke of the Jesuit Archives, Professor Iseult Honohan, Charles Lysaght, Dr Roisin Kennedy and Orna Somerville of UCD, Oliver Murphy, Peadar Nolan, Manus O'Riordan, Oliver Rafferty SJ, and Jeanne Winder. I also want to thank Barry Bowman, Frank Callanan SC, Hugh Hartnett SC, Roger Sweetman SC and Alice Harrison BL for their observations as experienced lawyers on Kevin's court martial, and Colonel Terry O'Neill PhD for his humorous recollections of the commemorative culture of the O'Connell School in the early 1950s. In America Aedeen Clements of the University of Notre Dame, in Britain Dr Jan Glaser of Stonyhurst College and in India Professor Jyoti Atwal of Jawaharlal Nehru University answered last-minute queries. In Ireland Dr Ciara Breathnach, Dr Patrick Callan, Professor Anne Dolan, Professor John Horgan, Dr Patrick McCarthy, Dr Deirdre McMahon and Daithí Ó Ceallaigh all read the final drafts, each identifying problems that needed attention, most of which I hope I have addressed. Finally, I must thank my extremely patient copy editor Djinn von Noorden, editor Patrick O'Donoghue and publisher Conor Graham.

I thank the following institutions and holders of copyright for access to and permission to quote from collections of papers and other material: Richard Barrett (the J.V. Joyce diaries, since deposited in the Military Archives); the Bodleian Library (the A.P. Magill papers); the British Library (India Office records and Sir Olaf Caroe papers); Brian Fitzpatrick (the John Fitzpatrick memoir); Carlow County Library and Archives (Carlow Union minute books); the Controller of Her Majesty's Stationery Office; the Director of the Military Archives; the Director of the National Archives of Ireland; the Director of the National Library of Ireland (the Liam Deasy, Florence O'Donoghue, James O'Donovan and Sean O'Mahony papers); the Imperial War Museum, London (the Lord French and Sir Henry Wilson papers); the Jawaharlal Nehru Memorial Library and Archives, Delhi (Oral History Transcripts); the Keeper of the Public Records of Northern Ireland; Kerry County Library and Archives (the Con Casey papers); the Kings College London Liddell Hart Centre for Military Archives (the Foulkes papers); Lambeth Palace Library (the Archbishop Davidson papers); Leitrim County Library, Ballinamore (oral history collection and McGoohan memoir); the Master, Fellows and Scholars of Churchill College in the University of Cambridge (the Amery and Strang papers); Monaghan County Museum (the Thomas Brennan and Father Marron papers); New York University Tamiment Library (the Seán Cronin papers); the Parliamentary Archives, London (the Bonar Law and Lloyd George papers); the Patrick and Katherine Kavanagh Trust (lines from 'News Item); the People's History Museum, Manchester (the Palme Dutt papers); the Royal Irish Academy (the Kevin B. Nowlan papers); UCD Archives (the Kevin Barry, Kevin Barry Memorial Committee, Katherine B. Moloney, Patrick Barry Moloney, Richard Mulcahy and Moss Twomey papers; Villanova University Library (the Joseph McGarrity papers); and the Westminster Diocesan Archives (the Cardinal Bourne papers). Over the years Kevin Barry, Louise O'Donovan, Síofra O'Donovan, Celie O'Rahilly, Michael O'Rahilly and Ruth Sweetman showed me important family material, and Fiona Maher kindly sent me a characteristically light-hearted letter from Kevin to Kitby, now held in Trinity College Dublin Manuscripts and Archives. Finally, I am grateful for access to Dan Breen's journals, which are in private hands.

Eunan O'Halpin
June 2020

Abbreviations

BL	Barrister at Law
BMH	Bureau of Military History
CB	Commander of the Order of the Bath
CBE	Commander of the Order of the British Empire
CMG	Commander of the Order of St Michael and St George
DMP	Dublin Metropolitan Police
DSO	Distinguished Service Order
ESB	Electricity Supply Board
GHQ	General Headquarters
IRA	Irish Republican Army
IRPDF	Irish Republican Prisoners' Dependents' Fund
KC	King's Counsel
MC	Military Cross
MP	Member of Parliament
NCO	Non-Commissioned Officer
OC	Officer Commanding
PC	Privy Counsellor
PTSD	Post-Traumatic Stress Disorder
QC	Queen's Counsel
RIC	Royal Irish Constabulary
ROIA	Restoration of Order in Ireland Act 1920
SC	Senior Counsel
SJ	Society of Jesus (Jesuit Order)
TD	Teachtaí Dála (Dáil deputy)
UCC	University College Cork
UCD	University College Dublin

Introduction

In 1990 the distinguished political scientist Richard English of Queen's University Belfast reviewed *Kevin Barry and His Time*, by Kevin's nephew Donal O'Donovan. He quite fairly asked whether a book was merited: 'there is really very little to say about Barry [who] thought, wrote and did nothing of any great significance. For it is only his significance as a republican martyr which justifies his being discussed at any length.' He criticised O'Donovan for the lack of 'analysis of the republican cult of the dead'. He also complained that Donal had not explored 'the precise mechanics by means of which propagandist value is derived from tragic figures such as Kevin Barry'. Kevin is referenced several times in English's *Armed Struggle* (2003) and *Irish Freedom* (2006),[1] suggesting a continuing appeal within contemporary republicanism as a 'republican martyr' in Richard's term: yet other evidence, including parliamentary proceedings at Westminster, indicates also that even in the twenty-first century the name Kevin Barry still has a register for a wider constituency.

A great deal of what was said of Kevin after death was uttered in the spirit of *De mortuis nil nisi bonum* ('Of the dead, say nothing but good'). There are many accounts of Kevin's bravery, his boyish humour, his diligence as a Volunteer, his kindness to his friends, his quiet faith and his stoicism in adversity. Such language may now appear as cloying, almost reverential, and the tone embarrassingly idealising, but that was the prevailing custom. Take tributes such as 'his sterling character – a character of singular sweetness, modesty and simplicity, but also of playful humour and moral strength …'

and 'We see a life nurtured by love and happy memories running on smoothly like some clear unpolluted stream ...' Consider 'the secret of his winning personality is shown in the letters written about him ... he treated all men as his friends, and met the world with open arms ...' Reflect on a teacher's verdict: 'I had always the highest opinion of his character – rugged and fiery at times, but always absolutely straight.' These phrases may read like a selection from the many panegyrics of Kevin to be found in the press, in commemorative literature, and in Bureau of Military History (BMH) statements of former mentors and comrades. In fact they refer to past pupils of Harrow, Eton and Stonyhurst who fell in the Great War – the Stonyhurst boy just eighteen when he died in France in 1916.[2]

I have visited only a few British public schools – Glenalmond, Radley, Winchester – but in each the warrior dead are ubiquitous. What strikes me about how Kevin Barry was invoked by his comrades, his teachers and his friends is not any quintessentially Irish, republican or Catholic quality, but rather how absolutely typical are the language and sentiments of a generational phenomenon in the United Kingdom and across Europe and the wider world scarred by the Great War. As Jessica Meyer observed of British commemorative culture, the dead 'were not simply heroes ... Through their deaths they had proved themselves to be superior to all other men ... even members of their own families.' The dead were 'constructed not merely as virtuous but as a source of pride for the bereaved'.[3] Adrian Beatty has written of the distinctive characteristics of Irish separatist and Zionist constructions of the heroic male dead in that era, but it appears to me that even in their explicitly religious elements these are not greatly different from how the fallen of the Great War were remembered and revered.[4]

What does distinguish Kevin from Britain's Great War dead is that, whereas the poppy has over the decades become a symbol of collective loss and remembrance of the Great War, his solitary image remains the dominant icon of youthful patriotic sacrifice for the War of Independence.

Kevin's very appearance – those photographs in a hooped sports shirt in his school and club colours – and background resonated in Britain because he resembled not some wild Fenian dynamiter or hungry peasant bent on shedding a land agent's blood, but one of the thousands of public-school boys and Oxbridge men Britain had just lost in the Great War.

The interplay of status and class in the British psyche was illustrated just a few weeks after Kevin's execution. The IRA's shooting in Dublin on the morning of Bloody Sunday, 21 November 1920, of a dozen officers and one civilian believed to be involved in intelligence work was received in Britain as a ghastly rerun and reminder of the Great War slaughter of gilded youths destined to be the ruling elite. *The Times* reported how the 'Officers' Last Home Coming' saw their funeral procession leave Euston Station, the coffins on gun carriages accompanied by the 'Massed bands, pipes and drums of the Grenadier Guards, Coldstream Guards, Scots Guards and Irish Guards', watched by 'men, women and children in their thousands ... instinctively massing themselves into a vast crowd ... inspired with a profound unusual sympathy'. In Westminster Abbey and in Westminster Cathedral, King George was represented respectively by his aides-de-camp General the Lord Horne and Lieutenant General the Lord Cavan.[5] Does anyone seriously believe that, if the IRA had killed a dozen British private soldiers or police constables in Dublin on Bloody Sunday morning, however ruthlessly, these would have received such elaborate public ceremonial funerals?

If Kevin has a parallel in British memory, it is surely Rupert Brooke, whom W.B. Yeats thought 'the handsomest young man in England'. Unlike Kevin, Brooke left a body of work by which to be remembered, in particular his poem 'The Soldier' (1914) with its declaration that 'If I should die / think only this of me:

/ That there's some corner of a foreign field / That is forever England.' That, together with two lines from 'Grantchester' (1912), an irritatingly clever faux-wry hymn to the halcyon world of Edwardian Cambridge – 'Stands the church clock at ten to three / And is there honey still for tea?' – were sufficient to secure his place at the apex of English Great War commemorative culture at least until 1939. Kevin Barry published nothing and the most famous song commemorating him, 'Kevin Barry', is little more than doggerel. Yet, on the basis essentially of a single ballad and a few photographs – all taken more than a year before he died aged eighteen years and nine months – he remains a vibrant icon of patriotic, idealistic death. *Dulce et decorum est pro patria mori* ('To die for one's country is a sweet and honourable thing') could be his epitaph, whereas Brooke, who expired tamely on a Greek island from an infected insect bite, never saw battle, and his death was seen as evidence of the waste of war.[6] By the time of the centenary of the Great War, Brooke had been eclipsed in British public memory by more interesting and finer writers and poets such as Robert Graves, Siegfried Sassoon and especially Wilfred Owen, men who had actually fought with distinction and wrote of war from experience.

There is an additional reason for studying Kevin Barry: his story tells us something about the young men who joined the IRA to fight against British rule, and later each other, between 1917 and 1923. Roy Foster suggests that the coterie of writers, poets, actors and social activists who were a key element in the planning and mounting of the 1916 Rising, were of a different breed to many who fought between 1919 and 1921: 'the actual fighting, particularly in the latter stages of the Anglo-Irish War and the Civil War, was often undertaken by people from a somewhat different background, owing allegiance to more straightforwardly Fenian and rural-agitation traditions'.[7] In the same vein, Sir Peter Rawlinson, who as attorney general in Edward Heath's Conservative government of 1970–74 prosecuted IRA men and was also a target for Angry Brigade bombers, made a startling contribution to a Commons debate following the Birmingham pub bombings in 1974: it was quite wrong to compare those Irishmen who had risen in 1916, 'fighting openly and manfully', with 'the sneaking riff-raff who take a bomb into a public house or a shop and then leave before it blows innocent people to pieces'.[8] Rawlinson's contribution raises an obvious question: can you quite like the rebels who engineered the Easter Rising, with its elements of theatricality, its aspirations for overt army versus army combat, and its poet-speckled leadership, yet deprecate the Soloheadbeg ambush of January 1919, where two policemen were killed in controversial circumstances, or the ruthless killings of unarmed British officers on Bloody Sunday and the Volunteers who pulled the triggers on those occasions?[9] The 1916 Rising, centred on a battleground chosen by the insurgents in the midst of a densely populated city centre, resulted in significantly higher civilian fatalities – 55 per cent of the dead – than did the War of Independence (where the 39 per cent civilian figure includes about two hundred people killed in intercommunal conflicts in Belfast where republican violence played only a very limited and largely defensive part).[10] Again, what was so different about rebels shooting unarmed policemen and civilians on the sunny morning of Easter Monday 1916 and the assassinations, one November Sunday morning four years later, of unarmed officers in their digs? Are they not all of a piece? Can one episode of Irish insurrectionary violence be implicitly approved, yet the succeeding phase be deprecated even though organised and led by the survivors of the first?

If nothing else, Kevin's example helps to challenge the presumption that those who planned the Rising and fought in Dublin in 1916 were different in motivation, intellectual formation and outlook – more high-minded, modern in aspiration and chivalrous in combat – than the trench-coated 'gun-boys' and baby-faced assassins of the War of Independence or of those on either side of the civil war who killed former comrades in cold blood.

This argument applies equally to British forces, whose departures from the accepted norms of combat in Dublin in 1916 were brushed aside as understandable overreactions in the heat of the moment, and whose adoption of targeted killing in 1920 was not simply condoned but applauded by key ministers in Lloyd George's coalition, particularly the prime minister himself and his ever-impetuous colleague Winston Churchill.

The difference between 1916 and 1919–23 in Ireland is not the people and groups who did the fighting – with the exception of northern loyalists, who were silent in 1916 but who wreaked havoc especially in Belfast from 1920 to 1922 – but rather the ways in which they fought.

This brings us back to Richard English's question: is Kevin worth writing about at all? And if he is, is it because he was somehow exceptional, or because he was typical of young Volunteers who fought against British rule between 1919 and 1921? And how different was he to the people against whom he was fighting?

CHAPTER ONE

The Barrys in Context

Kevin's story has been framed for posterity by two things: a catchy political ballad, which came into circulation in the year of his death and has stood the test of time despite – or perhaps because of – its clumsy words and trite melody; and a meticulously composed witness statement submitted to the Bureau of Military History in September 1952 by his eldest sister Kitby, or Mrs Kathleen Barry Moloney as she is described on the cover. Kitby dealt briefly with her own and with Kevin's progressive radicalisation, leading up to the day of his capture:

> On Monday, 20th September [1920], Kevin was to sit for an examination at 2 o'clock. He had come up from Tombeagh some days before and, on instructions, had not stayed at home [but] with [our] uncle, Patrick Dowling, 58 South Circular Road. About 4 o'clock that Monday afternoon I was in Mr. Aston's office in Abbey Street. I got a telephone call from my uncle's manager. He told me that they had just had an intensive military raid [and] Kevin had been arrested. From that moment I knew by some obscure instinct that Kevin was finished.[1]

Violence had intensified markedly in some parts of Ireland over the course of the summer of 1920, but Dublin city remained relatively quiet. H Company of the 1st Battalion, Dublin Brigade, was something of an exception in the Dublin IRA, because on 1 June they, along with some other Volunteers, pulled off a major coup at the King's Inn.

The carefully planned operation to disarm soldiers guarding the King's Inn worked like a dream. The various Volunteers from C and H companies – raiders, covering parties, drivers to take away the captured weapons – all performed their roles exactly as planned. They seized twenty-five rifles, two invaluable Lewis guns and a large amount of ammunition and military equipment. The operation took under seven minutes, one less than planned. All the material was driven away to safe houses. Kevin emerged from the guardroom carrying a Lewis gun, 'his boyish face ... wreathed in smiles ... he looked like a child clasping a new toy to his breast', saying excitedly to a comrade "Look Dinny, what I have got!"'.[2]

Some parts of the country became increasingly violent in the spring and summer of 1920 as IRA units stepped up action against police and military. Crown forces instituted an informally sanctioned policy of reprisals against the general public, embodied in the depredations of the newly recruited Black and Tans and Auxiliary Cadets, resulting in widespread destruction and a wave of terror across rural Ireland. Yet in Dublin, apart from a handful of targeted shootings of detectives, there was no great upsurge in IRA activity. The summer saw few clashes in the city between the military and the IRA. Six British soldiers – only one of them older than twenty – died violent deaths in the city between January and August 1920, but they were all victims of accidents. This reflected inadequate training and poor discipline. Slackness was everywhere. Individual soldiers in uniform were free to wander the streets; encounters with Volunteers in pubs often led to deals, with soldiers agreeing to sell weapons and ammunition for cash.[3]

It was in the course of completing one such clandestine transaction in the North Richmond Street area that two Volunteers from G Company noticed that, regular as clockwork, a military lorry arrived at a nearby bakery twice a week to collect bread for Collinstown Camp in north Dublin. Although guarded by an armed party, this was evidently a routine exercise and the NCO in charge did not take even the elementary precaution of posting a sentry beside the vehicle, instead leaving the guard sitting in the back of the lorry while the bread was carried out, or else allowing them to slip across the road to buy cigarettes or sweets.

Hearing of this opportunity, John Joe Carroll and James Douglas of H Company investigated further. Guided by a friendly carpenter, Carroll had a good look around the bakery and its approaches, noting that there were two exits, one through the yard on Church Street and one down a corridor, which led to the bread shop at 38 North King Street. He drew a rough map of the premises, which was then used to plan the raid. When he told his comrades about the opportunity, 'we thought this a "pudding" and decided to do the job'.[4] As with the King's Inn operation, the raid was carefully planned. Everyone – lookouts, cover parties, the two sections who would actually hold up the soldiers on the lorry, the men who would spirit the captured weapons and ammunition away – knew their roles, and the enemy would be taken completely unawares. Withdrawal and dispersal in the maze of nearby streets, lanes and alleyways would be easy. What could go wrong?

But the raid was a disaster. It saw the unplanned death of three young soldiers, one just a lad of fifteen summers, a bungled withdrawal and the arrest and eventual execution of Kevin Barry, a process which saw him transformed into a leading icon of the Irish revolution.

In what follows I explore how it came to pass that Kevin became an active Volunteer; how his family influenced him and were influenced by him in life and in afterlife; and how and why he became synonymous with revolutionary self-sacrifice. I am mindful of issues which arise in the exploration of such a short life, where there is no great body of work to analyse, and when most of the sources were created in the knowledge of Kevin's tragic end and extraordinary legacy.

Early accounts and recollections of Kevin made him appear implausibly virtuous. Donal O'Donovan's 1989 book disclosed a far more credible and interesting young man, whose religious habits and generally good conduct were balanced by a wholesome interest in women, on occasion a more-than-wholesome interest in drink and a general humorous irreverence.[5] It also brought out his extraordinarily close relationship with his eldest sister Katherine (born Catherine Agnes but styling herself Katherine or Kathleen, and usually known as Kitby within the family). I am conscious of what has been termed 'the dynamics of remembering within families' where collective memory 'proceeds in an extremely selective and reconstructive manner' to meet the needs of the present.[6] Kitby controlled the narrative of Kevin's story within the family, in terms alike of intergenerational transfer, and of the formal record: alone of Kevin's six siblings, she gave a lengthy and powerful witness statement to the BMH. It has become the template, and in a way also a straitjacket, for all subsequent writers. It was used by others who wanted to write about Kevin – her brother-in-law Jim O'Donovan, Seán Cronin in 1965, her nephew Donal O'Donovan in 1989, and now by her eldest grandson.

Kitby also ensured that Kevin's story would be the only one of consequence in the family, the only one worth sharing with succeeding generations.

Kevin Barry was born in Dublin on 20 January 1902, in the family home and dairy at 8 Fleet Street, in the city centre just a hundred yards south of the river Liffey. He was the fourth child and second son of Mary Dowling (1872–1953) and Thomas (Tom) Barry (1852–1908), who had married fewer than seven years earlier when Mary was just twenty-four and her husband about forty-four (his age is given as fifty in the 1901 census, and his death certificate in 1908 reports him as fifty-six). Mary was to bear a further three children before her husband died of heart disease at home in February 1908.

Number 8 Fleet Street was the Barry's Dublin base, but their ancestral home was the farm at Tombeagh, Hacketstown, Co. Carlow. Kevin's nephew and namesake Kevin and his family still live there. In Kevin's time the Barrys would have been regarded as 'strong farmers' thanks to the energies of his forebears. Tom Barry, Kevin's father, was an astute dairy farmer who saw the potential of the Dublin market. Assisted by his formidable sister Judith, he acquired first a dairy in Pimlico in the inner city, and then a lease on 8 Fleet Street with a dairy yard at the back. This meant they could sell the milk produced at Tombeagh in Dublin. They also rented additional grazing land on the periphery of the city in Crumlin and Templeogue. Fleet Street became the family's Dublin base.

Throughout Kevin's childhood he and his siblings moved between Carlow and Dublin, experiencing both town and country. In Carlow, where he attended primary school, he lived the hardy life of a farm boy; in inner-city Dublin, he became accustomed to navigating his way through crowded streets between his Fleet Street home, a succession of secondary schools, and the home and shop of his mother's brother Patrick (Pat) Dowling at 58 South Circular Road, near Leonard's Corner. The 1911 census indicates that Pat Dowling, then thirty-four, already employed three live-in assistants, suggesting a reasonably substantial establishment. It also suggests that the Dowlings, in common with the Barrys, had a certain amount of drive and ambition, and probably some capital. This may well explain why the family coped so well after the calamity of Tom's death in February 1908, when Kevin had just turned six.

Neither 8 Fleet Street nor the Pimlico dairy yard were owned outright by the Barrys, but rather leased for a fixed period. In 1937

Mary Barry wrote that 'in 1912 my lease lapsed and the Corporation would not renew' because the building was in poor structural condition. She was left in situ on a year-to-year basis, paying £50 annually. By the mid-1930s 8 Fleet Street was so decrepit that the Corporation had to spend £35 'securing dangerous portions of the structure', which Mary had to repay at £5 a year. By then she had sublet the downstairs shop and rooms for £136 a year, leaving a net annual profit calculated as £70 6s.1d. She was fearful that the building would shortly be condemned, leaving her with no source of income other than Tombeagh, upon which her son Mick depended for his living. It was a curious descent from 1921, when by her own account she had been in comfortable circumstance despite having a large young family to support.[7]

The Barry Family in Context

The Barrys came to Carlow from Cork, where they had been dispossessed of their land during Cromwell's time. Despite the disabilities placed upon Catholics, the Barry clan gradually acquired a good deal of land in north Carlow, initially as tenant farmers of the Earl of Wicklow. In 1861 the earl sold 12,000 acres to John Henry Parnell, who passed it on to his youngest son Henry, brother of Charles Stewart Parnell. In 1874 Michael Barry bought Tombeagh outright, probably availing of land-purchase legislation. The farm expanded through purchase in the succeeding years, and by the time Kevin was born in 1902 it extended to eighty-six acres, bounded on one side by the river Derneen. The two-storey farmhouse at Tombeagh, although extended to the rear, remains recognisably the same as it was when Kevin was born. Donal has written about the family tree, including a Kevin born in the late eighteenth century, a younger son who had an unfortunate end, dying on board ship on his way home from America. His ghost is said to have haunted Tombeagh ever since: our Kevin's sister Kitby certainly believed in ghosts to the end of her days, and expected to become one herself.[8]

The family tree indicates some rebel blood. On Mary Dowling's side, John Hutchinson, of Dualla, Co. Tipperary, is said to have been a yeoman officer who turned coat and joined the rebels in the Battle of Hacketstown in 1798. If so, he was fortunate to survive defeat. His daughter Margaret Hutchinson married Laurence Dowling of Ballyhacket House, and their son James Dowling (1821–1907) married Ellen McCardle (1838–1920). Their daughter Mary was Kevin's mother. The Barrys believe there is also a link to Michael Dwyer, the elusive Wicklow rebel who so troubled the Crown following the 1798 rebellion before accepting paid exile.[9]

Marriage to a man almost twice her age cannot have been all that easy for Mary Dowling. She bore her husband seven children in fewer than twelve years. Her grandchildren have fond memories of a kind and warm-hearted woman, to them 'Nana', who in her last years moved from the decrepitude of Fleet Street to a rather dark upstairs flat in 3 Molesworth Street. Her grandson Michael O'Rahilly recalled how the floorboards quivered when the grandchildren ran around. Nana once put him on the windowsill and showed him the statue of Queen Victoria, which was then still ensconced outside Leinster House. She pointed out the headquarters of the Masonic Order on the other side of the street, and told him that when she was newly widowed and trying to get a grip on the Fleet Street dairy, she was particularly supported by Jews, Masons and Quakers who would look in from time to time to make sure that things were going well. Ruth (O'Rahilly) Sweetman has similarly positive memories of a loving old woman who was interested in her grandchildren. She did not play the mother of the martyr or anything of the kind, or invoke her dead son endlessly. Her O'Donovan grandsons Donal and Gerry remembered her as affectionate and playful, and fragmentary correspondence suggests a well-grounded person with a quiet sense of humour.[10]

There was perhaps more to Mary than she cared to show. Kitby was emphatic that it was her mother's wish that Kevin should be supported unconditionally in his determination to offer no defence at his court martial and not to make a plea for mercy, and from time to time after his death there are signs that her will prevailed in family matters. Yet she definitely leaned a lot on her eldest daughter. In 1932 a priest visiting from the United States thought her 'a quiet, retiring mother who does not like to talk of her supreme cross … "Aah," she said, "it would be too hard for me to talk about Kevin. Kathleen will have to do that for you."' She 'appeared relieved that she is saved the anguish of the narrative'.[11]

Kitby, was born in 8 Fleet Street on 12 November 1896, just under a year after her parents' wedding on 28 November 1895 in St Andrew's, Westland Row. She went on to dominate her mother and younger siblings. Sheila, the Barrys' second child, was born in October 1898. She was generally known as 'Shel', although named in the censuses of 1901 and 1911, and in the register of births, as 'Julia Mary Josephine'. Her daughter Triona Maher maintained that Shel was 'always overshadowed' by Kitby, who 'was just that kind of person. She didn't mind responsibility and she took it. The others didn't stand up to her.' In fairness to Kitby, decades later she told her son that on her eleventh birthday (November 1907) her ailing father, knowing he had a serious heart condition, 'asked me to look after Mother if anything happened to him'.[12] In 1901 came the first boy, Michael, or Mick. Quietly humorous in manner, as the eldest son it was his destiny to run the farm at Tombeagh. On 20 January 1902 Kevin arrived, soon followed by Eileen, or Elgin, born on 13 November 1903. Elgin was an undemonstrative, self-contained person quite unlike her livewire eldest sister. Two more girls completed the family: Mary Christina (Monty), born in 1905, and Margaret Dolores (Peggy), in 1906.

The younger children can barely have known their father. Tom was just fifty-six when he died in Fleet Street on a Saturday in

February 1908 from 'vascular disease of [the] heart', despite the expensive attentions of Sir Christopher Nixon, physician to the lord lieutenant.[13] Mary was left a widow at the age of thirty-six, with seven children ranging in age from twelve to one. She also found herself responsible for running the Dublin dairy, the Tombeagh farm and the cattle-grazing operation.

Tom Barry's estate was valued at £2,714 9s., a considerable sum though scarcely a fortune. In his will he appointed his 'dear wife' guardian of his children, as was customary, and he expressly instructed his executors to sell his interest in 8 Fleet Street and the dairy yard at Pimlico together with his cattle in the city and county. He left £300 outright to Mary, £250 to his sister Judith and £30 in bequests to religious causes.[14]

Tom wished that the family would live a rural life: 'I desire that my wife and children during their minorities or until marriage as the case may be shall reside on my said farm at Tombeagh... [which] shall be worked for maintenance of my said wife unless and until she remarry.'[15] But in the event his wishes were circumvented: the lease on the Pimlico dairy yard was sold for £90, and the cattle and rights to grazing around Dublin for £1,470 17s. 10d., but 8 Fleet Street remained a family bastion. Aunt Judith, who had built up the Dublin dairy business, and perhaps did not relish the prospect of spending the rest of her life in bucolic isolation, believed that she could keep things going. Donal O'Donovan cites legal documents, which show how the letter but not the spirit of Tom's will was honoured: the executors simply sold Tom's interest in 8 Fleet Street to Judith for £100, and things continued much as before although the dairy's milk supply now came from Tombeagh by train.[16]

In Dublin Aunt Judith was apparently the force behind the dairy business, although Mary is listed as the proprietor in the 1910 *Thom's Directory*.[17] When Judith died in 1912, Kitby, in her words, 'became my mother's chief adviser in all affairs'. Although her word was generally law amongst her younger siblings, Kevin

had a way of poking fun at her and winning her around, just as
he did the servants in Tombeagh despite constantly 'playing tricks
on them'.[18] The division of the family between Dublin and Carlow
did not suit everybody: Triona Maher recalled that her mother Shel
resented being despatched to supervise the household in Tombeagh
in 1915 instead of staying in Dublin. All the girls recalled Kevin as a
playful and generous brother. His easy way with girls, unusual enough
in the Edwardian era, was to stand to him in his teenage years.

That Kitby was born to leadership is not in doubt. Her marriage
in 1924 changed nothing. She seems to have dominated her husband
Jim Moloney (1896–1981) and her five children as effortlessly as
she had her own siblings.

First Schooling

Kevin began his education at the age of six at the Convent of the
Holy Child in Clarendon Street in Dublin, an unusually central
location for a school, which required children to take their exercise
in a rooftop yard. Not long after Tom's death Mary decided that
the five younger children should go to school in Tombeagh. Kevin
and Mick attended Rathvilly National School, three miles from
Tombeagh, sometimes making the trip by pony and trap, sometimes
getting a lift from their kinsman Jimmy Barry, who drove the cart
carrying milk to Rathvilly station for consignment to Dublin. Local
recollections of Kevin from neighbours and relatives are uniformly
positive and affectionate. These include a little girl whose plaits he
soaked as she carried water home in buckets: 'I made up a story
to my father about how my hair got so wet to keep Kevin out
of trouble.' (Her father Ned O'Toole was the local schoolmaster
and, in retirement, a serious student of the landscape who wrote,
amongst other things, about a standing stone on the Barry farm.)[19]

There was no suitable secondary school near Tombeagh, so in
January 1915 Kevin came back up to live in Dublin. This raises the

question of where his political opinions were formed. The Barry and Dowling families were strongly nationalist – Carlow and Wicklow being scarred by the memory of the 1798 rebellion – and electrified by the rise and fall of Wicklow's Charles Stewart Parnell. In attempting to trace the roots of Kevin's political outlook, it is important to consider his older brother Mick's trajectory. Michael received no secondary schooling, instead going to work full-time on the farm in Tombeagh. But in 1917 he joined the Rathvilly company of the Volunteers, and quickly became an officer. By 1920 he was the battalion adjutant, the second most senior position. This is notable, because across Ireland it was not that common for the eldest son of a farming family to play a major role in the IRA. This was particularly so in Mick's case, with his father dead and the weight of the family's well-being on his shoulders. Typically, it was younger brothers with fewer responsibilities who could find the necessary time for and take the inherent risk involved in IRA membership.

Kevin's sister Shel recalled that the older children were told rebel stories 'over and over ... Father & Auntie [Julia] & Mother always spoke with ... pitying contempt of anyone (policeman, schoolteacher etc.) who had to work for the British Government'. This clashes with Kitby's grand narrative. She attributed the children's political views primarily to Kate Kinsella, an illiterate Dubliner who was the heart of the Fleet Street house. Kitby recalled that

> when the firing started on Easter Monday [1916], she [Kate Kinsella] went out into the street ... dashed past me, lit two candles on her little altar ... I said, 'What are those candles for, Kate?' She said, 'For the boys in the Castle' [presumably a reference to the Irish Citizen Army party, which had attacked but failed to capture Dublin Castle] and from that until her last breath she was an uncompromising republican.[20]

Yet as we see from Mick's story and Shel's recollections, rebel currents were at least as strong in Tombeagh as in Fleet Street.

Kevin's first recorded excursion to a separatist event came in November 1915. Through St Mary's College schoolmates, he got his hands on tickets for a Manchester Martyrs' commemoration concert in the Mansion House. Kitby accompanied him. Eoin MacNeill, president of the Irish Volunteers, took the chair and Bulmer Hobson, co-founder of the Fianna Éireann and a senior figure in the IRB (Irish Republican Brotherhood), made a powerful separatist speech. Kitby recalled that 'we felt then that we had found our proper atmosphere, although outside of Bobby Bonfield and the McNeill boys there was no single person in the packed Mansion House that we knew. From that on, we were always discovering people among our friends who had the same ideas ... I was 18 years old.'[21] Bobby Bonfield became a dedicated 4th Battalion Dublin Brigade Volunteer while studying at UCD. In December 1922 he reportedly assassinated the pro-Treaty shopkeeper and former TD James Dwyer in Rathmines. On 29 March 1923 (Holy Thursday), having escaped from custody, he was arrested on St Stephen's Green by plain-clothes security men close to University Church, which President Cosgrave was visiting as part of his Easter observances. He was driven away and shot dead in a field in Clondalkin.[22]

Kitby's son Paddy, presumably guided by his mother, wrote in the *Belvederian* in 1945 that the Manchester Martyrs meeting so inspired Kevin that he 'wanted to join the Fianna Eireann: but he was so young at 13 that his family thought it unwise'.[23] Kevin's sister Elgin, on the other hand, believed that Kevin did join the Fianna, while keeping quiet about this at home.[24] It hardly matters: it seems clear that he and his older siblings had grown sympathetic to advanced nationalism even before the Rising, as a result both of Carlow and of Dublin influences.

The Rising and its aftermath undoubtedly further radicalised Kevin, Kitby, Michael, Shel and Elgin. Mary lamented that 'the few souvenirs and things from Easter week that Kevin had treasured were done away with' during raids on Tombeagh following his execution.[25] It appears that Kitby, who by then had an office job, was in 8 Fleet Street when the rebellion broke out. It is likely that most of the family were down in Carlow for the Easter weekend and so missed the immediate excitement and the danger. Kitby wrote that from 1916 onwards, the way was clear: 'As a family we were in full sympathy with the Republican movement and gave every help, such as contributing to the collections, selling flags, keeping things for people.'[26] The Barry brothers both joined the Volunteers the following year, Mick in Carlow, and Kevin in Dublin a few weeks after the death following forced feeding of Thomas Ashe in October 1917.

Amongst the rebel dead was The O'Rahilly, who had opposed the Rising then bravely joined it when he realised that it was going ahead despite Eoin MacNeill's order to cancel it. He was mortally wounded by machine-gun fire in a desperate charge towards a British barricade on Moore Street. The O'Rahilly's eldest son Richard, 'Mac', was to marry Elgin Barry in 1935. From the day of Kevin's execution Elgin remained an unwavering though undemonstrative republican, whereas Mac, perhaps reflecting on his own father's doubts, became critical of the physical force tradition: by the late 1970s he maintained to me and others that the Rising could not be justified, and argued that its impact upon subsequent developments had been exaggerated. Like some historians, he pointed to the conscription crisis of 1918 as the crucial episode which produced a somewhat awkward unity within Irish nationalism.[27]

Considerable efforts were made between July 1917 and April 1918 to negotiate an agreed home rule settlement through the Irish Convention. Chaired by Sir Horace Plunkett, the Convention met in Trinity College Dublin. It was the last throw of the dice for John

Redmond, the leader of constitutional nationalism, who died in March just as the Convention foundered on the Ulster Unionists' insistence that they be excluded from the application of home rule. With unfortunate timing, the Convention's final report more or less coincided with the opening on the western front of the last great German strategic initiative of the war, the so-called 'Ludendorff offensive'. The aim was to deliver a crushing blow to the British and French armies before the United States, which had joined the war months earlier, could send significant reinforcements across the Atlantic.

The initial success of the German offensive caused the British government to panic. Faced with an acute manpower shortage, Lloyd George's government decided to introduce compulsory military service in Ireland, hoping to sweep up 150,000 men, sweetening the measure by promising also to bring in home rule for twenty-six counties. The decision was taken in a panic, and against the clear advice of the Royal Irish Constabulary (RIC) inspector general, the Viceroy Lord Wimborne, the leading Ulster unionist Edward Carson and the Chief Secretary for Ireland H.E. Duke, who warned the prime minister that 'conscription will produce a disaster'.[28] C.P. Scott, the influential editor of the *Manchester Guardian*, tried to dissuade Lloyd George: such a step was 'no part of statesmanship and may even prove a disastrous turning point in your career'. He might have added 'and Ireland's history'.[29] The decision was announced on 9 April 1918.

Chief secretary Duke was proved wrong, but only in the sense that the measure was never introduced; otherwise he was prescience personified. The threat of conscription unified nationalist Ireland in opposition as 1916 had not done. The institutional Catholic church, hitherto generally hostile to Sinn Féin and the Irish Volunteers, joined in the chorus of condemnation. The government reluctantly backed down. Field Marshal Lord French, the rakish Anglo-Irish cavalryman who had failed in battle in France in 1914–15, was now given the opportunity to play the strong man in Ireland as the new Viceroy; Lloyd George believed 'he would be excellent for the job'.[30] He would run the country on no-nonsense lines, stamping out sedition and bringing sense to the childish Irish by his tough methods.[31]

The conscription crisis transformed nationalist politics: it occasioned a huge surge in support for Sinn Féin, it provided motivation for young men and youths to join the Irish Volunteers as the Barry boys had already done, and in the December 1918 election it led to the near annihilation of the Irish parliamentary party (despite, as Mac O'Rahilly was fond of pointing out, Redmond's candidates receiving about 22 per cent of all votes cast). Sinn Féin, committed to a policy of abstention from Westminster, won 73 of the 105 Irish seats, one of them going to Kitby's future father-in-law, P.J. Moloney of Tipperary. Sinn Féin was pledged to establish a sovereign Irish assembly, Dáil Éireann, which was duly inaugurated in Dublin's Mansion House on 21 January 1919. A declaration of independence was issued, together with a proclamation 'to the Nations of the World!' By chance, on the same day Volunteers of the Third Tipperary Brigade, which had been established at a meeting in P.J. Moloney's home in Church Street, Tipperary in 1918, killed two policemen who were escorting a cargo of gelignite to a local quarry. 21 January 1919 is now taken as the day that the War of Independence began, though at the time things were not so clear-cut.

But it was not the threat of conscription which had radicalised the Barry brothers – they were already Volunteers. Kevin was only fifteen when he joined, and prudently did not mention this new commitment to his mother, who was safely out of the way in Tombeagh.

CHAPTER TWO

The Education of a Rebel

In 1915 Kevin was sent to secondary school in Dublin. From January to June he attended O'Connell School on the North Circular Road, where he left no particular trace. Colonel Terry O'Neill, who attended the school in the late 1940s and early 1950s, recalled how the staff would make occasional reference to two old boys who had died fighting for contrasting causes. One was Frank Flood (1901–1921), the UCD engineering student and friend of Kevin's executed in 1921, of whom we shall hear more; the other was Brendan 'Paddy' Finucane (1920–1942), who was an O'Connell's pupil until his family moved to London in 1936, and who thereafter had a dazzling career as a Royal Air Force fighter pilot, becoming the youngest officer to reach the rank of wing commander at the age of twenty-one before being shot down over the Channel in 1942 (in October 1941 Prime Minister Churchill thought 'the pilot Finucane might be a great figure' for propaganda purposes relating to Ireland). Somewhere or other in the school Finucane had carved his initials, and this evidence of mild delinquency became an object of abiding interest to the boys.[1]

During his brief stay there, Kevin overlapped with others also to rise to prominence in republican circles. These included future Taoiseach Seán Lemass (1901–1971), one of over a hundred pupils and past pupils of O'Connell School who participated in the 1916 Rising, and Ernie O'Malley (1897–1957), later to become

a powerful memorialist of the Irish revolution, one of its least
abashed killers, and a self-educated man of the visual and literary
arts. In classrooms or corridors Kevin may even have bumped into
a future First Lord of the Admiralty, as Brendan Bracken (1901–
1958), then a tempestuous Tipperary teenager, was also enrolled in
the school for a few months. He was then consigned to boarding
school under the care of the Jesuits at Mungret College in Limerick,
from which he absconded repeatedly (and where he overlapped
with Paddy Moloney, killed in 1921, whose brother Jim was to
marry Kevin's oldest sister Kitby in 1924).[2]

The Christian Brothers' 'intensely nationalist' approach to
education can scarcely have influenced either Kevin or Bracken
in the diametrically opposite political choices which they later
made, one towards radical nationalism and an early death; the
other into the centre of the British commercial and political
establishment. Bracken made his name and money in financial
journalism, ultimately becoming chairman of the *Financial Times*,
and following election as a Tory MP in 1929, he was one of
Winston Churchill's closest confidants during the wilderness years
from 1935 to 1939. From 1941 to 1945 he was in the cabinet,
first as Minister for Information – a suitable role for a man who
had successfully 'spun' his life story so as to make himself appear
an Australian orphan – and, for a few weeks in 1945, First Lord
of the Admiralty.[3] Kevin's time in O'Connell School was, like
Bracken's, so brief that the Christian Brothers seem immediately
to have forgotten the connection: a full front-page tribute to Kevin
in the October 1921 edition of their publication *Our Boys* made
no mention of his months as a Christian Brothers pupil, and stated
incorrectly that Kevin attended St Mary's College for two years
before entering Belvedere.[4]

O'Connell School was well-regarded academically. It was
customary for middle class boys – the sons of doctors, lawyers and
the like – to be enrolled there for a time in order to get a good

academic grounding, before being moved for their final years of secondary education to more prestigious institutions where they would acquire a suitably bourgeois veneer. What is surprising in Kevin's case is that he was moved after only a few months. From what we know of his character, it is unlikely that he had failed to settle in O'Connell School. Nevertheless, he moved or was moved in the autumn of 1915 to St Mary's College in Rathmines. The most likely explanation is that Kitby perceived social advantages in sending Kevin to a more exclusive school. She had exceptionally finely tuned social antennae, and St Mary's College, run by the French Spiritan or 'Holy Ghost' order, catered in general to a somewhat more elevated cohort of the Catholic middle classes than did the Christian Brothers. The school was located in the heart of genteel Rathmines, just south of the Grand Canal, in one of the city's most desirable quarters.

One or two pieces of memorabilia tell something of Kevin's year at St Mary's, and of his developing political outlook. One is a textbook, *The Ideal Book of Poetry (For the Young)*, edited by Holy Ghost Father J.A. Kingston, a 'collection of English and Anglo-Irish verse for the young'. Writing in 1915, Father Kingston lamented 'the cold treatment accorded to the writings of our Irish poets'. His solution was to include 'Anglo-Irish poets who may not be equal to the best masters of English verse' but who would 'appeal most feelingly to the children of their own race' until 'Ireland has built up for herself a literature truly Gaelic and National'. His selection mixed established British poets including Shakespeare, Pope, Burns, Keats, Macaulay and Tennyson with Irish writers such as James Clarence Mangan, Thomas Davis, Katherine Tynan Hinkson, Ethna Carberry and W.B. Yeats, poets calculated to sentimentalise rather to radicalise the youth of Catholic Ireland. Kevin was thus exposed to Macaulay's retelling of how Horatius saved Rome from false Sextus and Lars Porsena 'in the grand old days of old', to Davis's invocation of 'A nation's voice, a nation's voice – It is a solemn thing!', to Mangan's consolatory 'My Dark Rosaleen / Do not cry, Do not weep / The priests are on the ocean green / They march along the deep', and to the Scottish poet Thomas Campbell's *Lord Ullin's Daughter* (which another eminent poet, Patrick Kavanagh, was to recite effortlessly in Kitby's Rathgar drawing room when he married her daughter Katherine in 1967). We cannot assess the impact of this *pot pourri* upon Kevin's outlook, save to note that he treated the volume itself with no great respect, marking lines and pages, scribbling notes and random words in pen and ink here and there, repeatedly using a rubber stamp to imprint his name, executing a crude drawing of a warship, and writing the German Great War slogan '*Gott strafe England*' on a blank page:[5]

His propensity to doodle is also evident in a surviving homework copybook from his year in St Mary's, where a 'St Mary's Gutty' and 'Rathvilly Gutty picking up fags and orange peels from the lawn' are unkindly sketched. His essays addressed a range of set topics. On 'Kingship', he wrote of a time when 'all believed or were forced to believe in the divine right of kings. When all believed that men – for the most part drunken libertines and besotted fools – had been sent by God to rule the millions, few of which were worse in morality or intelligence than they.'[6] Writing on 'Prejudice', he showed an awareness of racism, 'a subject on which every Irishman should be able to discourse eloquently'. Kevin identified two categories of prejudice, which, when combined, were the underlying cause of conflict: 'That of the white man against his coloured brother, for brother he is whether black, red or yellow, and that of the white man against his fellow white man of a different nation ... The American people ... look down' on the Black man 'as a work beast, as an animal without a soul. A white American refuses to travel or eat with a negro. Even for the slightest offence he is punished and in former days and even [in] latter [days] ... has been "lynched by the mob" of "Superior white men".'[7]

Onwards and Upwards: A Jesuit Education

St Mary's College closed in 1916. There were a number of Catholic secondary day schools in Dublin where Kevin could have been enrolled. The family could have chosen O'Connell School or Synge Street, or perhaps the Catholic University School (CUS) in Leeson Street. But Belvedere College SJ carried by far the greatest social cachet. In Belvederian James Joyce's highly autobiographical *A Portrait of the Artist as a Young Man*, Stephen Dedalus's father justifies the family's decision to enrol Stephen in a Jesuit school: 'Christian brothers be damned! ... Is it with Paddy Stink and Mickey Mud?'[8] Todd Andrews, a Christian Brothers School Synge Street pupil and proud of it, would not have been surprised at such an attitude: he took it as natural that at UCD he should be only on nodding terms with Kevin, despite each knowing the other was in the IRA, because 'he was a rugby player and had been to a Jesuit school'.[9]

It is likely that Kevin was sent to Belvedere College SJ because the family, or at any rate Kitby, recognised an opportunity to elevate him further in the social hierarchy. It was then the most prestigious Catholic boys' secondary day school in Dublin. Mrs Barry paid four guineas a term for Kevin to attend, or £12 3s. a year. To put this outlay in a Carlow context, in 1918 a male attendant in the Carlow Workhouse Schoolboys' ward was paid 10s. a week, or £26 a year, while a 'wardsmaid' was on an annual salary scale of £15 to £20. In 1921 the post of laundress at Tullow Workhouse, probably much coveted in the locality, was advertised at £36 a year, or £18 with 'rations within door'.[10]

James Joyce's experiences at Belvedere from 1893 to 1898 are immortalised in fictional form in *Portrait*. Father Joseph McDonnell, who had supervised Joyce's religious development, was still spiritual director in Kevin's time there. Kevin joined the venerable Sodality of the Blessed Virgin Mary, founded in 1563, of which Joyce as the elected prefect had been 'virtual captain of the school' in 1896–7 until he felt he had to choose between his obvious spirituality – he was invited to consider becoming a Jesuit – and his sexual interests, which in themselves did not greatly perturb his Jesuit mentors.[11] While an observant Catholic (he joined the sodality in due course) Kevin does not seem to have felt any comparable tension between his religious observance and his growing fascination with girls.

Belvedere's city centre location resulted in its being caught up in the events of the Rising. Buildings were hit by gunfire, though not seriously damaged, and Jesuits went to the aid of local people. Two former pupils died: Joseph Plunkett, the mannered aesthete who had overseen the calamitous military planning for the rebellion, was executed, while Reggie Clery, a solicitor's apprentice and former school rugby star, was shot by rebels on Haddington Road as his column of army reserve volunteers returned to Beggars Bush Barracks after a route march. Another Belvederian, Cathal Brugha, was badly wounded in the South Dublin Union fighting alongside his future civil war opponent W.T. Cosgrave, whose young half-brother was killed there.[12] But the Great War hit Belvedere far harder than did the rebellion. Like other elite schools in Ireland and Britain, it had a strong tradition of producing boys for military careers. Between 1914 and 1918, forty-seven Old Belvederians died in British service. Its sister school Clongowes lost ninety-five of the 604 former pupils who went to war. Many scions of the other Irish Jesuit schools also served and died. Jesuit priests became prominent as military chaplains. Father Francis Browne SJ, who was living in Belvedere when Kevin was executed, won the Military Cross and Bar for succouring wounded men under fire. The rector of Belvedere's Jesuit community during Kevin's time, Father Charlie Doyle, was brother of Father Willie Doyle, who after his death in France in August 1917 became almost an unofficial saint for many Irish Catholics. It was a biography of Doyle that gave my father Paidín 'the much-needed push in the day of my indecision' to apply to become a Jesuit in 1940.[13] The school community offered prayers for the safety of Old Belvederians at the Front, and for the souls of those who had died. *The Belvederian* of 1919 also carried the happy news of 2nd Lieutenant Jock Burke, who had been presumed dead only to turn up 'looking fit and well' in Dublin, though with one 'helpless arm'; it also gave accounts of the war experiences of various Belvederians and carried photographs of them in uniform. Yet the times were changing; there was also a large photograph of Cathal Brugha (in civilian dress), and an account of how he had been chosen as chairman of 'the Dáil Eireann' because of his fluency in Irish.[14]

From that we can see that Belvedere was no longer a bastion of Castle Catholicism and unquestioning loyalty to king and country. The failure of the British government to honour its promises on home rule, the repression following the Rising and the conscription crisis had all contributed to a shift in attitudes amongst many Irish Jesuits and lay teachers. This may explain why Kevin was allowed to express consistently radical and often anti-British views in his written work. Yet it would be wrong to treat his surviving doodles as sacred texts, or to parse their arguments too closely. Homework was homework, after all.

Kevin was a strong pupil generally but inclined to sloppiness. His chemistry master Tom Counihan, then a Jesuit Scholastic, reproved him for poor presentation: 'Finish your notes. Sketch incomplete. Your notes are to be entered in more careful handwriting.'[15] The propensity to doodle and scribble seen in his St Mary's days remained evident. The top of the first page of *Grammar and Composition on La Belle-Nivernaise* has 'K Barry loyalist of Irish Republic' scrawled across it, while the flyleaf records 'League Final 1918. Mountjoy beat Blackrock 7–6.' The title on the cover of *Henry V* has been changed to *VI*, and amidst scribbles on the flyleaf is a small sketch of a twin-engine aircraft.[16] Around Latin exercises 'UP the Republic!' appears several times. While his essays vary in quality and tone, they certainly show flashes of personality, of a general irreverence, of some knowledge of world affairs and of a sustained hostility towards British rule in Ireland. One, which he submitted to George Dempsey, the school's longest-serving master who had been James Joyce's English teacher, addressed 'Industrial Unrest'. Kevin's views and sympathies could not have been clearer: 'We are today passing through a crisis ... which is unparalleled in the history of the world. It is the culmination of four years of starvation, privation and misgovernment – the nemesis which awaits war profiteers, place hunters and grasping capitalists. It is probably the beginning of the end of aristocracy ...' The reasons for the strike were plain:

> In nine cases out of ten ... the cause is hunger. This itself may arise from two causes, bad wages or misgovernment ... There is no remedy for a strike except to accede to the demands of the strikers ... we here in Dublin had ... a strike ... all over the world backed them ... we received a forcible demonstration of the power of Labour... and the power of agitation in the person of ... James Larkin and his able lieutenant, COMMANDANT JAMES CONNOLLY.

He received a mark of 60 per cent, without comment on his radical tone.

Where Kevin's ideas and information came from is unclear. His mother may have passed on her open-minded attitude towards people of other religions. In Carlow the Barrys were on good terms with their Protestant neighbours around Rathvilly (which, as we will see, did not prevent Kevin exchanging shots with the local Church of Ireland rector in 1920).[17]

In a later essay, possibly written in 1918, Kevin wrote about kingship in an expansive passage, which intertwined biblical themes, the French revolution and anti-colonialism with his own republicanism, while displaying a certain naiveté about political conditions in South America:

> what did God say when the Israelites asked him for a king? His answer form[s] the basis of one of the best arguments for Socialism. There is absolutely no necessity for a king ... when the labourer [sic] – the backbone of every nation – has the same vote as the nobleman ... France, America, The Argentine and Brazil are four of the greatest and richest nations of the world, ruled by the chosen representatives of the people ... 'Liberté, Egalité, Fraternité' the motto of [the] 2nd greatest Republic in the world will shortly become the war cry of all and we hope our little island will not change her views upon the subject of Kingship.

In another essay entitled 'the Fault, dear Brutus, lies not in our stars, but in ourselves, that we are the underlings', Kevin wrote:

> There are people who say that the reason Ireland is not free is because Irishmen are not united. Well, they can't give that reason any longer because Ireland is united, or at least it is so unanimous that the dissenters do not count. But a word on this unity before passing to other things ... No matter how bleak things look at present a brighter day is coming and if everyone does his share, instead of submitting to present circumstances, instead of being satisfied with present conditions, there is no doubt but that 'at a no far distant date' we may be celebrating our—— [a note in Kevin's handwriting follows: 'Deleted by censor']18

This effusion secured a mark of 40 per cent, and the marginal note 'piffle' beside the paragraph quoted. But a piece on 'Imagination', which offered the ringing conclusion that 'Certain it is that the Irishman is much more imaginative than the phlegmatic Sassenach,' received 85 per cent.

Bold statements and platitudes are littered throughout Kevin's copybooks, in his writing and on the margins. His tone became increasingly politicised and passionate. But he could be distracted: an essay on the minor characters in Shakespeare's *Henry V* is most notable for a large doodle on a blank page of a full-busted 'Kathy when she's 50' chastising a young boy holding a spoon in a jar marked 'Jam' and saying 'I'm ... sorry.' Another is of 'Shel when she's 48' reproaching an impudent boy who shouts 'Yah' and sticks out his tongue: 'I'm sick of you! Can't you behave?'[19]

Kevin's essays clearly indicate political conviction. 'Nine times out of ten' the cause of revolution 'is bad government. In ... every country there has been a period of oppression and tyranny, a period of despotic rule by monarch or ministers.' Everywhere 'a time came when the people decided that they would not stand it no longer and a revolution took place. If it were successful everything was all right. If not, it was only deferred for a few years so that in the end the people triumphed'. That naive conclusion was immediately qualified: 'The great remedy for revolutions is to use an English-made Irish bull, a preventative. Revolutions may be very easily prevented ... by a constitutional government by the representatives such as was supposed to have been the case in England.' A penultimate paragraph, scored out, of this scrawled four-page essay runs: 'Of course I do not include the revolutions of S. America – no sane person would call them revolutions' with 'S. America' crossed out and '1916' written over it in pencil.

Kevin signed this essay '*Caomhín de Barra*', as is used sporadically throughout his St Mary's and Belvedere copybooks. This brings up the wider question of his knowledge and use of the Irish language. It is hard to be definite about this: while many separatist-minded people took to using Irish versions of their names, rendered in the Gaelic script, they did not all internalise Irish. It is doubtful whether anyone in Fleet Street or Tombeagh spoke Irish routinely: Kate Kinsella certainly didn't, and in the 1911 census only Kitby and Shel, based in Dublin, are shown as knowing the language (presumably through classes at secondary school, which in Kitby's case was the Dominican Convent on Eccles Street). During and after the War of Independence some of Kevin's siblings sometimes signed their names in Irish in the Gaelic script, but there is little to suggest that it became the domestic vernacular for them or for their families. Kitby's future father-in-law, P.J. Moloney, is solemnly recorded in the proceedings of the first meeting of Dáil Éireann as P.J. Ó Maoldomnaigh TD. Yet, as he ruefully reflected in Barlinnie jail in Glasgow in 1916, he had just been embarrassed by a visiting Jesuit priest of Irish extraction, 'who spoke to me in the Gaelic tongue. I was ashamed that my laziness prevented me from learning to speak & understand my own language.'[20]

Friendships and Fitting In

It can be hard to switch schools in mid-teens, but Kevin did so twice, effortlessly. Tom Counihan taught Kevin maths and chemistry and was also his rugby coach. Over time he became an important mentor to Kevin, whom he summarised as at once good-humoured and 'a dour kind of lad ... once he got down to something he went straight ahead'.[21] Another Jesuit, Tom Ryan, wrote in rather more sentimental terms of Kevin's 'special quizzical smile ... he was a natural leader and drew others to him without effort but never put himself forward'. Ryan made him rugby secretary for the senior team in 1918–19, during which he wrote letters twice a week to other schools to confirm fixtures. He was given ten shillings to cover postage, and at the end of the season, 'what was my [Ryan's] surprise when he ... handed me a half-crown saying: "Sir, here is the change from your 10s."'[22]

Kevin's integration into the school must have been helped by his interest in sport: like another Belvederian revolutionary, Cathal Brugha, he threw himself into every sort of organised physical activity available, playing rugby, cricket and hurling.[23] It was through sport that he formed a particularly close friendship with Gerry McAleer from Dungannon, who like himself was something of an outsider. Gerry, who stayed in digs on the North Circular Road during term time, never really knew why Kevin befriended him: 'Perhaps it was my Northern accent or because we shared the name Gerard. Kevin was always in an honours class: I was in a pass. He was a brighter boy than I was. I think I worked harder because I had to.' Either way the friendship, which saw Kevin holidaying in Dungannon with the McAleers, who owned the Commercial Hotel, continued into their time as medical students in UCD. On one visit Kevin left his mark, literally, by carving the initials KGB into a freshly cemented windowsill. During the spring of 1918 Kevin wrote Kitby a cheery letter from Dungannon. He found Northerners extremely friendly, and he had 'got several motor drives last week. The motor man and I are great pals because he is a Meath man and looks down on all Northerners. The longer I stay ... the better I like it.' Kevin also sought cash, as he had had to spend most of his money to replace a bicycle chain, which had broken on a trip to Pomeroy. Proof of his penury was provided by the envelope, which he had posted unstamped, costing Kitby a thruppenny delivery charge.[24]

Kevin turned out to be a reasonable rugby player, though no star. Gerry remembered him as 'a fairly solid fellow, broader than I was. We were both forwards ... He was a demon for eating chocolate bars at school. He would eat it morning, noon and night.' A bit of bulk was probably no harm in scrums and rucks, though it would hardly enhance a boy's speed.[25] Kevin's efforts saw him make the squad but not the team for the Leinster Junior Cup in 1917, when to everyone's great surprise Belvedere beat Blackrock College in the final. *The Belvederian* wrote of 'K. Barry (forward) – though rarely brilliant always plays a good, hard game; a fair tackler; works well in the scrum.'[26] The team's prodigious 13-year-old scrum half Eugene Davy (1904–1996) 'watches the ball very keenly and frequently comes around on the opposing half' – he went on to an outstanding international career (1925–1934) as an out-half.[27] Two years later Kevin was on the senior cup team: 'No forward deserved his place better. Showed great dash, and tackled like a demon. This player improved very much … A useful hooker.'[28]

In the same season, 1918–19, Belvedere took up hurling, an innovation in a school which otherwise emphasised the same field sports as most British public schools: rugby and cricket. Hurling was already played in Belvedere's sister school Mungret in Limerick, but its adoption in Dublin suggests a wider shift in the cultural wind. Kevin was selected, along with Gerry McAleer and Eugene Davy. The first match was an away game against Terenure College. It did not go well: Belvedere lost by ten goals and two points to two goals and one point, or twenty-three points to seven. Kevin's interest in sport was crucial after his death in contributing to his iconography as a youthful Irish rebel. Three of the four most-circulated images of him came from the 1918–19 experimental hurling team photograph, from the senior rugby 2nd team of 1918 (wearing a white shirt), and from one taken of the Old Belvedere Rugby Club 2nd team in 1919. The fact that in two of these he was wearing the distinctive Belvedere hooped jersey contributed to the image of a healthy, athletic, all-round young man, a team player not an egoist. In reporting pleas for clemency in Ireland and Britain on 30 October 1920, the *Freeman's Journal* carried the 1919 photograph over the caption 'Master Kevin Barry'.[29]

The fourth image widely circulated after his death is somewhat different: Kevin is in the midst of a group of senior boys, wearing a trench coat, shirt and tie, with a slither of hair hanging down his forehead. This was a detail from a photograph, first published in *The Belvederian* of 1919 and captioned 'Pillars of the House', which had been taken by chance. Father Fearghal McGrath was 'in the playground at Belvedere' and 'happened to have a plate to spare & snapped ... a few of the bigger boys'. When an image of Kevin was sought in 1922 for memorial cards, to be sold by Belvedere boys to raise money for charities, he sent the picture for copying to Keogh Brothers photographers. When the image was enlarged, Keogh's 'wished to touch out the wisp of hair, but K's mother objected. She said it was characteristic.'[30]

As a Jesuit-educated medical student Kevin was almost indistinguishable from thousands of young British officers who had died in the Great War. Jay Winter has written of the profound sense in post-war Britain that 'the deaths of thousands of educated and privileged young men' constituted 'a lost generation': the flower of England, fresh from the public schools and universities, had been sacrificed. This sentiment is echoed in the words of one Winchester and Christchurch, Oxford man, Olaf Caroe: 'almost all my own friends and contemporaries fell on the Somme or round Ypres, in Gallipoli or Mesopotamia ... My own survival must be attributed to the fact that I went to India and not to France or Gallipoli.'[31]

University Student

Kevin entered 1st Medicine in UCD in October 1919. As the holder of a Dublin Corporation scholarship and living in the city centre, he had no transport costs and his scholarship income more than covered his needs. While not neglecting his IRA duties both in Dublin and in Carlow, he seems to have had plenty of time on his hands, and plenty of friends with whom to spend it, while also attending about three quarters of his scheduled lectures – in those days the college kept a register – and doing some study. Dancing, drinking, betting, flirting and attending the cinema were his main pastimes. The introduction of a midnight curfew limited but did not eliminate the city's night life.

During the day Matassa's coffee house was a favourite haunt. What Dublin pubs he drank in we do not know. Kevin did not have to go far to meet new girls. He attended céilis in UCD and in other venues and, according to the abstemious Gerry McAleer, also 'had nights out in those "low down" dance halls', mixing in a rather different social milieu. Kevin wrote to his Athy friend Bapty Maher of being eyed up by 'a peach of a tart' in a train journey up to Dublin, and on a drunken outing from Tombeagh to Glendalough he spent time 'lying on a sofa in the Royal Hotel with a Belgian girl drinking'.[32] Perhaps more interestingly, however, he could treat young women as people rather than simply as objects of unrequited or requited lust. In his generation of young Catholic Irishmen, that in itself was probably unusual. His ease with girls is reflected in a gentle valedictory letter to his friend Kathleen Carney, written the evening before his execution. It ends: 'Now I'll shut up. I wish you every success in love and business. Give my adieux to Des [her brother] and your mother and say a little prayer when I cash in. Your pal, Kevin.'[33]

CHAPTER THREE

Training and Military Service, 1917–20

By the time of his capture outside Monk's Bakery, Kevin was an unusually experienced Volunteer. He operated both in the least populous county in Leinster, Carlow, with a population of 36,252 in the 1911 census, and in Dublin, which with 477,196 people was by far the largest. In Carlow he was involved in a number of minor disruptive operations: the burning of an abandoned RIC barracks, and armed raids on houses; in Dublin, he participated in two armed confrontations with the military. He fired his weapon in two engagements, and he killed at least one person.

It would be wrong to assume, despite Sinn Féin's resounding electoral success in December 1918 in a first-past-the-post, single-seat system, that nationalist Ireland had converted en masse to physical force republicanism. That victory obscured the fact that many Irish people, nationalists as well as unionists, had voted against the separatist movement. In most of Ulster, including Monaghan, Cavan and Donegal, the Redmondites, buttressed by the powerful and pugilistic Ancient Order of Hibernians (AOH), remained a significant political force. In the south-east, although the Redmondite party was all but annihilated in terms of parliamentary seats, at grass-roots level, notably in Waterford where the Redmondite tradition and organisation remained resilient, there was a strong counterweight to Sinn Féin.[1]

In Carlow, as elsewhere across hitherto Redmondite Ireland, those preparing actively to fight against continued British rule were in a small minority. The majority who supported Sinn Féin and saw Dáil Éireann as the legitimate legislature of a free people were not itching for violence, but for politics. There was also a significant Protestant population of about 10 per cent, most of whom, by 1919, could be termed quiet unionists seeking to avoid trouble. Thus Carlow's Irish Volunteers, as they evolved into the IRA, were by no means guaranteed popular support for armed action. Even the first minor disruptive operations they undertook – the cutting of telegraph wires, the burning of abandoned police barracks, a handful of attacks on police and raids on houses for weapons – ran the hazard of discommoding and antagonising rather than enthusing the general public, nationalist as well as unionist, Catholic as well as Protestant.

Induction and Training

Kevin joined C Company, 1st Battalion, Dublin Brigade, Irish Volunteers in the autumn of 1917. Always an active fellow, moving in and out of the house on errands and missions of one kind or another arising from school and sports activities, or meeting up with his friends, he was able to keep his military commitment secret both from the family and from his wider circle in Dublin. During vacations in Tombeagh in 1919 and 1920, he was attached to C Company of the 3rd Battalion, Carlow Brigade, in which his brother Mick was also serving. Everyone in the locality, including his mother, must have known.

As with other aspects of people's recollections of him, we have to be careful in handling testimony about Kevin's commitment and efficiency as a Volunteer. But evidence certainly indicates that he was an enthusiastic participant. He definitely attended almost all 'parades' where training took place, usually one evening a week, when in Dublin. Furthermore, he must have made a positive impression because although very young, he was promoted to 'Section Commander' in 1919. He was also sworn into the Irish Republican Brotherhood (IRB), the venerable secret society through which Michael Collins developed his particular grip upon some of the most active elements within the Volunteers. How seriously he took this additional commitment to republicanism is unclear. Kitby's future husband Jim Moloney, who while a pharmacy student in Dublin in 1919 joined the IRB in a Parnell Street pub and paid a weekly 6*d*. subscription thereafter, maintained it was an irrelevance to rank-and-file young Volunteers at the time.[2]

C Company, which after a time was reorganised with Kevin assigned to a new hived-off H Company, met in various locations, including the O'Flanagan Club in Ryder's Row, off Bolton Street, in the Tara Hall in Gloucester Street, and in 44 Rutland Square, the building which now bears his name.[3] None of these venues was especially secret: 44 Rutland Square in particular was a hotbed of separatist activity of all kinds including fundraising dances, céilis and cultural events.

In composition H Company resembled the Dublin units of the pre-Rising Irish Volunteers. The members were mostly tradesmen, labourers, clerks, apprentices and shop assistants, with a leavening of students. Kevin stood out on account both of his youth and of his being a Belvedere College boy, about which he was teased.[4] Volunteer training followed a GHQ-prescribed regime. GHQ's general approach was set out in the monthly journal *An t-Óglach*, which carried 'Training Notes':[5] the 16 December 1918 issue, for example, gave detailed instructions on musketry, on how to tap and to cut telephone and telegraph wires, and on different types of signalling, although 'owing to the limited space at our disposal, we are … unable to give the Morse and semaphore alphabets, special signals, particulars of flag drill etc'. Instead, they recommended 'the text-book on "Signalling" by Captain E.J. Solano, 1918 edition, to be had from Ponsonby's, Grafton Street, for 1s 6d'.[6] This nicely illustrates the point that GHQ envisaged the Irish Volunteers as operating on the assumptions, practices and aspirations of a conventional army as much as those of a guerrilla force.

How much useful military knowledge or experience a part-time Volunteer could acquire through this sort of training is debatable, particularly once it became necessary to carry out such activities largely in secret. The reality was that in Dublin in 1920, as Joost Augusteijn baldly put it, 'most Volunteers did little' and few saw any action or heard a shot fired in anger.[7] The average Volunteer simply showed up for training at the appointed time and place.

The pre-1916 Irish Volunteers custom of training and drilling at company strength, and organising route marches when such activities were neither secret nor illegal, had had obvious advantages: drilling and marching instilled a sense of cohesion and discipline, helped each Volunteer to see himself as one part of a larger organisation and as a legitimate soldier, acculturated men to await and to obey orders automatically, and made an impression upon the general public. But open drilling also facilitated observation, enabling the police to form an accurate picture of the strength and composition of units.

In addition to drills, basic training embraced tactics, signalling, information gathering, elementary first aid, preparation of explosive charges, sabotage, maintenance and use of arms, and tactics in street and open fighting. It is unclear what tactical training Kevin received for urban operations, where Volunteers needed to act in small groups, assembling for action and then dispersing and disappearing individually into the general population. Equally, we do not know whether specific training was given to ordinary Volunteers in techniques of close-up killing, though such targeted killing required a somewhat different approach than conventional fighting. In Dublin city in 1920–21 the IRA mainly operated in small groups, relying on pistols and handheld 'bombs' (what might also be termed grenades), which were easy to conceal but required close proximity to the target and were often unreliable. The one major exception to the rule that the Dublin IRA went out to fight in small parties, the attack on the Custom House on 25 May 1921, was a disastrous shambles. It resulted in the immediate deaths of five Volunteers and the capture of over seventy.

Firearms training was constrained by several factors: the chronic shortage of weapons and ammunition; the wide miscellany of weapons acquired and used by the IRA, which made maintenance and resupply difficult and prompted improvisation in the manufacture of ammunition, often leading to malfunctions; and the problem of finding suitable locations in or near the city where firing during training would not attract the attention of Crown forces.

We do not know how extensive Kevin's firearms training was, whether it took place mainly in Carlow or in Dublin, or whether he had ever previously handled and fired a Mauser automatic, the prized but somewhat temperamental weapon he used in the Church Street operation. Nor is it clear how much instruction and practice he had in the use of rifles: these weapons, far more powerful and accurate in combat than revolvers or automatic pistols, were highly suitable for rural fights because an enemy could be engaged from a distance, whereas revolvers and automatic pistols required the user to be close to his target and were therefore far more vulnerable to detection and to return fire. In rural areas IRA units had to rely largely on shotguns: these were legal and plentiful because of their routine use in pest control, but they, like pistols, were lethal to human targets only at very close range, even when improvised 'slugs' were used (which scattered lead shot in a wide arc) rather than conventional cartridges.

What we do know about rural Ireland, however, may explain a surprising aspect of the conflict between 1919 and 1921. The anomaly is this: about 44 per cent of British military fatalities of all kinds were self-inflicted, or 'own goals' in contemporary British military parlance. The great majority of these were through accidental shootings. By contrast, only about 11 per cent of IRA deaths were self-inflicted.[8] One reason for this surprising disparity between the professional, full-time army and police forces in 1920, and their ragtag part-time IRA opponents is that the latter – or at least rural Volunteers – were intimately familiar with the hazards of mishandling firearms. They grew up in a world where almost every farm had a shotgun and a 'rook rifle' for vermin control, and so the rituals associated with the safe handling of firearms were second nature to them. A further, likely explanation is that most of the time even the most active Volunteers did not carry weapons: they kept them in hides or 'dumps' and retrieved them only for specific operational or training reasons, whereas most soldiers on duty were expected to carry weapons and ammunition at all times.

In built-up areas where the enemy controlled the streets and where successful attacks depended upon concealment of weapons and intentions until the last moment, and upon Volunteers being able to merge into the general civilian mass once firing had ceased, rifles were of little use because they were too long to be easily concealed by anyone carrying them. The somewhat shorter Thompson sub-machine gun, designed for close-quarter trench warfare, began to arrive in quantity from the United States in the early summer of 1921. It was more suitable for urban operations, but it was only used in a handful of attacks before the Truce (producing one fatality, John Rossiter, a groom and father of nine from Dublin, who died when a train carrying troops was fired on from Ballyfermot railway bridge on 24 June 1921).[9]

As the conflict intensified, so too did GHQ's strictures on training. Some of these suggest a disconnect between the theoretical requirements of a conventional army, and the exigencies of a guerrilla movement operating in both rural and urban settings. One instance of GHQ's penchant for senseless instructions is

General Order no. 25, which ordained that 'purchases' of weapons 'shall in future be made by no Volunteer outside his own area', an edict which made higher organisational sense but was meaningless: why should a Limerick IRA man passing through Dublin not buy a revolver from a drunken soldier if he had the chance?[10] Few GHQ instructions, however, were as out of touch with realities as the Training Order of 1 July 1921, which solemnly ordained that 'Officers commanding all Units will ensure that all officers, NCOs and men are able to swim', detailing how the 'best swimmer in each Company' should instruct everyone else. Officers should ensure that training took place 'only at perfectly safe reaches of river, lake, or sea and that proper lifesaving appliances are available'.[11]

Too Young to Die, but Not to Kill? Kevin's Age in a Military Context

Kevin was only fifteen when he joined the Volunteers, the same age as Todd Andrews,[12] and just eighteen years and nine months when he was executed. The issue of his age merits consideration, particularly because one of the arguments adduced in favour of commutation of his sentence was his youth.

Such youth in a fighter was by no means uncommon in either conventional or unconventional conflicts in the early part of the twentieth century. During the Great War, eighteen was the minimum age for conscription into the British armed services, but in practice youths could volunteer at an earlier age by the simple means of lying. In Germany the minimum age for recruitment was seventeen years, but again youths could and did enlist voluntarily at a lower age. Recruiters were notoriously unfastidious about the matter. Field Marshal Sir William Robertson, Chief of the Imperial General Staff from 1916 to 1918, had been underage when enlisting as a trooper in the 16th Lancers in November 1877.[13] John Condon from Waterford, a Royal Irish Rifles private who died fighting on

24 May 1915, is termed the 'youngest known battle casualty of the war' by the Commonwealth War Graves Commission, although there is considerable doubt whether he was really just fourteen as claimed.[14] He was one of thousands of youths who lied about their age on enlistment; another was James Tormey of Westmeath, who joined the Connaught Rangers in February 1915 aged fifteen, winning promotion to lance corporal before being discharged as underage when his parents wrote to the War Office a year later. He was of the Athlone Brigade IRA when killed in February 1921 in an engagement with Crown forces, not long after his older brother was shot dead near the wire fence in Ballykinlar internment camp.[15] Michael Joseph Sheehan CBE (1899–1975) of Kanturk, Cork, who retired as a brigadier general in the Indian army in 1947, was commissioned as a 2nd lieutenant in the Royal Munster Fusiliers in 1915, and is said to be the youngest British officer to serve on the Western Front in the Great War (his father Daniel Sheehan MP (1873–1948) also fought, and his two brothers were killed).[16]

There was also a separate military category of boy soldier, under which youths of fourteen and upwards could be recruited for non-combat roles such as band boys and buglers. They did, however, receive weapons training in anticipation of progression to full soldiering.[17]

Within the separatist movement, the Fianna Éireann initially admitted boys as young as eight. As they grew older, they received some arms training. As with analogous militaristic youth organisations elsewhere in Europe they were not intended to engage directly in combat until of military age, but rather to perform support roles such as scouting and carrying despatches. Two Fianna boys died during the Rising, their uniforms giving them the appearance of combatants to their enemies.[18] In June 1917 the Fianna's Eamon Murray mortally injured DMP Inspector Mills – 'I killed the man' – by striking him on the head with a hurley during a fracas, and in March 1919 unidentified uniformed youths shot and killed ex-soldier Alfred Pearson following a scuffle during an arms raid at his home on Richmond Road: a witness pleaded with them not to kill her, saying she was a Sinn Féiner herself.[19] Less than a month after Kevin's execution, 16-year-old Pat Deasy was killed during the West Cork IRA's ambush at Kilmichael on 28 November, one of three Volunteers shot during that celebrated and controversial engagement.

The War of Independence in Carlow

In Carlow even more than in Dublin, the armed wing of the independence movement developed slowly following the Rising and its aftermath of countrywide arrests of activists. John McGill, who joined the Rathvilly company on its formation in 1917, recalled that 'we had no arms. Our training was mainly drilling, field exercises and lectures on military subjects.'[20] Carlow was no different to the majority of counties in the slow pace at which the Irish Volunteers evolved into the IRA, moving, in Joost Augusteijn's phrase, from public defiance towards guerrilla warfare.

Operations in rural Carlow presented quite different challenges than in the city: other than the railway there was no public transport, and Volunteers travelled mainly by bicycle or on foot, or occasionally by pony and trap. They had to know the lie of the land, or to be guided by somebody who did. In 1920 Carlow was a quiet county: there were very few ambushes or armed confrontations with Crown forces, and almost no aggressive patrolling by the police. The main feature of the year was the progressive withdrawal of police from small vulnerable outlying stations, part of a policy pursued across the country. This enabled the Carlow IRA to destroy abandoned police barracks, exercises which had considerable propaganda value. If well planned and executed, these operations involved little risk and strengthened both the morale of the local IRA and their prestige and authority. Across Ireland the greatest hazard involved in such destructive operations was not Crown forces, but the highly flammable petrol used by the incendiaries to destroy abandoned buildings.

There were just three conflict-related deaths in the county during 1920, all the responsibility of the IRA. On 8 September Volunteers held up a RIC patrol outside Tullow. The intention was apparently only to disarm the police, but when they resisted constables Timothy Delaney and John Gaughan were shot and killed outright: *The Wicklow People* claimed that the two men had already submitted their resignations from the force.[21] John Doyle, a farm labourer, father of seven children, and suspected informer from Wexford, was abducted, held for a night, interrogated, court-martialled and killed just inside the Carlow county boundary at Knockroe on 20 September. This was the work of the North Wexford Brigade.[22] A further three alleged civilian spies were killed in Carlow in 1921: a businessman who had stood up to the IRA and his solicitor who were killed in a raid; and an ex-serviceman, Michael Hackett, who was abducted, shot and secretly buried.[23]

In terms of deaths arising from political conflict, Carlow, the smallest of the twelve Leinster counties, was the fifth most violent per head of population.[24] Of the thirteen deaths attributable to political violence in Carlow between 1919 and 1921, the most significant blow struck was in March 1921 at Mullanagaun, when the Carlow Brigade's ASU was caught off guard, while training in open country, by a combined police and military patrol. One civilian and three Volunteers were killed and six captured, and the unit was effectively destroyed just as the armed campaign entered its most violent phase.[25] Similar calamities caused by lax security in other small counties had a similar effect: in the same month at Selton Hill in Leitrim, Crown forces surprised a newly established ASU intended to ginger up the local IRA, killing six Volunteers, capturing three and wounding others. In May 1921 the West Cavan Brigade ASU was smashed at Lappinduff when one Volunteer was killed and a dozen were captured and sentenced to death, including experienced Belfast men sent down to galvanise the local battalion. Those setbacks put an end to any chance of significant IRA activity against Crown forces in those two counties.[26]

Dublin was not immune from such disasters where large numbers of Volunteers assembled for training purposes. On the eve of Kevin's ill-fated Church Street operation, chief of staff Dick Mulcahy and other senior GHQ officers who were observing a trial of new munitions narrowly escaped capture at Kilmashogue mountain, when Auxiliaries surprised an entire IRA company nearby who were engaged, unarmed, in drilling: one Volunteer was killed and over forty were arrested. The very fact that as late as September 1920 the Dublin IRA had thought it safe to gather openly in such large numbers near the city is itself a reflection of how relatively quiet the city had been up to then. All that was, of course, soon to change dramatically.[27]

Students as Part-time Soldiers

There is no evidence to suggest that university students were any more or less suited to Volunteer life than any other segment of Irish society. Students had certain advantages: unlike men in regular employment, or tied to a farm, or with families to support, they had a good deal of free time during the day, and it was easy enough to dodge a lecture or two if needs be. Most were in their late teens or early twenties.

In UCD medical and engineering students were proportionately more likely to join the IRA than were those studying law or the arts. According to Donal O'Donovan, four medical students were among the twenty-six Volunteers assigned to the Monk's Bakery operation: Kevin, Tom Kissane, Liam Grimley and Mick Robinson.[28] Various UCD medical, dental and veterinary students became significant military and paramilitary figures, some

eventually choosing the life of a soldier over the profession for
which they were preparing.

At 9 a.m. on 14 April 1920, Detective Henry Kells was walking
down Camden Street on his way to work. At the corner of Montagu
Street, two young men stepped out and shot him dead. One of
the killers was 20-year-old Hugo MacNeill, like Kevin a medical
student, who had joined the Fianna in 1916 and the Volunteers in
1919. MacNeill went on to take part in the equally cold-blooded
killing of a suspected intelligence officer on the morning of Bloody
Sunday, 21 November 1920. He never finished his studies – partly,
he claimed, for financial reasons – instead becoming a pro-Treaty
officer and fighting with distinction during the civil war. Some say
he commanded the firing squad which carried out the Cosgrave
government's decision to execute without trial on 8 December 1922
the four leading anti-Treatyites Liam Mellowes, Dick Barrett, Rory
O'Connor and Joe McKelvey captured in the Four Courts in the
first days of the civil war. Whatever the impact upon MacNeill of
his experience of close-up killing, it did not prevent him having an
exceptional career. His leadership abilities were quickly recognised,
and he was one of six officers sent to the United States for command
and staff training at Fort Leavenworth in 1926–7. He returned with
his reputation for cerebral soldiering enhanced. Selected to lead the
1st Division of the hastily expanded army in 1940, tasked with the
northward defence of the state from aggression, his possible Nazi
sympathies caused security and diplomatic headaches for the state;
but no one impugned his professional competence.[29]

Other medical students who took easily to clandestine warfare
included Bobby Bonfield, who Kevin had known since his year in
St Mary's in 1915–16; Seán Dowling, a would-be writer pushed
into the dental profession by his family, who was a Dublin Brigade
officer during the War of Independence, was 'out' on Bloody
Sunday, held senior rank on the anti-Treaty side in the civil war
and retained his links with extreme republicanism for decades

while tending to his patients' teeth; Andy Cooney, who was 'out' on Bloody Sunday, made his name as a GHQ organiser in Kerry in 1921, briefly became chief of staff of the anti-state IRA in the 1920s and ended up practising in the United States; and Seán Hyde, who attempted to establish an anti-Treaty mounted unit during the civil war, and became a vet.[30] Dr Con Ward of Monaghan, already in practice in Castleblaney by 1919, was a formidable, unrelenting presence within the leadership of the Monaghan IRA under Eoin O'Duffy, in a county where the IRA was responsible for as many civilian as police and military deaths.[31]

To that list can be added UCD's Martin Finn and Michael O'Hanlon (involved on Bloody Sunday), both of whom went on to qualify, and Dan Bryan (1900–1985) from Kilkenny, whom I knew well in his last years.[32] Entering UCD as a medical student in 1917, by 1919 Bryan was, in the words of his one-time army intelligence subordinate Douglas Gageby of *The Irish Times*, full-time 'at the game' of intelligence to the detriment of his studies. 'Out' on Bloody Sunday at Mount Street Bridge in an intelligence role, Bryan became a professional soldier. He developed an unparalleled reputation both within the army and amongst the Allied intelligence community for his sophisticated management of counter-espionage and security problems during the Emergency.[33] Another medical student to make his mark on the conflict was Galwayman Louis Darcy, dubbed 'the Michael Collins of the West' by police intelligence chief Ormonde Winter. Darcy, who had studied at the College of Surgeons before becoming a full-time revolutionary as a GHQ organiser, was OC Headfort Battalion, Galway No. 1 Brigade when, possibly through treachery, he was captured. He was killed by Auxiliaries, supposedly while attempting to escape, at the spot where an RIC constable had been shot some time before.[34]

The most celebrated of all UCD medical students-turned-warriors was Ernie O'Malley (1897–1957), a man who like Seán Dowling combined a yearning for a literary life with an appetite for clandestine warfare. He was variously revered and dreaded for his work as a GHQ organiser in different parts of the country from 1919 onwards. O'Malley was diagnosed with neurasthenia (otherwise known as shell shock or PTSD) by a New York psychiatrist in the 1930s. He became a close friend of Kitby Barry and her husband Jim Moloney, for whom he gave the pensions board a powerful reference: Moloney was 'always eager to fight' and next to the battalion OC, was 'the best officer' in the 4th Battalion, Third Tipperary Brigade.[35]

We might also note the case of South African-born Brendan Muldoon, initially a Volunteer in the 1st Battalion, Carlow Brigade while a student at Knockbeg. He came to UCD to study engineering in 1919 and joined the Dublin Brigade. Amongst his actions were an attack on a military lorry near North Frederick Street in which he was slightly hurt and his comrade, fellow UCD engineering student Dermot O'Dwyer, was mortally wounded. In a subsequent operation Muldoon lay in wait in a house on Donore Avenue to kill a spy, although the target did not materialise.[36]

From such instances it appears that university students were as willing to become accomplished close-up killers as were young men of lesser education and prospects. An example from University College Cork (UCC) is Cormac Ó Cuilleánain (1900–1970), a Volunteer in the 5th Battalion, Cork No. 1 Brigade. In 1942 he wrote somewhat testily that 'if the [Pensions] Board believes' that his poor results in his first and second years of study for his BA were due to 'drink, women or dogs and not to my activities' they would be mistaken, as he was engaged full-time with the Riverstown company. Otherwise 'by now I should have been a first-rate Gaelic scholar – not the third-rate one that I am'. On one occasion he and a comrade captured and 'executed' two 'Cameron bucks', i.e. soldiers caught sneaking up the railway line from Queenstown at night, presumed to be assassins but possibly deserters. He later took part in the execution of 'a small rat of a fellow ... captured

... during [the] Truce', and in June 1922 that of ex-RIC constable Thomas Williams, kidnapped in Laois and brought back to Cork because the IRA wrongly thought him implicated in the March 1920 killing of mayor Tomás MacCurtain. When he died in 1970 the *Cork Examiner* simply stated that this 'noted Gaelic scholar' had begun his studies 'at a very troubled period of the country's history' before waxing eloquent upon his academic achievements.[37]

In Kevin's case, of course, he had taken the decision to fight and if necessary, to kill and to die two years before he had even left school for university.

The British Response to Increasing IRA Activity

The early months of 1920 saw not simply a significant increase in violence in different parts of the island but major changes in how the protagonists pursued their aims. The IRA largely acted along lines laid down by GHQ to make large parts of the country ungovernable by emasculating the police. Attacks on small remote RIC barracks led to their abandonment and to the concentration of police in larger barracks in the towns. The RIC thus ceased to be an everyday presence in large parts of rural Ireland, particularly in Munster, reducing contact with the public, leaving large areas without any law enforcement and reducing the police's ability to accumulate local information.

The last months of 1919, marked by the IRA's dramatic attempt on the life of the viceroy Lord French, saw the culmination of lengthy disputes within Dublin Castle on how to cope with the rise of Sinn Féin, the establishment of Dáil Éireann and the growth in disorder and violence. The RIC Inspector General Sir Joseph Byrne, a Catholic career soldier who had been brought in to the RIC after the Rising, had been critical of the military's failure to support the police effectively, had opposed the introduction of specially recruited temporary police, and had argued that the government's strategy should be to open channels of communication with moderates within the Sinn Féin movement. He was pushed out on the grounds that he had 'lost his nerve' (he was later vindicated and rehabilitated by Sir Warren Fisher of the Treasury, but did not return to Ireland).[38] Byrne was replaced by a more pliable officer from Belfast, T.J. Smyth, who raised no objections to the introduction of temporary constables recruited from the ranks of unemployed ex-servicemen. Thus the 'Black and Tans' were born.

When the ill-prepared Black and Tans were mixed in with the regular RIC from January 1920 onwards, the results were as General Byrne had warned: discipline largely collapsed and police restraint in the face of provocation disappeared. On 22 May 1920 Inspector General Smyth told Dublin Castle he feared the force would either collapse or run amok. But by that time the government in London had decided effectively to coerce the general population across nationalist Ireland.[39] On 6 February 1920 the Chief of the Imperial General Staff Sir Henry Wilson noted that 'Lloyd George [is] all out for blood in Ireland', determined to crush Irish disorder while the Government of Ireland bill made its way into law: French's private secretary, a highly partisan Ulster unionist, told Wilson that 'no man's life is safe, spies and murderers everywhere … Johnny French [is] brave as a lion, but so erratic and unbalanced'.[40] Some ministers, particularly Winston Churchill (Secretary of State for War until mid-February 1920, and thereafter colonial secretary), were convinced that violence was the only way to crush Irish separatist disorder, and that such violence should be meted upon the population generally. The spread of unofficial police reprisals, including targeted killings in Cork, Tipperary and Limerick as well as indiscriminate coercion of the civilian population and widespread destruction of property, was quietly applauded and encouraged in London even as it began to shock British public opinion. To that end a new elite gendarmerie, the Auxiliary Cadets, recruited from battle-hardened ex-officers, was introduced into Ireland in August 1920.

In March 1920 Sir Hamar Greenwood was appointed Chief Secretary for Ireland in succession to Ian Macpherson, who, although in favour of coercion, was considered to have lost his nerve. Greenwood, a dim Canadian lawyer who had returned to the colours and fought throughout the Great War, became the butt of opposition fury and derision in the House of Commons, where his job was to defend the government's conduct in Ireland. Shortly after Greenwood's appointment, the higher echelons of Dublin Castle were purged of political partisans and a cadre of very able officials were sent over from London under the leadership of Sir John Anderson, who as Joint Under Secretary took effective control of administrative affairs. Their main tasks were to overhaul the decrepit machinery of Irish government, in preparation for a political solution falling short of complete independence; to provide dispassionate advice to London about conditions in Ireland; and to open secret lines of communication to the separatist leadership, in anticipation of an eventual agreed cessation of violence and negotiations leading to a final settlement. But this new cohort of civilian officials had no control whatsoever over the security forces, police or military.

Ulster diehard though he was, Wilson was appalled by the unfolding shambles in Ireland. He advised General Sir Nevil Macready, appointed as General Officer Commanding (GOC) in Ireland at the end of March, to get a grip on affairs and curb unofficial reprisals by publishing 'lists of the head Sinn Feiners and shoot by roster' in retaliation for IRA violence.[41] Only by such means could the army maintain its own discipline, and rebel activity be penalised in a focussed way rather than through punishing the public generally.

Macready's greatest problem was that a new police supremo, General Hugh Tudor, was appointed in May, over whom he had no control. Neither in practice did the incompetent, inconsistent blusterer Lord French, as Henry Wilson observed: 'poor little man he is so weak and pliable and then has such inconsequential gusts of illogical passion. He is an Imperialist, a Democrat, a Home Ruler all at the same time. Poor man.'[42] Tudor, who looked to Churchill rather than to Hamar Greenwood for policy guidance, saw his job not as containing police excesses, from reprisals against towns to targeted killings, but as directing them: indeed, Henry Wilson was taken aback in September when in the course of a long talk with Tudor and Churchill, Tudor 'made it very clear that the Police and the Black and Tans and the 100 Intelligence Officers are all carrying out reprisal murders'. Wilson was 'glad that I am in no way responsible for Tudor and that I have protested for months against this method of out-terrorizing the terrorists'.[43]

Macready's intentions and actions were to prove significant for Kevin. What he wanted above all was to see IRA men caught and punished through the legal system, if needs be through military courts, rather than shot out of hand or while supposedly trying to escape. He also argued for reprisals against property to become government policy, which would enable these to be carried out in a contained and targeted fashion. By the time that London agreed to a system of 'official reprisals', however, rioting police had set fire to towns such as Lahinch, Trim (whose destruction Wilson termed 'a fatal policy and the negation of government' in September), Tubbercurry and Balbriggan, while the burning of Cork city centre in December showed that, even when troops retained their discipline, the police were beyond Macready's control.[44]

Macready needed to see IRA men tried, convicted and hanged. It was Kevin's misfortune to be the first Volunteer to become available for such treatment.

Into Action in Carlow and Dublin

Kevin, of course, was not privy to British debates about how to control Ireland in 1920. He was busy with his studies, his social life, and his Volunteer activities. His IRA experience was somewhat unusual in that he was an active member of two units at once, operating in very different conditions: in Dublin he was a section leader in H Company, 1st Battalion, Dublin Brigade; when in Tombeagh during university vacations, he was in C Company, 3rd Battalion, Carlow Brigade. In comparison with most elements of the IRA nationally, both units could be classed as having been fairly active during his time with them.

Kevin took part in one or two minor operations in Carlow such as the cutting of telegraph wires, but it was in Dublin that he first saw significant action. In May the Dublin Brigade decided to mount a raid for arms on a military outpost in the King's Inn at the top of Constitution Hill. Joe Dolan of 'the Squad' reconnoitred the buildings, noting the general laxity of the soldiers. The IRA waited for a fine day, when it was expected that soldiers would be wandering around the grounds rather than sitting in the guardroom. The carefully planned operation eventually went ahead on 1 June.[45] (Kevin's participation in the action meant he missed an examination in UCD, but he made little of this academic hiccup.[46])

The King's Inn raid disclosed extraordinary military slackness, but also a high degree of organisation by the IRA: the operation had taken only six minutes instead of the expected seven, and the raiders got clean away with their haul. But for months the obvious message about the need for constant alertness did not really sink in; for most ordinary soldiers, duty in Dublin continued to be a matter of routine. The army itself was not yet an IRA target, and serious street attacks on troops were a thing of the future. Furthermore, as Henry Wilson noted bitterly at the end of March, the army in Ireland was composed chiefly of 'wholly untrained raw children'.[47]

The continuing laxity of barracks life in Dublin is well illustrated by events in Richmond (Portobello) barracks on 20 September, the very morning of the Monk's Bakery operation that saw Kevin's capture. Sergeant George Pollington, a highly decorated Great War veteran, had been discharged from the army in 1918 suffering from shell shock. A year later he was permitted to re-enlist in the Worcestershire Regiment, and was posted to Dublin. He was drinking in the NCOs' mess with May Fitzpatrick, a young woman whom he had kept in the barracks, contrary to regulations, for the previous two nights. Out of his mind from drink, he announced his intention to kill her. The barman hid Pollington's rifle, but the sergeant went out and found another, returned, and shot dead a fellow NCO who tried to intervene. Another NCO then stepped in front of May declaring, 'If you shoot her, you shoot me.' Pollington killed him, but May Fitzpatrick managed to escape through a window. That such events should unfold in a well-guarded barracks supposedly supervised by orderly officers says little for British military discipline and morale in Dublin.[48]

A few weeks after the King's Inn raid Kevin, on holiday in Tombeagh, was prominent in his first significant operation with C (Rathvilly) Company, 3rd Battalion, Carlow Brigade. The company's first major action, the successful destruction of the recently abandoned Hacketstown RIC barracks, had taken place in April.[49] In July they received GHQ sanction for a raid on the late John Redmond's lodge at Aughavannagh in Co. Wicklow. This was occupied by Redmond's son Captain William Redmond MP, his sister Johanna Green and her husband Max. The company had received permission to burn down the building, for fear that it might become a base for Crown forces (there might, of course, also have been an element of spite against Redmondites in the planned action). GHQ officer Mick McDonnell, already an experienced assassin, took part, along with the Barry brothers and other Volunteers of the Rathvilly Company under OC Matt Cullen. In the return of activities submitted by former officers of the Carlow Brigade in the mid-1930s to facilitate the administration of the 1934 Military Service Pensions Act, ten men including the Barry brothers are listed under 'Attack on Aughavannagh Military Barracks, July 1920'.[50]

Cullen recalled how on a wet night the party cycled the fifteen miles across the mountains to Aughavannagh. Finding the main door securely bolted, they smashed a pane of glass in a back door: 'Kevin ... got in through it, head first.' Willie Redmond confronted him, carrying a club, but 'the sight of Kevin's automatic vanished the pluck of the Captain'. There followed a row in which Johanna Green took a spirited part. Redmond 'asked us to go through the place and see the loss: pictures and valuable papers etc.', which would be destroyed were the house to be burnt down. He said that as an MP he was in a strong position to prevent the house being requisitioned by Crown forces. The Volunteers withdrew and considered the matter, before returning. They told Redmond that they would spare the building but would hold him responsible and kill him if the building was taken over by military or police. Such a threat was clearly in breach of the Volunteers' own rules, which laid stress on honouring 'the laws of war'. It illustrates the point that the realities of conflict, even at a relatively early stage and in a quiet area, were more brutal and morally ambiguous than republican rhetoric and propaganda would admit.

Similar ambiguity surrounds Kevin's last big operation while in Tombeagh. Although the IRA was short of weapons, the country was not. In addition to the shotguns ubiquitous in rural Ireland, thousands of weapons had been brought home by individuals as souvenirs of war. Furthermore, many rifles remained in the hands of people who had served in the National Volunteers and the Ulster Volunteer Force before the Great War; these weapons being the private property of their holders.

GHQ, expecting that the British authorities would soon compel people to hand in weapons for safe keeping, directed the IRA to commandeer as many as possible while these were still in private hands. This general raid for arms was to take place across the country on the night of 31 August/1 September. Although not intended as political or sectarian acts of intimidation and expropriation, in practice most of the homes raided by armed parties of Volunteers were those of people who were regarded as hostile to the separatist movement – sympathetic families had either already made their weapons available to the Volunteers or had been deprived of them by the authorities.

In some areas raids went off without trouble. In others they were fiercely resisted: across county Monaghan four Volunteers were killed while raiding Unionist and Redmondite farms, and overall the action greatly accentuated sectarian tensions there.[51] In Carlow things were far calmer. Thirteen houses were reportedly raided, some weapons being seized without trouble. It was, however, very different at the Church of Ireland rectory in Tullow, home of the Reverend Charles Stuart Stamford Ellison. Matt Cullen recalled how he, Kevin and another Volunteer marched up to the door and demanded admittance. Instead, 'the minister let down the window' and, presumably thinking that the IRA had come to burn his home, or to kill him, or both, fired with a shotgun at 'point blank range'. Although no one was hit, 'some of our men got a fright'. Cullen recalled that 'Kevin with an automatic, Mike Mac[Donnell] and myself with revolvers' replied. They took cover, firing for some time before withdrawing. He explained that 'we did not like' to shoot a clergyman without orders, which begs the question of why they returned fire in the first place. They did not revisit the rectory, as the military took away Ellison's gun for safe keeping.[52]

Had the clergyman been wounded or killed, the consequences would surely have been severe. Whatever the attackers' motives, the shooting of a Protestant rector defending his home would have been seen as a shocking sectarian act. Between 1919 and 1921 just three Irish clergymen were deliberately killed. In 1920 Auxiliaries shot two Catholic priests, young Father Griffin in Galway and elderly Canon Magner in Cork. In 1921 in Bawnmore, Cavan, the elderly Church of Ireland Canon John Finlay was killed by a blow to the neck from a maverick Volunteer during a house-burning in Cavan.

Canon Magner's killer was convicted of his murder but found insane, while the man who killed Finlay was shunned by his comrades and condemned from the pulpit by his parish priest.[53] The killing of clergymen was perhaps the only matter upon which the Irish churches were ecumenical in their denunciations.

Curiously, the Carlow IRA's fight with Ellison received little press attention, whereas a 'dastardly' attack the same day by armed men on the house of a Church of Ireland rector in the adjacent county of Kilkenny, was discussed by a number of newspapers – ironically, the perpetrators there were three drunken ex-soldiers, who were probably lucky that the police caught them before the IRA did. Yet the shooting at Canon Ellison's home must have sent shivers down the spine of every Protestant in Carlow: when might the IRA come for them?[54] It was probably fortunate, during the campaign to save Kevin from the gallows, that his record of activism in Carlow was either not known to or not publicised by the British authorities. It would have made useful counter-propaganda.

Kevin's next significant IRA engagement was to be his last.

CHAPTER FOUR

Church Street

The Plan

Donal O'Donovan writes that the plan arose from the observations of two Volunteers who, loitering in the Church Street area for other reasons, noticed that a military lorry with an armed party of soldiers called regularly twice a week to Monk's Bakery at around 11 a.m. to collect bread for the army camp at Collinstown, north of the city. By O'Donovan's account, John Joe Carroll of H Company reconnoitred the bakery, and saw that in addition to the Church Street entrance a corridor accessible from the bakery yard led to a shop at 38 North King Street. This made the site an attractive one for an operation, which would depend on speed, timing and a quick getaway, as British troops were stationed in the nearby North Dublin Union.[1]

Carroll informed Seamus Kavanagh (1897–1962), captain of H Company, of this opportunity. Recalling the ease with which the King's Inn raid had been carried out, Kavanagh, a 23-year-old carpenter and cabinet-maker who had fought with credit as a company commander in 1916 in St Stephen's Green and the College of Surgeons, was keen to mount another coup.[2] He made his own reconnaissance, and was shown around the bakery and yard by a fellow carpenter who worked there. The purpose would not be to kill soldiers, but rather to take them by surprise and seize their weapons before they could resist.[3] The ploy had already been tried elsewhere, with success. Charlie McGoohan recalled how ten Leitrim Volunteers mixed with people leaving Mass near Drumreilly in order to approach a bogged-down military lorry, which was being guarded by six disconsolate soldiers: 'We were singing and indulging in some horseplay amongst ourselves. As we were about to pass the lorry we turned and rushed the soldiers … The whole thing was a rather tame affair. We got 6 rifles, the first that any of our company had ever seen, and we were really thrilled by their appearance.' While 'the poor Tommies' walked back to Ballinamore, the Volunteers set fire to the lorry and carried off their booty.[4]

Kavanagh's account of events as given to the BMH was along much the same lines as Carroll's, though he accorded himself a more prominent role in developing the scheme. Twenty-five men would take part, assigned to various tasks: guarding against enemy reinforcements, covering the raiding party, moving the captured weapons, disarming the soldiers, taking control of the bakery office and disabling the telephone. The lorry would be enveloped right and left by harmless-looking young pedestrians coming along Church Street, who would suddenly produce their weapons and force the cooped-up soldiers to surrender without a fight. The NCO and two soldiers who would be collecting the bread in the bakery itself would be unarmed, and therefore easy to subdue for the Volunteers assigned to enter the office and disable the telephone. The captured weapons could be carried through the bakery yard to the side passage, which led onto North King Street, from where they would be loaded into the waiting transport and whisked away while the Volunteers dispersed amongst the general throng. If the operation went as planned, the signal to withdraw would be a whistle blast from Kavanagh; if, however, there was any shooting, Kavanagh said that Volunteers were to disperse without any signal from him.

This is an important and controversial point, because Kevin maintained that he took cover because he heard no signal to withdraw. Other Volunteers differed over the question of whether there was an agreed withdrawal signal in the event of a fight. Furthermore, Seán O'Neill claimed that Kavanagh had not even known of the initial scheme, which 'we thought a "pudding" … [until] we had to acquaint him of it' after receiving clearance from the Dublin Brigade commander, Dick McKee. But Kavanagh said that it was he who secured the permission first of his battalion, and then of McKee, to carry out the operation as it was just outside H Company's area. Kavanagh said McKee subjected him to a 'severe cross-examination' of every detail of his plan before approving it and fixing the date for Monday 20 September.[5] Who are we to believe, and why do their accounts differ on fundamentals?

The Barrys certainly felt that Kavanagh had let Kevin down by not giving a signal to retreat. Their view of him may also have been coloured by the fact that he had in their eyes proved to be a turncoat during the civil war, initially joining the anti-Treaty forces before becoming an intelligence operative for Tom Cullen and Liam Tobin and eventually securing a commission in the Free State army. Yet as the former captain of H Company he played a leading part in organising annual masses and other functions commemorating Kevin over the years.[6] Whether handshakes were accepted or refused on such occasions, at which pro-Treatyites and militant republicans mingled annually, and which Mary Barry attended for many years along with her family, is unknown.[7]

The Operation

H Company had clear advantages going into the operation: they chose the target, the location and the time; they had the experience of the King's Inn success behind them; they had the benefit of complete surprise; and, armed with pistols, they were better equipped for an engagement at close quarters than the party they were attacking. Although six of the soldiers carried rifles, five were cramped in the

back of the lorry with their weapons upright between their knees –
two on each side, and one with his back to the cab; the sixth was in
the cab beside the driver. Furthermore, no guard was posted beside
the vehicle. But the operation did not go as planned and it failed
in its original objective of capturing arms. It occasioned the deaths
of three young soldiers and of one Volunteer, and the wounding of
another.

It is not unusual for witnesses to differ about details of events
which they experienced, particularly after an interval of more than
three decades. But the discrepancies between Kavanagh's account
and that of O'Neill are on major points. All IRA sources agree that
Kevin was a few minutes late when the party assembled: Kavanagh
said Kevin explained that he had had to call into UCD to find out
about his repeat examination scheduled for that afternoon (whereas
family sources maintained that he had been at Mass). He was issued
with a .38 Mauser semi-automatic and Parabellum ammunition
rather than the Webley revolver with which he was more familiar:
'he was not pleased with this, and the other Volunteers chafed him
about it'.[8] On the face of it, the Mauser was superior in design and
operation to the Webley: sleeker, better balanced in the hand and
with a larger magazine. The gun was much coveted: J.J. Lawless of
the Dublin Brigade, an experienced armourer, thought it 'an ideal
weapon' for city fighting, although Bill Stapleton knew some to be
'tricky and unsafe'. Others noted that it required careful preparation
and handling. Leitrim's Charlie McGoohan, a Great War veteran
who was a noted marksman, loved the weapon, as it had 'a nice
smooth trigger action and [was] very accurate', but it was prone to
jamming if loaded with 'poor ammunition ... I believe it was one of
these weapons ... which was responsible for the capture of Kevin
Barry.'[9] Seán O'Neill recalled that Kevin 'did not like' the weapon:
'If you have not all the ammunition with the [same] mark and date
it causes a jam.' Loading and fitting the magazine correctly was
also a more complicated exercise than with a revolver.[10]

On 20 September the lorry was later than expected so the Volunteers had to loiter around the area, trying to look inconspicuous. When it arrived, the NCO in charge went in to check that the bread was ready, then came out and ordered two bandsmen on fatigues duty to follow him back in to collect it. None were armed. According to the evidence presented at Kevin's court martial, six soldiers and the driver remained sitting in the lorry, meaning that there were ten soldiers involved.[11] But Seamus Kavanagh claimed he counted nineteen soldiers in all, and Seán O'Neill said there were twenty-three. Kavanagh said he eventually gave the order to move, using his handkerchief as the signal, because he was concerned that the military might notice so many young men hanging around. As three groups moved towards the lorry,

> one of the Volunteers (not Kevin Barry) as a result probably of over anxiety ran out in front shouting 'hands up' and fired; it was now obvious we were in a fight, as most of the British troops were standing up grasping their rifles and watching us.
>
> I gave the order to fire ... We drew our guns and charged, shouting as we ran forward. Some of the troops put their hands up, others returning the fire ... I saw some of the British falling ...
>
> We began to retreat as arranged firing as we went. I could see more ... soldiers falling as if shot or trying to take cover behind their dead and wounded comrades. Their officer was certainly hit, as I saw his head and arm slumped over the side of the cab [there was no officer present].[12]

Seán O'Neill, by contrast, stated that when ordered, 'everyone' on the lorry kept their hands up 'for about 10 seconds, but when they found only one man covering them ... they grabbed their rifles'.

Either way, in the fight that followed one soldier was killed by a shot to the chin – 15-year-old Private Harold Washington, whom Kitby in one account maintained that Kevin said he killed with his fourth shot before his gun jammed for the third time. Private Thomas Humphries and Private Marshall Whitehead were mortally wounded.[13]

The first recorded witnesses to the attack were Bandsman Smith and Bandsman Noble, both of whom were in a corridor in the bakery when they heard shots outside and were then fired on from the yard. The attackers 'were all very young men, and of different sizes, up to 5' 10", clean shaven some with caps and trilby hats'. The bakery office staff – the manager Mr Fehily, the clerk Mr Molloy and a Miss Byrne – only realised something was amiss when two armed men came in, one seizing the telephone receiver before leaving, when he ran into Lance Sergeant Bank, who struck him with his fists before being pistol-whipped on the head. 'Immediately afterwards' Molloy 'heard a number of shots outside, and became frightened, when he with the Manager and the Lady Clerk ran upstairs. They cannot describe the men, except that they were good looking, and respectably dressed, and they would not know them again.'[14]

Capture and Interrogation

Lance Sergeant Banks returned to the yard and armed himself with Private Washington's rifle. He then spotted Kevin lying face down under the front of the lorry with a gun and ordered him to come out. Kevin did so, dropping his weapon and putting up his hands. Placed in the lorry beside the dead Washington and the seriously wounded Humphries and Whitehead, he was driven to the North Dublin Union. It must have been a somewhat awkward journey. A bystander helped Bandsman Noble to the Union, and Smith walked with him.

The prosecutor asserted that at some point, when asked to explain what he had been doing by a lieutenant of the Lancashire Fusiliers, Kevin stated that 'We were after the rifles,' and later that he had been ordered to take part by an officer.[15] Kevin's own account of his experiences in the hours immediately after his arrest does not mention this, and the claim was not tested during his court martial because no questions were asked of the prosecution. But his own account, given in an affidavit prepared at GHQ insistence, is convincing precisely because of the matter-of-fact, understated way in which he described his interrogation.

It was not until 28 October that Dick McKee told Kitby that Kevin must make a statement outlining his ill-treatment during interrogation after arrest. This affidavit, compiled by solicitor Seán O hUadaigh and Kevin with help from the Auxiliaries guarding him on military nomenclature, was a sober and credible account. The term 'torture' was applied to it by British sources – *The Times* of 30 October summarised it under the heading 'Alleged Torture in Ireland' – and Hamar Greenwood used the same term when disputing the affidavit's veracity in the House of Commons. Kevin never uttered that word himself and seems, probably rightly, not to have thought of the mistreatment in those terms.[16] What he described was bad enough:

> after I was placed in the defaulters' room two commissioned officers came in. They both belonged to the 1st Lancashire Fusiliers. They were accompanied by three sergeants of the same unit. One of the officers asked my name, which I gave. He then asked the names of my companions in the raid or attack. I refused to give them ... I persisted in refusing. He then sent a sergeant ... for a bayonet. When it was brought in the sergeant was ordered ... to point the bayonet at my stomach. The same question ... was repeated, with the same result. The

sergeant was then ordered to turn my face to the wall and point the bayonet to my back ... The sergeant then said he would run the bayonet into me if I did not tell ... I was turned round again. The same officer then said to me that if I persisted in my attitude he would turn me out to the men in the barrack square, and he supposed I knew what that meant with the men in their present temper. I said nothing. He then ordered the sergeant to put me face down on the floor and twist my arm. I was pushed down ... after my handcuffs were removed by the sergeant who went for the bayonet ... one of the sergeants knelt on the small of my back. The other two placed one foot each on my back and left shoulder, and the man who knelt on me twisted my right arm, held it by the wrist with one hand while he held my hair with the other to pull back my head.

My arm was twisted from the elbow joint. This continued to the best of my judgement for five minutes. It was very painful. The first officer was standing near my feet, and the officer who accompanied him was still present. During the twisting of my arm the first officer continued to question me as to ... my companions, and also asked me for the name of my company commander and any other officers. As I still persisted in refusing to answer these questions I was let get up, and I was again handcuffed. A civilian came in, and he repeated the questions with the same result. He informed me that if I gave all the information I knew I could get off. I was then left in the company of the military policeman, the two officers, the three sergeants and the civilian leaving together. I could certainly identify the officer who directed the proceedings ... I am not sure of the others, except the sergeant with the bayonet. My arm was medically treated

by an officer of the RAMC ... the following morning, and
by the prison hospital orderly afterwards for four or five
days.[17]

The treatment Kevin described was not dissimilar to that
endured by hundreds of suspected Volunteers across Ireland.
Edward Balfe gave an account of the handling of prisoners
by the Devonshire Regiment in 1920 in Enniscorthy, Wexford,
a quiet town in an extremely quiet county. He recalled that 'the
soldiers on either side began using their bayonet[s], stabbing
me all over the body'. He also received 'several clouts' and was
punched in the face in the barracks. He and other prisoners had
to undergo the 'terrible ordeal' of a daily 'bath' of cold water,
administered in the freezing yard by bucket and excruciatingly
painful rub-downs with a rough brush.[18] What is most surprising
about Kevin's initial interrogation is not that he was badly
roughed up and threatened – 'violently interrogated', as Liz
Curtis puts it in her sympathetic study of Irish nationalism, or 'ill
usage' as Frank Gallagher termed it – but that this phase ended
so quickly.[19]

It is striking that, once Kevin's identity was established,
no effort appears to have been made to ask the RIC in Carlow
about his activities there during his visits home in the university
vacations. This probably reflects the fact that the Dublin Military
District had not yet adopted a structured approach to the handling
of prisoners, whereby these would be questioned systematically
and repeatedly in order to elicit information and insights. Kevin
suffered physically from the brutality inflicted after his arrest, his
arm in a sling and his elbow requiring medical attention for some
days. Although the popular song records 'turn informer or we'll
kill you' and a warder reported that Kevin was offered thousands
of pounds to betray his comrades the night before his execution,
he was not subjected to any physical coercion thereafter. As with

other aspects of his story, his disinclination to dwell on the physical abuse, and also the manner in which he downplayed the fact of his refusal to yield to his man-handlers, makes his restrained account all the more credible.

CHAPTER FIVE

Defending Kevin

The Legal Route

GHQ's slow and uncertain reaction to news of Kevin's impending trial has to be seen in the context of the many other important pressures at the time. GHQ was bent on intensification of the military campaign. On 1 November GHQ organiser Ernie O'Malley indiscreetly wrote, in a notebook later seized by British forces in Tipperary, that 'England [is] to go up in lumps [a reference to a planned bombing offensive there]; also intelligence officers in Dublin' (the systematic killings of suspected British operatives, which eventually happened on Bloody Sunday, 21 November).[1] Furthermore, GHQ was aware that the Dublin Brigade was making plans to rescue Kevin from prison by force. If those succeeded, there would be no need for recourse to legal stratagems.

Kevin's was but one instance where the lives of Volunteer prisoners were in imminent danger. In London, Terence MacSwiney was approaching the end of his lengthy hunger strike, an exercise which, through skilful exploitation of his title of Lord Mayor of Cork, was commanding worldwide interest. In Cork jail, hunger-striking Volunteers Michael Fitzgerald and Joseph Murphy, to whose plight neither republican propaganda nor the newspapers devoted much attention, were wasting away. In India, no fewer than fourteen soldiers of the 1st Battalion, Connaught Rangers, were under sentence of death for mutiny.

Kevin's case was obviously of importance not simply in itself, but because he was the first republican to face a capital charge before a military court since 1916. It followed that GHQ had a wider interest in ensuring that his trial saw a rigorous and challenging testing of the new legal apparatus. Although he did not wish to be defended – and his family had accepted this – GHQ could, and did, initially overrule his objections (it is unclear whether Kevin's refusal to be represented predated GHQ's decision that he should be).[2]

The first formal stage in the investigation of the deaths of the three soldiers took place at the King George V military hospital in Arbour Hill, Dublin – now St Bricin's – on 21 September. Inquests were held in succession on John Doyle, the Volunteer killed in the Dublin mountains on 19 September, then on the two NCOs killed by their comrade in Portobello barracks on 20 September, and finally on the three soldiers who died as a result of 'the Church Street affray'. In their case, a sixteen-man jury unsurprisingly found that they died from gunshot wounds 'fired by some person unknown'. As the military had captured one of the gunmen concerned, 'J. Berry, 58 South Circular Road, Medical Student', the Crown had a ready-made defendant for a capital charge.[3]

The soldiers who died were themselves extremely young: twenty, nineteen and fifteen. Although unattended by government ministers or Church potentates, their families may have drawn slight consolation from large public turnouts for the burials. The cortège for 19-year-old Marshall Whitehead, an only son of a Boer War veteran who had enlisted in October 1918, passed through streets 'thronged with people' in Halifax en route to the cemetery. His parents thanked everyone for their messages of sympathy 'and floral tributes', the military for arranging the funeral procession, and the police band for the 'beautiful music'.[4] 20-year-old Thomas Humphries, whose widowed mother had remarried, was buried with military ceremony in Bradford: *The Leeds Mercury* carried photographs of the funeral procession, of his coffin and bearers, and a portrait of him with a young girl (presumably a stepsister). He was also described as a 'youth', showing that Kevin did not have a monopoly on that term in describing those who died as a result of the Monk's Bakery clash.[5]

The portents for Kevin were inauspicious. Macready wanted a death sentence, which would send a message not only to the rebels but to Crown forces that the law would be upheld and applied rigorously. Sir Henry Wilson fully supported him, and endorsed the views of the Adjutant General, Sir George McDonough, who on 18 October wrote that if reprisals

> are necessary they must be recognised & controlled by competent authority. The present system of uncontrolled reprisals, not approved but yet condoned by the Gov[ernmen]t, is to be condemned in every way. It must lead to great hardship even to loyal citizens, & offers every opportunity to evil disposed persons to commit crimes & satisfy their own private animosities. Its effects on the discipline & morale of the troops must be disastrous.[6]

From Macready's point of view, the execution of a convicted IRA killer would be a modest but positive step in retaining control of his own forces, showing that the law could in due course deliver retribution for murder. Macready's view was that Kevin's death sentence should stand so that the increasing lawlessness of Crown forces could be contained. It would demonstrate to the army that the law was effective, and so reduce the incentive to conduct unofficial reprisals.

In his report for the week ending 31 October Macready called for corrective propaganda regarding 'the man Barry'. The significance of the soldiers' recorded ages – two were nineteen and one was twenty – was noted by Castle and military authorities and put into the scales in the propaganda war, but this had no impact in Ireland or internationally. It might have been different had the army known that in reality Private Washington was only fifteen, born in Salford on 24 October 1904, and that he was the second of his parents' sons to die in action.[7] The British might also have made much of the point that Kevin and his comrades had launched their attack while dressed as civilians. Thus he could scarcely claim the conventional privileges of a prisoner of war, being, rather, a *franc tireur* – a combatant dressed in civilian clothes and so indistinguishable from the general public – and therefore not entitled to the same legal protection as a captured uniformed combatant.[8] It was extremely seldom that IRA men fought or were captured in uniform, because civilian clothes were a necessary part of their cover. If Kitby's recollection is correct, her employer Ernest Aston was told by Hamar Greenwood that Kevin, though 'a child in years ... is a long time mixed up with that crowd'.[9] A press report, presumably relying on official sources, also stated that while very young he was already a 'corporal' in his unit.[10] It is curious that, having this knowledge about the extent of Kevin's military experience, the British did not disseminate it more effectively.

Not everyone was moved by Kevin's youth. The widow of Alan Bell, an elderly retired resident magistrate employed by the Castle to make secret inquiries who was hauled off a tram and shot in Ballsbridge in March 1920, asked a Castle official if Kevin had been one of his assassins: 'she said she would die happier if she thought that one of that gang had been wiped out'.[11]

Military officers made indifferent judges. The *Manual of Military Law* of 1914 stated that 'The object of military law is to maintain discipline among the troops and other persons forming part of or following an army.'[12] Officers were accustomed to act as members of what were essentially disciplinary tribunals with unusually severe powers, endowed upon them within a framework designed not for dispensing dispassionate justice but for maintaining order within the armed forces. An effective defence of Kevin by a skilled lawyer might not have affected the verdict, but could well have thrown up issues and considerations more or less beyond the comprehension of a court of officers, generating uncertainty about the new and untested law and procedures under which Kevin was tried. The court-martial process also left the exercise of clemency in the first instance in the hands of the General Officer Commanding (GOC) in Ireland, rather than with the head of government in Ireland, the viceroy Lord French. That undoubtedly made it harder for the government in London to interfere when representations were made directly to them, even if they had reservations about the utility of hanging so young a man who maintained that he had acted not as an assassin but merely as an ordinary soldier obeying orders.

In fact there was a parallel discussion in official circles in London about the nuances of the power of granting commutation to Irishmen convicted by court martial of a capital offence. This arose in respect of the fourteen Connaught Rangers who had been sentenced to death in the Punjab following the July 1920 mutiny. The India Office and the War Office differed about where discretion ultimately lay, the former maintaining that it was a political matter and the Indian army that it was an internal military issue.[13]

Kevin's case did receive a good deal of preparatory legal attention, but only from the Crown side.[14] There was acute dissatisfaction in London with the inability of the Dublin Castle authorities to bring a single successful prosecution for the murder of a policeman or soldier since 1916. In June, in anticipation of the Restoration of Order in Ireland Act (ROIA), Macready had directed that 'there should be the utmost speed in bringing civilians to trial by courts martial and that a roster of qualified officers should be drawn up in each command to facilitate this'.[15] The military authorities prepared the prosecution case against Kevin with particular care precisely because they knew it would be an important test of the new law and of the judicial procedures adopted, and that its course would probably have implications for other IRA prisoners, who would inevitably be charged with similar offences.

Kevin's determination not to be defended at his court martial presented his family, and particularly Kitby, with an appalling dilemma. Should she have argued or pleaded with him to get legal advice and to accept representation, in the interests of others who would assuredly be tried in due course under the same legislation? It was one thing for Kevin to say that he did not wish to be defended; quite another for him to be without legal guidance for almost a month. Given GHQ's masterly inactivity, one wonders why the family did not hire a solicitor themselves – not necessarily to persuade Kevin to change his mind but to make sure that he and everyone else understood the possible ramifications. A lawyer might also have been able to advise Kevin on how to comport himself, as this could have a bearing on the view the court would form of him. Until Kitby met Tim Healy KC (1855–1931), the leading barrister and sometime Irish Party MP, she and Kevin may have been under an illusion about the likely outcome of a court martial not only in terms of conviction but of the sentence and the speed with which it would be carried out.

Kevin was left unrepresented and uninformed about the nuances of his situation until solicitor Seán Ó hUadhaigh took over his case and met him for the first time just two days before the trial. Responsibility for that deplorable gap lies not with the British authorities, but with GHQ and with Kevin's family. For some days following his arrest, the family had obeyed GHQ's instructions not to visit Kevin lest this confirm his identity. Given that various fellow students from UCD did go to see him, GHQ's logic appears weak. The absence of contact with his family may have contributed to the solidification of Kevin's decision not to allow himself to be defended. So too may the absence of legal advice about the likely consequences of that course, not only for himself but for those

Volunteers who assuredly would follow him on capital charges before military courts.

On 30 September and 4 October, Kevin was brought from his cell to hear the sixteen witnesses who would be called by the Crown during the trial give depositions of their evidence. As David Foxton QC observes, his participation in this exercise suggests that he may not yet have decided to go undefended and to enter no plea.[16] He put twenty-six questions to five of the witnesses. It was hardly the action of someone determined not to defend himself, though it was also naive: Roger Sweetman SC, husband of Kevin's niece Ruth O'Rahilly, observed that 'it is a given amongst defence lawyers that you never cross-examine witnesses on deposition since it involves showing your hand to the prosecution and giving them the opportunity to mend theirs before trial'.[17] Was it this dispiriting episode which convinced Kevin not to mount any defence? Yet there were surely rich pickings for any competent lawyer to exploit in cross-examination in the various Crown witnesses, especially when appearing before a court of military officers, most of whom would not know one end of a statute or legal procedure from the other.

At some point 'during these weeks', Kitby recalled that she was instructed to go to see solicitor Eamon Duggan TD, who would be 'in charge of the defence'. Although Kevin had 'sent out messages to everybody that he was not to be defended', Duggan said he was acting on GHQ instructions, so Kevin and the family would have to comply. Evidently Duggan and Kitby did not hit it off when they met on Saturday 16 October. She said he complained to her about her brother's obstinacy, although he had not even spoken to Kevin. We have to proceed with some caution here: Duggan was to be one of the signatories to the Treaty of December 1921, which Kitby abhorred. It may be that her post-Treaty antagonism coloured her recollections of their encounter.

Kitby said that Duggan had only discovered that day that the trial was to take place the following Wednesday, just four days later.

Yet the original notice informing Kevin of the date of his trial is dated 12 October, and the signatory, a Captain Barrett, stated that 'I have by same post written to Mr Edmund Duggan, and I hope to be able to send him and you, tomorrow, a copy of the charge sheet and Summary of Evidence.'[18] This shows that Duggan was known to the military authorities as Kevin's solicitor by 12 October at the latest, and suggests that he received the summary of evidence no later than the next day. Duggan wrote seeking an adjournment, as he was involved in a case before the House of Lords on 20 October. On Monday 18 October he told Kitby that no adjournment had been granted, and he abruptly entrusted the entire file to Kitby to bring to fellow solicitor Seán Ó hUadhaigh, who he informed her would be taking over the case. Kitby later learned that Duggan was also availing of his London commitment to get married.[19]

Kitby called to see Ó hUadhaigh, who in turn despatched her with the summary of evidence to Tim Healy. Healy, however, was deeply pessimistic about Kevin's chances of acquittal. He tearfully advised Kitby, who had reported Kevin's 'fierce resentment at having to recognise the court', that unless allowed to plead his client's insanity, he could not mount a defence: Kitby 'refused this [option] out of hand, without consulting anybody'.[20] Consequently, Healy maintained it would be better if Kevin was not legally represented at all, as this 'would throw on the English conscience the responsibility of hanging an eighteen year old boy who refused to defend himself'. Healy expanded upon the essential 'badness of the English people' and remarked that 'if Bonar Law were premier he might be able to do something, but that Lloyd George was an unspeakable cad'. Kitby believed Healy thought her 'odd' because she would not join him in weeping: 'towards the end ... I was trying to cheer him up. I felt so sorry for an old man who could not understand a young soldier's point of view.' Healy 'gathered up a lot of hothouse fruit from the sideboard for my mother' and had one of his sons drive Kitby back to Ó hUadhaigh's office.[21]

It seems somewhat odd that in so grave a matter an experienced barrister did not furnish a carefully considered view in writing to his fellow professional Ó hUadhaigh. If such a document was written, it has not survived. Furthermore, Healy did choose to defend other Volunteers charged with capital offences before courts martial. He mounted an unsuccessful defence for Seán Allen of Tipperary town, who was executed in Cork prison on 28 February 1921 for simple possession of a firearm and a seditious document, and in March 1921 he secured the acquittal of two Galway Volunteers charged with the murder of Constable Timothy Horan on 30 October 1920.

The fact that Kevin was only eighteen years old – well under the age of majority, though by no means too young to bear arms – raised the question of his fitness to determine his own fate. Could he have been persuaded of the importance of adopting a different approach to his own prosecution, not to save his own skin but in the interests of those who might otherwise follow him to the gallows under the same new legislation and procedures? The hazards of being unrepresented in any legal proceedings were obvious: in the case of a court martial, they were increased, because of the judicial inexperience and likely bias of the judges involved. These were military officers rather than trained jurists, and were far more likely to adopt an unnuanced, cut-and-dried approach to their task.

Kitby's account of her discussion with Healy also suggests that at that point Kevin was willing, however reluctantly, to obey GHQ's orders to enter a defence. So what changed his mind? Was it Healy's prognostications to Kitby that Kevin had no chance of acquittal anyway, unless he allowed a plea of insanity, and that he might do better not to be defended at all?

Other Irishmen Awaiting Their Fate

By the time of Kevin's arrest, the case of Terence MacSwiney, on hunger strike in Brixton prison following his conviction and two-year sentence for possession of a police cipher, was attracting widespread interest and sympathy. MacSwiney had been elected Lord Mayor of Cork in March 1920 in succession to Tomas MacCurtain, who had been assassinated in his home by masked police, one of three such reprisal killings that night after an RIC constable had been shot dead by IRA gunmen acting without orders. MacSwiney had also succeeded MacCurtain as commander of the IRA's Cork No. 1 Brigade. This was a point that became entirely lost in the propaganda war surrounding the hunger strike for unconditional release upon which he embarked on 12 August.

The death of Thomas Ashe resulting from force-feeding during a hunger strike in 1917 had caused the British authorities to lose their nerve when Irish political prisoners adopted the tactic. In April 1920, scores of hunger-striking prisoners had been unilaterally released from Mountjoy. The overstretched prison authorities blundered, releasing convicted men as well as ones not yet tried, a debacle which led to the clearing out of the reactionary and incompetent old guard at the top of the Irish administration.[22] In London the following month, 175 untried Irish detainees were released from Wormwood Scrubs prison following a hunger strike lasting twenty-three days. One of the last two released was P.J. Moloney TD, later to be Kitby's father-in-law. It can have been no joke for a man of fifty whose third such protest in three years it had been: 'with their release the great strike was brought to a triumphant close'.[23] Thereafter the British authorities decided that hunger-strikers should be left to die rather than be released, triumphant and unrepentant, on compassionate grounds.[24]

By early September Ireland's most senior judge, the Lord Chancellor Sir James Campbell, feared 'a general massacre' if

MacSwiney died in jail. But Sir James Craig was also fearful that Orangemen might embark 'on something like a general massacre in Belfast' should the government back down.[25] The British government had in any case to tread warily in MacSwiney's case. If convicted men could continue to gain freedom simply by going on hunger strike, how could order be maintained?

Supported by his formidable sisters Annie and Mary – the latter of whom thwarted an attempt by MacSwiney's young wife Muriel to have the Lord Mayor of Dublin issue a public appeal to give up the strike – MacSwiney adamantly refused sustenance unless released unconditionally, and yet lived on and on far beyond his predicted demise. The prime minister was supplied with copies of the prison doctor's daily reports, though he can scarcely have relished reading them – 'his bowels were opened yesterday ... It was about a teaspoon of brownish slime – probably bile.' Sir Norman Moore (1847–1922), the son of Irish parents, a convert to Catholicism and a distinguished physician who particularly enjoyed the company of 'native Irish speakers', was called in, his fee presumably met by Muriel. He told the prison doctor, who in turn informed the Home Office, that the sisters were 'quite obdurate in their determination not to influence McSwiney [sic] to take food. In his own words "they seemed even more determined if possible than he was".'[26]

There is a marked contrast between MacSwiney's story and those of Michael Fitzgerald and Joseph Murphy, both of whom died in Cork jail while MacSwiney's fate still lay in the balance. Fitzgerald, who had been arrested in the City Hall with MacSwiney while attending a meeting of Cork No. 1 Brigade officers, was awaiting trial on charges arising from the 'Wesleyan raid' in Fermoy of December 1919 in which a soldier had been killed. He lasted sixty-seven days without food before his death on 17 October.[27] He was followed eight days later by the American-born Joseph Murphy, held on a charge of possession of a Mills bomb. Murphy survived for seventy-six days, two days longer than did MacSwiney, yet outside Cork there was limited interest in his and Fitzgerald's cases as they weakened, and the revolutionary government's formidable propaganda operation made only limited effort to broadcast their plight. Dublin Castle official Mark Sturgis noted how in death Murphy 'is robbed even of an heroic advertisement as the papers this morning are full of MacSwiney'.[28] It was only the latter's fate which was brought to the world's attention.[29]

This was because of the resonance of MacSwiney's titular position as leader of Cork civil society, rather than because at the time of his capture he had been of the IRA's Cork No. 1 Brigade. The point was that he was Lord Mayor of Cork, a title held under a royal charter, and that he was starving himself to death not five miles from Buckingham Palace. In addition, as Lord Mayor he was successor to Thomas MacCurtain, a man who, as was accepted even by so hostile a figure as Bishop Cohalan of Cork, had been assassinated by a police murder gang.[30] It probably also helped that MacSwiney was a figure of recognisable respectability: a teacher in a commercial college, married into a wealthy Cork family. Such social considerations did not apply for Fitzgerald, a mill worker, and Murphy, a council employee, as they approached their lonely deaths in Cork prison.

There are parallels between how the MacSwiney sisters stood by their brother, and the way in which Kitby and her mother supported Kevin in his decision and resisted GHQ instructions to change tack. It is also clear that some people felt the sisters rather overshadowed MacSwiney's wife Muriel and watched her closely lest she try to persuade her husband not to leave her a widow with a young child. It is perhaps not surprising that Kitby and Mary MacSwiney became firm friends in later years.[31] So far from leaving them sorrowing in the shadows, the deaths of Kevin and of Terence cast them each into limelight unusual for women within the revolutionary movement. This they both came to accept, if not necessarily to relish.

The Trial

Did Kevin receive a fair trial? It is unarguable that his defence was inadequate, because he chose not to participate, not to be represented by counsel, not to accept any legal advice beforehand, and not to put any questions to witnesses when invited to do so during proceedings. What this meant was that anything produced in evidence against him went unchallenged. IRA GHQ surely failed in their duty of care towards him. Initially, they overruled his wish that no defence be mounted, but ultimately left the decision with him. Furthermore, GHQ must have understood that the case was important not only for Kevin, but for other Volunteers who would inevitably follow him into the dock throughout the country.

Kevin was the first Volunteer to be charged with a capital offence under the ROIA, and the first to be brought before a military court for such a crime since 1916. In some respects GHQ's belated and uncertain response to the issues raised by his capture, trial and conviction was a foretaste of how successive republican leaderships were to handle comparable dilemmas in the decades ahead. There are analogies with the struggle of republican women in Armagh prison in 1980, and with the series of hunger strikes in 1980–1, which led to the deaths of ten republican male prisoners and had a transformative impact upon nationalist politics in Northern Ireland. In those cases the strikers took the initiative, as did Kevin in 1920. Over time, some of those involved and their families grew sceptical about whether the military and political leadership of the republican movement had the best interests of the prisoners in mind. Of course, in the cases both of Kevin and MacSwiney, the families, or at any rate the most powerful personalities in those families, appeared determined that there should be no last-minute wavering or change of course.[32]

The British intelligence chief General Winter afterwards suggested that Kevin died essentially because the IRA leadership wanted a martyr.[33] But it is clear that GHQ's dilatory and confused approach to Kevin's case was not the product of a ruthless calculation that an executed young Volunteer might be of more use than a live one in prison. Rather, they had a great many other things on their mind, from ramping up the military campaign to handling the issue of MacSwiney's London hunger strike to deliberations on the targeted killing of British intelligence agents in Dublin. The extraordinary risks that senior officers and rank-and-file Volunteers of the Dublin Brigade were desperate to take to rescue Kevin also make a lie the idea that someone senior had calculated that a dead Kevin was a prize worth having.

On the eve of the trial, Ó hUadhaigh's firm wrote protesting against the procedure adopted – they incorrectly assumed the trial would be held in camera – and seeking an adjournment 'on the grounds that the time allowed to us to prepare the Defence is totally inadequate'. The second part of the summary of evidence had only reached them the day before. This protest was ineffectual.[34]

The panel of officers selected to try Kevin could hardly be faulted in terms of their military records and distinctions. Four of the seven held the Distinguished Service Order (DSO), an award second in status only to the Victoria Cross. The president, Brigadier General Cranley Onslow CB CMG DSO, had been serving in Ireland with the 2nd Battalion, the Bedfordshire Regiment, when the Great War broke out. Shipped directly to France, he fought in the crucial early defensive battles of Mons and the Aisne. After recovery from wounds, he commanded the 7th Brigade at the battles of the Somme, Ypres and Messines in 1916–17. His CMG indicates that he had cooperated closely with Britain's French and Belgian allies. Kitby recalled him as 'a very tall man with a dark melancholy face and a lot of dark hair'.[35] Onslow was a kinsman of the 4th Earl of Onslow, whose nephew Cranley (1926–2001) became familiar to followers of British high politics as a canny chairman of the influential Conservative Party backbench MPs'

1922 committee, immortalised by Alan Clarke MP in his diaries recounting the intrigues and heaves against Margaret Thatcher, which culminated in her resignation as Tory leader and prime minister in 1990.[36] Curiously, another Onslow garnered footnotes in the story of two more recent Mountjoy prisoners, the bank-robbing Littlejohn brothers. They claimed that it was through the good offices of a prison visitor, Lady Pamela Onslow, that they first made contact with British intelligence officials. These officials allegedly encouraged their plans to rob banks in Ireland. The brothers were eventually extradited from Britain and jailed for a 1972 bank hold-up on Dublin's Grafton Street (only to escape from Mountjoy in 1974, one of them remaining at large in Britain until the following year). The 'Littlejohn affair' was an acute embarrassment for the British government, and was anxiously watched by Prime Minister Edward Heath.[37]

The full court which heard Kevin's case was as follows:

Brigadier Cranley Onslow CMG CBE DSO (Bedfordshire Regiment)

Major H.P. Yates DSO (South Wales Borderers)

Lieutenant Colonel C.F. Phipps DSO (Royal Garrison Artillery)

Major E. Morton CBE (Cheshire Regiment)

Lieutenant Colonel F.C. Pilkington DSO (15th Hussars)

Lieutenant Colonel B.H. Chetwynd-Stapylton (Cheshire Regiment)

Major S.J. Watts (Royal Engineers)

With the exception of Major Watts, certified as 'a person of legal knowledge and experience', the men who determined Kevin's fate had no legal or judicial training. If military stereotypes are any guide, the keenest minds on the board would have been Phipps, an artillery man, and Watts, a Royal Engineer – a corps for which, as one veteran recalled, 'you had to be jolly good at mathematics'. By the same logic, Lieutenant Colonel Pilkington was probably both the wealthiest and the dimmest member: cavalry officers required considerable private means to augment their army salaries, and in such regiments, brains were rather frowned upon.[38]

Mary, Kitby, Gerry MacAleer, Seán Ó hUadhaigh and three other friends attended proceedings in Marlborough Barracks (now McKee Barracks) on Blackhorse Avenue off the North Circular Road. They and the court of officers turned up promptly at ten, but for some time there was no sign of the prisoner. The armoured car taking Kevin from Mountjoy had broken down en route – more evidence of military casualness – and a replacement had had to be secured. When Kevin finally arrived 'he looked well and cheerful and desperately amused when he saw the table full of British officers'.

Seán Ó hUadhaigh – or 'Mr Wood, solicitor, Kingstown' as the *Dublin Evening Mail* iconoclastically reported him – sought an adjournment to consult his client, explaining that he had only been brought in at the last minute and had had no time to prepare a defence. He was allowed fifteen minutes. Ó hUadhaigh then said he wished to lodge a complaint about Kevin's treatment after capture. He said he took it that this would be investigated. As prosecuting counsel observed, this was procedurally dubious: Ó hUadhaigh had no standing to raise anything with the court once Kevin had declared himself 'a soldier of the Irish Republic' and had refused to recognise the court and to plead. Nevertheless, Ó hUadhaigh's sleight of hand worked: the question of ill-treatment had been raised and was picked up by the press.

Although he had withdrawn from the case, Ó hUadhaigh remained as a spectator. A plea of 'Not Guilty' was entered on Kevin's behalf. Brigadier General Onslow, in Kitby's words, 'very kindly tried to explain to him the gravity of the situation': Kevin 'did not answer but took out of his pocket a copy of the previous day's *Evening Telegraph* which he proceeded to read'.[39] Thereafter neither members of the court, nor prosecuting counsel, exerted themselves unduly to protect his interests. It is generally accepted that many 1916 rebels had been fortunate in the approach of their prosecutor, Lieutenant W.E. Wylie, who had practised at the Irish bar and who regarded it as his professional duty to ensure that undefended defendants were fairly treated by the military courts. It is said that his advocacy secured W.T. Cosgrave's life (Cosgrave was sentenced to death, but this was immediately commuted to life imprisonment). Crown counsel displayed no such consideration towards Kevin.[40]

The Crown produced and examined a succession of sixteen witnesses, fifteen of them soldiers. The transcript of proceedings indicates that in each case Kevin declined to ask any questions with a brusque 'No', whereas we have seen that he had shown some interest during the swearing-in of their witness statements. When invited to put a question to the eighth witness, he replied, 'Don't bother asking me that question any more, I'm not interested in the proceedings,' to which the president replied, 'I have got to ask you, it is part of my duty.' Kitby's recollection was that 'the President flushed very dark red but said mildly, "It is my duty to ask you. I think that as a soldier you can appreciate that." "Righto," said Kevin, "if it facilitates you, I have no questions."' Thereafter Kevin reverted to a simple 'No'. No member of the court was inclined to step in to play devil's advocate. During the testimony of the sixteen witnesses, the president raised just one point in clarification, asking of Lance Sergeant Banks's evidence: 'Has this witness actually identified the accused?' The prosecutor's next question secured an affirmative reply.

The transcripts suggest that there were several aspects of witnesses' evidence where a defence counsel might have sown some doubt about the extent of Kevin's direct culpability for the killing with which he was charged. Skilful cross-examination, while it might not have altered the verdict, would surely have exposed inconsistencies in the evidence on various matters including the positive identification of Kevin as the man who had shot Whitehead or anyone else, the chain of custody of the weapon allegedly seized from him and the bullet presumed to have killed Whitehead.

On that point the evidence was somewhat problematic: the surgeon Colonel Palmer described how Whitehead had 'a bullet wound of entry, without any exit, on the left-hand side of his abdomen'. His bowel was also perforated in several places, 'the most dangerous wound any man can receive'. The cavity of the abdomen was 'full of blood, clotted blood', which was 'roughly removed with the hand'. He found no bullet. As soon as Whitehead's wounds were sewn up, he was taken away and Humphries was brought in. There was no time to clean up the theatre between the two patients. By the time Humphries was dealt with, according to the theatre attendant, it was in a 'very bad' condition, 'All blood and swabs of every description.' When cleaning the operating table he heard something fall, 'some light article'. He afterwards found 'a small little bullet' on the floor, as well as several instruments and some blood. He put the bullet in his pocket, and later handed it over to an officer.

Evidence regarding the captured weapon and ammunition indicated that the bullet which hit Whitehead was an orthodox one, whereas of the three undischarged Parabellum rounds still in Kevin's magazine, two were factory-produced flat-nosed nickel-cased ammunition, which would produce 'a worse wound'. The third round, copper-coloured, was 'identical' to that produced in court as having killed Whitehead. Cumulatively, cross-examination on these points might have planted sufficient doubt in the court's collective mind to lead to a sentence of imprisonment rather than of death, or offered them some leeway in light of the youth of the defendant.

Barry Bowman, an experienced solicitor who has acted in many courts martial since the 1970s, reviewed the trial proceedings, material collated by the prosecution in preparing their case, the regulations governing courts martial in 1920 and Kitby's witness statement. His view is that 'the court martial was carried out in accordance with the rules and procedures then in being'. The same held good for the court treating Kevin as a member of the Lancashire Fusiliers, which was a requirement of the Army Act. Bowman was, however, critical of the defence 'even though the court was not recognised. There was no evidence against Kevin having shot any of the soldiers,' although he had stated under interrogation that he was acting under orders 'and as a co-conspirator was liable for the full penalty'. Frank Callanan SC, Hugh Harnett SC and Alice Harrison BL, experienced barristers who saw the same documents, are all of a mind that the case was hopeless no matter what stratagem had been adopted.[41]

During an afternoon adjournment, Kevin was allowed to mix with his family in the barrack yard. In her BMH statement Kitby recalled how he drew her aside, quietly gave her his version of what had happened at the bakery, explaining how his gun jammed on the first shot. He cleared it, and fired twice more, killing a soldier, before it jammed again. He took cover under the lorry to clear the blockage, caused by the fourth round he had attempted to fire. He had heard no signal to withdraw. He was 'amused' that the military were unable to work out that it was he who had killed Private Whitehead. However, Donal O'Donovan writes that Kitby had given a somewhat different version to his father, stating that Kevin fired twice before his gun jammed, cleared that blockage, fired again and 'got this man', before the weapon 'jammed again on the fifth round'.[42]

Quite what Kevin made of the fact that, for legal reasons, the court martial was required to deem him to be a soldier of the Lancashire Regiment, we do not know. But it could be argued that he therefore died as a soldier, albeit a British one (although unlike the Connaught Rangers mutineer Private James Daly, executed a day later in India, the Commonwealth War Graves Commission does not record his place of burial). The soldiers who died were never a topic of any interest within the family until Donal's book appeared in 1989. If Kevin was shocked at the youth of the soldiers killed, he kept this to himself. His recorded reaction to participation in close-up killing is very much as indicated in contemporary military psychology studies: while a small minority may be immediately traumatised by their deed, most combatant killers report an immediate 'exhilaration'. Reflection, humanisation of the dead enemy and eventual acceptance of responsibility tempered with an element of regret at the necessity of the act of inflicting death, come over time.[43]

Despite the presence of the press and of his family, Kevin did not take the opportunity to address the court. Just before his execution, he explained to his friend Kathleen Carney that 'I believe the usual thing done ... is to make a speech from the dock or something but I wouldn't be serious long enough to do it. Besides anyone who ever knew me would never believe that I wrote it.'[44]

But thanks to his affidavit, a composed account of his treatment immediately after capture was already in the public domain, to the great benefit of republican propagandists and the enduring discomfort of the British authorities.

The court was adjourned without pronouncing a verdict. Kevin, his family, and for that matter those of the soldiers who had been killed, who presumably kept an eye upon proceedings in Dublin, had to await both judgement and sentence. On the first there could be little doubt; the second was a different matter.

The Politics of Punishment for Political Crimes in Ireland, 1916–21

The question of the punishment to be meted out to persons convicted of political killings remained fluid surprisingly late in Ireland. In July 1919 Sinn Féin adherent John Ward was tried for the unprovoked killing of Anthony Herron, a middle-aged farmer and father of six young children. Herron was shot in Donegal in December 1918 during the general election campaign, after rival groups of supporters had exchanged words on the road following a Redmondite election rally in Glenties. On conviction Ward surrendered his gun, bought for £5 in Glasgow, and his sentence of six-months' imprisonment was set aside because of time already spent in custody. That killing is still remembered by locals and by Herron's family.[45]

An even more extraordinary example of judicial leniency occurred just two months before the Church Street attack. In July 1920 18-year-old Volunteer John Lacey was tried for killing 61-year-old Ellen Morris, a mother of thirteen children, during an IRA raid for money on her Wexford home. When Lacey fired a warning shot into her kitchen ceiling, Ellen went to push him out: he plaintively told a court that when 'she raised the spade to hit me' his gun went off, killing her outright. He pleaded guilty to manslaughter, saying that he had fired unintentionally in 'an unconscious, impulsive act'. For this he received just eighteen months' hard labour. So far from being outraged at such a remarkably mild sentence, Lloyd George was delighted: it was a case where men 'turned King's witness in order to save their own lives ... a boy of 17 who ... went to the house but the woman there beat him off with a spade and he shot her. He was caught and in terror confessed the whole plot.' There was hope that many other youngsters would follow his example. Following the killing, the OC of the North Wexford Brigade was court-martialled for failing to control his men and reduced to the rank of private for three months before being reinstated: 'I was not allowed to sulk ... and ... I did more work.'[46]

Another matter was the age at which people could be executed for capital crimes. Gavrilo Princip (1894–1918), the Serb nationalist whose killing of Archduke Franz Ferdinand in Sarajevo in June 1914 triggered the competing mobilisations that led to the Great

War, escaped the death penalty because, aged only nineteen when he committed his crime, he was underage by one month under Hapsburg law (he died of disease in prison in 1918, four years into his twenty-year sentence). In Britain and Ireland, however, there was no such legal impediment, and there was recent precedent for the imposition of the supreme penalty by a military court. The shell-shocked Londoner Private Aby Bevistein (1899–1916) was only seventeen when executed for desertion on the battlefield in France on 20 March. The IRA themselves executed at least one aged 17 or 18, John 'Slag' O'Sullivan of Cork, in June 1921, after a court martial attended by the divisional commander Liam Lynch (1892–1923): the presence of so senior an officer was unusual at such proceedings, which even when the IRA troubled to hold them before killing alleged spies tended to be rather ad hoc affairs.[47]

CHAPTER SIX

Reprieve or Rescue

Making the Case for Reprieve

By the time Kevin was sentenced in October the political climate had significantly degenerated. The level of violence had grown markedly in some parts of the island, and the police and military were under severe strain. We should, nevertheless, note that by far the most violent places in Ireland in terms of deaths in the summer and early autumn were not Cork or Dublin, but the Unionist-dominated cities of Londonderry and Belfast. The bulk of the violence there was not directed against the British state and Crown forces, but occurred between the contending unionist and nationalist communities. The principle of indefinite partition on a six-county basis had been enshrined in the Government of Ireland act of June 1920: this escalated tensions and saw outbreaks of intercommunal violence, which the authorities could not control. Whatever was spurring loyalists to violence in Derry and in Belfast in those months, it was not the killing of British soldiers in Dublin.

It was only on 22 October that news of Kevin's death sentence became public. This had a galvanic effect, not only amongst republicans: the Irish Women's Franchise League sent a strong telegram, as did a meeting of the Women's International League in Manchester; fourteen students of Trinity College Dublin, all ex-officers, urged 'reprieve on humanitarian grounds ... As soldiers they feel forcibly that in the case of one so young obviously acting under orders of older men,' Kevin could be spared 'without compromising [the] prestige of the Crown'. From his alma mater UCD came many similar appeals from various quarters, including decorated ex-officers studying for degrees. Many individuals wrote or telegraphed calls for mercy to Dublin Castle, to the Viceroy and to the British government. One correspondent made the reasonable point that to hang someone on 1 November, the Feast of All Saints, a Holy Day of Obligation in the Catholic calendar and a day of 'respectful observance' in the Church of Ireland, would be unfortunate. A man from Monkstown wrote that Kevin 'is only a boy – with all the impulses of youth – deal leniently with him'.[1] The issue of Kevin's youth was perhaps more vexed than his protagonists allowed. The fact was that at eighteen and three-quarters he was not exceptionally young by the military standards of the time.

On 25 October Kitby's employer Ernest Aston told her that he planned to intercede 'at the highest level' and intended going to Britain with Lieutenant Commander John Francis MacCabe (1879–1950), a Local Government Board official 'who had distinguished himself ... for the sinking of German submarines' and was 'a friend of the Lloyd George family'. MacCabe, educated by the Jesuits at Stonyhurst and an engineering graduate of Trinity College Dublin, was a quintessential 'Castle Catholic', son of a doctor who had become a close friend of Gerard Manley Hopkins SJ during the poet's unhappy sojourn in Dublin. McCabe had won the DSO for his part in the sinking of a German submarine while captain of the minesweeper *Conan Doyle*, and was later mentioned in despatches for other operations.[2] Aston asked Kitby for a photograph of Kevin to bring to London, which she provided after checking with GHQ. An elated Aston returned to Dublin on 29 October, assuring Kitby that he had Lloyd George's personal word of honour that there would be a reprieve. On the same day the veteran Belfast MP Joe Devlin overcame his deep loathing of the prime minister sufficiently to speak to Lloyd George about Kevin's case and afterwards was 'certain our efforts would succeed'.[3] On 30 October the ailing Archbishop Walsh of Dublin was 'carried up' to Sir John Anderson's room in the Castle, accompanied by Lord Mayor Lorcan Sherlock. They did not plead the issue in terms of Kevin's age, but sought a reprieve 'solely on the bad effect his execution would have'. Mark Sturgis noted that this 'is the old argument that has been used over and over again'.[4]

There is little doubt that Kevin's sentence, coming on top of the long drawn-out nightmare of Terence MacSwiney's hunger strike, traumatised nationalist Ireland, already in shock at the growth of violence throughout the country and at the government's approach to suppression of republican violence by penalising and terrorising the general public.

General Macready was – correctly from a British point of view – irked by the way the press were covering Barry's story. He called for corrective propaganda: 'this man was conclusively proved to have shot a soldier with an expanding bullet', i.e. a 'dumdum' round forbidden under the 1899 Hague 'Declaration Respecting Expanding Bullets'.[5] The point that Kevin and the other attackers were dressed as civilians might also have been stressed. Yet the British propaganda response in Kevin's case was hesitant and ineffectual.

Upon Lord French's return to Ireland on 31 October, Macready, Sturgis and another official went to the Viceregal Lodge to seek a final determination. French began by stating that 'a life was at stake, and the proceedings were anything but perfunctory'. A minute by Lord Chancellor Sir James Campbell, arguing for a reprieve on grounds of Barry's 'extreme youth', was read out by an official. Campbell, memorably condemned by Sturgis as 'a poltroon of the most contemptible dye', had changed his views radically since the moment when, in 1913, he had been pencilled in as attorney general in the planned Ulster Provisional Government.[6] He was now on the realistic wing of southern unionism, and generally an advocate of coming to terms with Sinn Féin rather than attempting to eradicate the independence movement by fire and sword. French was not impressed: he ascertained from one official that Barry's age would 'not of necessity mean a reprieve' from a death sentence in England. He said he fully accepted the findings of the court martial, and 'heard the story from Macready' who said 'it was the sort of case which the soldiers and police rightly expected us to exact the full penalty'. French dismissed Campbell's pleadings, and minuted that 'the law must take its course'. Mark Sturgis thought this 'a very impressive interview'.[7]

French later complained to Hamar Greenwood about Campbell: 'It is most unfortunate that a man who can take such views should be the chief law officer in the country.'[8] He was also unimpressed by Archbishop Walsh and Lord Mayor Sherlock, who had 'called & urged me to remit the death sentences': 'They were very earnest … but they really showed a very poor case.' As ever, he chose to see only good arising from a firm executions policy – 'Macready tells me he has a few more coming on': 'these hangings may give rise to temporary disturbances [but] … there is no doubt that they will have a tremendous effect for good in the long run'. He was unmoved by a personal appeal from the Belvedere rector Father Francis Browne SJ, of whose outstanding war service as a military chaplain with the Irish Guards he was well aware.[9]

The day following the execution Campbell, who had lost a son during the Great War, wrote in fevered terms to his long-suffering friend Bonar Law (who himself knew all about the loss of young lives, as two of his three sons had been killed in combat). He argued that Kevin's circumstances were the consequence of having released unrepentant and determined men with blood on their hands after the Rising. These had gone on to become the godfathers of the revolutionary movement, moulding youths like Kevin to their will. He also had doubts about the legality and speed of the process by which the date of execution had been determined. On whose authority had this been done, he wondered, since nobody had asked him about it? Bonar Law was well used to letters from Campbell. What set this one apart was that for once this notoriously shameless, importunate place-seeker was explaining that he had sought a decision not for his own benefit but for someone else, and for the highest political reasons:[10]

> I had ... nothing before me but the fact of Barry's extreme youth, the inference that he was under duress more or less from the fact that he was accompanied by ... men much older than himself and that after the shots were fired the men left him & made their escape while he invited certain arrest by taking refuge under the lorry.

Campbell contrasted Barry's case with that of Thomas Ashe, who in 1916 had been responsible for 'ruthlessly shooting dead over 20' RIC men including 'the County Inspector whose body was so riddled with bullets that every bone was broken', and yet who within a year had been released for no good reason to resume his subversive ways.[11]

Rescuing Kevin

At this remove, and knowing how many other grave issues GHQ was addressing in October 1920, it is difficult to understand why such strong support was given to the Dublin Brigade's plans for a rescue operation. It is not as though Kevin was high in the counsels of the brigade, or that he possessed significant information about future plans and operations. Apart from Mick MacDonnell and Tom Ennis of the Squad, whom he had met during the Aughavannagh and Tullow operations, and the Dublin Brigade vice OC Peadar Clancy, he was not widely known to senior IRA men. It rather looks as though the entire Dublin Brigade, including its otherwise cerebral leadership, were as affected by the Dáil propaganda as the outside world.

Motivating forces for those who wanted to act was shame that Kevin had been abandoned by his comrades without warning, and embarrassment that the IRA had made such a hash of their plan to disarm the bakery fatigue party. The missed opportunity to mount a rescue while Kevin was being driven between Mountjoy and Marlborough Barracks for his court martial, particularly when his armoured car broke down en route, may have acted as an additional spur. John Joe Carroll's belief that in talk of rescue 'the "Brass Hats" were only play-acting and had no intention of risking their skins in any serious attempt at rescue' reflects both understandable suspicion, and the strength of feeling amongst Kevin's comrades that something had to be done.[12]

A number of rescue schemes were considered. The difficulties were, however, formidable. Mountjoy was a secure, purpose-built prison, to which access to and egress from was easily controlled. The streets outside were subject to frequent police and military patrols. Kevin was unusually tightly guarded, not only by warders and soldiers who could sometimes be bribed or intimidated, but by Auxiliaries. Nevertheless, one sympathetic warder, Patrick Berry, who had been smuggling messages to and from political prisoners since 1917, advised that there was one relatively simple means of rescue: an IRA party could use the arrival of the daily early morning milk cart to force their way in through a side entrance adjacent to the chapel, where Kevin would be at Mass, guarded by only one Auxiliary.[13] For whatever reason, this plan was not followed.

Rescuers would somehow have to trick their way in, find and grab Kevin, and quite possibly shoot their way out of the complex, then get through the security cordon outside. Crowds of well-wishers for Kevin might provide some cover but would also present a moral hazard as these civilians would be in danger should firing break out.

Dublin IRA men later took pains to record their mobilisation for the aborted rescue operations. Among them was John J. Lawless of E Company, 2nd Battalion, a 1916 veteran who went on to fight on the Free State side during the opening week of the civil war before working as a civilian in intelligence.[14] Charlie Bevan of C Company, who with his brother Tommy had been sentenced to death after the 1916 Rising, 'was mobilised on Sunday evening [31 October] about 7 o'clock, in North Frederick Street in Mark Wilson's place ... The plan miscarried.' Andrew Bermingham, another 1916 man involved, also recalled how 'it was called off'.[15] One plan involved the use of explosives to blast a hole in a side wall of the prison, near the hang house. Men would have immediately had to clamber over the rubble through clouds of dust, find their way into that part of the prison where Kevin was being held, rescue him and somehow get him out. This scheme was apparently abandoned when it was established that Kevin's Auxiliary guards had orders to shoot him should there be an escape attempt.[16]

Kitby recalled how on 30 October she was asked to participate in a rescue to take place that afternoon. The idea was that she and 'one girl who could be relied upon for courage and initiative' – she chose her sister Elgin – would call to Mountjoy to visit Kevin at 3.15 p.m. From previous experience it would be 3.30 p.m. by the time they reached the boardroom. They were to behave as normal with Kevin until, at 3.40 p.m., Kitby and Elgin would each 'tackle the Auxiliaries' to prevent them shooting Kevin as an expected IRA rescue party burst in. The party would have to be clear by 4 p.m., when a fresh tranche of troops would arrive at the jail. Kitby was unimpressed with this scheme, but she and Elgin were willing to go along with it. As they awaited admission to Mountjoy, however, a priest stepped forward and asked to be allowed to see Kevin. He was admitted ahead of them, thus disrupting the IRA plan. When the pair were finally admitted they sat ready to act, each having identified which Auxiliary they would attack: 'Until a clock struck 4, we were "ready for anything" as Captain Byrne had told us to be.'[17]

Kitby's account is, however, challenged by two others given to the BMH. Bernard C. Byrne of the 'Squad' said that the Dublin Brigade had arranged for an unnamed priest to make an unannounced visit to Kevin at 3.20 p.m. Elgin would then present herself at Mountjoy, so that Kevin would be kept in the boardroom awaiting her rather than being brought back to his cell. It was assumed that the military guards in the prison, due to be replaced at 4 p.m., would be 'fairly lax'. Kevin, apparently, knew what was afoot (although Kitby says she had refused 'categorically' from the time of his arrest to tell him his friends would somehow rescue him).[18] But 'our plan went slightly awry' as 'the Barry family were definitely reluctant to cooperate' and 'it was only after much persuasion that Miss [Elgin] Barry could be persuaded to come to the prison gates at all. When eventually she did arrive, she approached me and told me that she had definite information that Kevin would be reprieved during the weekend and that she would take no part in the rescue.' When Byrne 'told her that I could carry on without her assistance … she told me' that if he made a visit in her place 'she would create a scene'.[19]

A final scheme, described by Kitby, involved two of the most senior officers in the Brigade, Dick McKee and either Peadar Clancy or Oscar Traynor, disguising themselves as clergymen to trick their way in lieu of the Barry family group of Mary, Kitby and Mick. They would then have to overcome and silence the Auxiliary guards and warders in the governor's office, before making their way back out accompanied by Kevin. Traynor's recollection was that he and Clancy were to attempt the rescue: when he observed that it seemed 'a very desperate job', Clancy replied, 'typical of the man, to the effect that "desperate jobs usually bring success"'.

This plan bordered on insanity: quite apart from the operational hazards, these men knew all about the Dublin IRA's organisation, personnel and future plans. Bloody Sunday was in the pipeline, and no one should jeopardise that. The rescue was called off after a courier sent by McKee returned to say that Mrs Barry was strongly opposed: 'unless some guarantee as to its success could be given no extra lives should be endangered'.[20]

Kitby said that she, her mother and brother took the tram to Mountjoy willing to give up their last chance to see Kevin if the Brigade rescue was to go ahead, but that Jack Plunkett met them outside and told them to proceed as the plan had been abandoned. Plunkett supported this version of events in a separate statement. These arguments were assembled in 1949 when the family threatened to sue both *The Irish Press* and Traynor for stating in a lecture that the rescue attempt had been called off at Mary Barry's insistence. Traynor replied that his remarks had been incompletely cited, and that what he had said was that Mrs Barry had opposed the plan because of the likely loss of life involved. *The Irish Press* published the Barrys' protest, Plunkett's supporting statement and Traynor's clarification. Seán Ó hUadhaigh told the family that they could achieve nothing further without a perilous libel suit.[21] Traynor stuck to his guns in his Bureau witness statement, completed just a few months after the row.[22]

Dick McKee and Peadar Clancy outlived Kevin by only three weeks. On the night of Saturday 20 November they were arrested in the Gloucester Street home of John Fitzpatrick, another Dublin Brigade officer. McKee told his host he thought he had been followed there by a man 'with [a] Trilby hat'. McKee was unwell, and despite the danger of a raid Clancy 'said he would not go when Dick refused to'. The house was later raided: when Fitzpatrick gave false names for his companions, a British officer replied 'You are a fucking liar. One is the notorious Peadar Clancy, the other is the notorious R. McKee.' The three were taken to Dublin Castle, where

Clancy and McKee, together with young Clareman, Conor Clune, who had only come up to Dublin to deliver the account books of the cooperative which he managed for audit. McKee, Clancy and Clune (who may have been mistaken for a significant IRA man) were kept while Fitzpatrick and various other prisoners rounded up that night were sent to Beggars Bush barracks. As Fitzpatrick said goodbye, 'McKee said to me "if you get through give my love to my mother, sisters, brothers & all the boys". He looked very pale & sad.' Clancy just 'smiled goodbye'. Clancy, McKee and Clune were interrogated and killed in the Dublin Castle guardroom by British personnel, probably led by a Captain Hardy, an intelligence officer notorious for his brutality. Dublin Castle stated that they were shot while trying to escape on the morning of 22 November, but medical examination revealed broken bones and abrasions consistent with prolonged assaults, and bullet wounds to the head and body. John Fitzpatrick was later singled out in Beggars Bush by a British officer whom he described as 'a tall young fellow, good-looking, with a stiff leg', who said: 'I am after putting three bullets [sic] through your two fucking Sinn Fein pals' hearts and I am coming back to do the same to you in a few minutes.' Fitzpatrick was shown the three bodies in an effort to make him identify them. McKee's 'face was battered up a lot. He had big marks all around his face. Some marks looked as if pieces of flesh was knocked out of them. He had bayonet wound in side & his fingers were all cut where he had grabbed [a] Bayonette [sic].' Clancy's 'face looked as if it had got a good beating. His forehead was marked over the eye. Also it stuck out well over his face & it looked as if it was burnt. His face was all yellow.'[23]

While going through a collection of photographs following the death of Kitby's last surviving child, Helen, in 2011, I came across half an envelope. Written on the outside in Kitby's hand was 'Cmdt Peadar Clancy'. When I inverted the envelope, a lock of fine brown-reddish hair fell out. Clancy had known Kevin, and probably also Kitby. Todd Andrews, who only encountered Clancy once, was left with 'an indelible impression of the superman … Only once again in my life did I meet anyone whose personality had that overwhelmingly mesmeric effect on me.'[24] Perhaps Kitby had a grá for Clancy, or perhaps he was one of the many young men who seem to have fallen for her. Either way, the lock is now with Clancy's family.

Other Irish Rebels Awaiting Their Fate

There is a marked contrast between the way in which Kevin's name and image drew attention across the world before and immediately after his execution, while the fate of another young Irishman executed a day later achieved no significant register at all. On 2 November, in Dagshai prison in the Solon hill station in the Punjab in northern India, 21-year-old Private James Daly of the 1st Battalion, Connaught Rangers, was executed for mutiny. This followed a court martial in which, like some of his comrades, he refused to recognise the court yet cross-examined the majority of prosecution witnesses, and produced a witness in his defence. In total sixty-two soldiers were convicted and seven acquitted of a range of offences including mutiny. Shortly before Daly died, thirteen of his comrades found their death sentences commuted to life imprisonment. There was general relief in India that no other Irish units stationed there reported any signs of trouble. In fact the Leinster Regiment performed creditably in south-western India the following year during the bloody repression of regional unrest, what the British termed the 'Moplah revolt' and Indians the 'Malabar Rebellion'.[25]

E.S. Montagu, Secretary of State for India, made the point that 'if hereafter the relations between England and Ireland were ever happily adjusted, we might wish, as part of an amnesty which might then be granted, to reconsider the sentences. This would of course be impossible in the case of the one, though possible in the case of the 13,' but Daly's fate was sealed by three considerations: the fact that two soldiers had died during the mutiny; that he had 'maintained a spirit of flagrant defiance ... until arrested'; and most importantly, as the commander in chief, India, warned, because there would be 'disastrous consequences' for discipline amongst the native troops of the Indian army if all the white soldiers were spared. He would never again be able to execute any Indian soldier for any offence. He was also against delaying Daly's execution because such uncertainty would be unfair to a fellow soldier.[26]

Daly, whose re-enlistment in 1919 suggests that he had not held particularly strong nationalist sympathies, was not even named in the official communiqué announcing his death, which was accorded a brief paragraph in *The Times of India*.[27] He was clearly a young man of strong character, who died with dignity. His commanding officer and an army chaplain were quoted in December as saying that 'the boy met his death like a brave soldier' and that 'his last moment was marked by coolness and grace'. Daly's farewell letter, addressed from 'Heaven,' stated:

> It is all for Ireland. I am not afraid to die; it is only thinking of you. If you will be happy on earth I will be happy in Heaven. I am ready to meet my doom.
>
> The priest is with me when needed, so you need have no worry about me, as I am going to my dearest home. But I wish to the Lord that I had not started on getting into this trouble. But it is done now and I have to suffer. Out of 62 of us I am the only one to be put to death. God bless you all.[28]

Despite his execution for mutiny, Daly was buried in a small British military cemetery in Kirkee rather than in the prison grounds. His niece wrote that 'the sudden news of Jim's death ... prostrated my mother ... she never regained her health'.[29]

The story of a fellow mutineer demonstrates how difficult it is to generalise about the motivations of Irishmen who volunteered to serve in the British forces. William Coman from Cashel, who was released from prison in England after the signing of the Anglo-Irish treaty in December 1921, eventually re-enlisted in the Royal Engineers in 1937, was captured in France in 1940 and spent five years as a prisoner of war in Germany, from where he wrote asking the Department of Defence to suspend payment of the 10s. 6d. weekly Irish pension awarded to Connaught Rangers mutineers: 'I will have to leave my money with you until the war is over.' Whatever Kevin might have made of that example of tangled allegiances, he would have been amused by Coman's rakish civilian career, which included a five-year sentence for 'larceny by force, violence and armed assault' in Thurles in 1924, and shorter sentences for failing to pay a bus fare in 1947, for breaking and entering in 1950, and for theft of a bicycle and drunkenness in 1955.[30] Kevin could fairly have been convicted of at least one such offence during his student days.

Some of the mutineers sought to draw a parallel between their experiences and Kevin's. In 1927 a 'Connaught Rangers Mutineers Association' met for the first time in the Kevin Barry Memorial Hall in Parnell Square, and agreed to petition the government for compensation or pensions. Headed by a man who some former comrades regarded as a turncoat and informer, it did not draw much support from former mutineers outside Dublin, and that effort eventually fizzled out.[31]

CHAPTER SEVEN

Dying a Good Death

Awaiting the End

The family had only kind words for the prison officers, soldiers and Auxiliaries who guarded Kevin in Mountjoy as he awaited his fate: 'they were all very fond of him'.[1] Kitby said that on arrival in the prison Kevin had quickly 'established himself with the warders by giving one of them a tip – Busy Bee – for the race that was to be run on the Wednesday'. In the event he was not much of a tipster: Red Bee – not Busy Bee as Kitby had recalled – was an undistinguished also-ran in the Expert's Stake at the Curragh at the Irish St Leger meeting on Wednesday 23 September. However, his gaolers, his guards and his legal nemesis all seem to have been greatly impressed by his humour and his fortitude. Captain W.G. McKay of the Royal Artillery, 'who was in charge of Kevin Barry ... His job was to see he did not escape' was 'very struck with the high gallantry of Barry all the time'.[2] Kitby claimed when court martial officer Captain Barrett visited Kevin to deliver the court's verdict on 28 October, he 'handed him his sentence, burst into tears and left his cell'.[3] The original document, on 'Army Form W 3996', signed by 'CC Onslow Brigadier' at Marlborough Barracks, was dated 20 October.[4]

In accordance with prison rules, as a condemned man Kevin was permitted to choose two warders to be with him in his final hours. Donal O'Donovan identified one of these, Edward Proctor, possibly chosen because he was from Carlow. Kevin gave him a set of rosary beads, as a keepsake.[5] The identity of the other chosen warder is unknown.

Despite the security implications, after his trial and conviction Kevin was allowed plenty of visitors, whom he would meet in the governor's office. He seems to have been accorded far more visiting time than a conventional prisoner. Amongst his guests were fellow students from UCD, male and female, and a range of Catholic clerics, some of whom came on their own initiative and some, it appears, strangers to him. All the accounts of him after sentence, and indeed all his surviving letters, are of a young man determined to maintain a cheerful and irreverent attitude. Valedictions such as 'Yours till Hell freezes,' 'Yours till I qualify' and 'Over the top' in letters to friends confirm this. If any of his friends counselled a plea for mercy, he ignored them. On 30 October newspapers carried accounts of how, when passing other prisoners in the prison en route to meet visitors, he had cheerfully remarked to one of them that 'I am off on Monday.' At the time the press did not comment on the selection of 1 November, All Saint's Day, but it was an inept choice of date for an execution. As Donal O'Donovan put it, 'the English made a martyr of Kevin Barry'.[6]

When Father Albert emerged on the afternoon of 31 October, having talked his way into Mountjoy uninvited, he addressed the crowd: 'He spoke about Kevin's joy knowing that the students were outside.' Kevin had initially 'demurred' when asked for a message to relay, but eventually said 'The only message I have is: "Hold on. Stick to the Republic."' Kitby was irritated that 'Live for the ideal for which I am about to die,' 'palpable literary paraphrases', somehow appeared in the newspapers.[7]

Kevin's final meeting with family members was almost unbearable for them. Mountjoy was thick with soldiers and Auxiliaries, and there were armed warders as well as Auxiliaries in the boardroom. Kitby found it difficult to talk at first, 'because several of the warders were crying. My mother was composed but quiet, and my brother Mick was at no time a great chatterer.' When Kitby mentioned the students outside, 'Kevin rubbed his hands and said: "Oh, gosh, if I could only catch one more sight of them."' When Kitby suddenly dried up, he 'began to swing his foot and whistle "Steady Boys and Step Together", and he gave me a sideways smile, so I started talking again and gradually we were all talking quite naturally'. Then the deputy governor entered and said 'I am sorry, Mrs Barry. I'm afraid you'll have to go.' Kevin's last words to Kitby as he kissed her were '"Give my love to the boys in the Company." We turned at the door for a last look and he was standing at the salute.'[8] Kitby elsewhere spoke of 'that last night … Kevin was the bravest. He kissed us. He straightened up and said: "Don't cry. Let us be brave."' Forty years later, in explaining her emotional response to the last-minute collapse of her daughter Judy's wedding plans, she wrote:

> I haven't cried at all … Even alone I feel that if I started I couldn't stop …. I feel a bit as I did when Kevin was captured and during the awful six weeks – that if I broke down it would somehow affect him – that I couldn't until he was dead. Then I couldn't cry either – so I went for three weeks & then got 3 abscesses in my mouth & had to cry from pain.[9]

Dying a Good Death

In Ireland those executed after the Rising were all said to have died unflinching; War of Independence narratives similarly convey a sense that those facing death by the bullet or the rope, whether rebels or captured soldiers, policemen or alleged spies, generally took their fate well, whether resignedly or defiantly. Paddy Daly recalled that when the British agent J.C. Byrne was told that he was going to be shot, he 'jumped to attention immediately and said: "You are right. God bless the King. I would love to die for him." He saluted and there was not a quiver on him.'[10] In Clare, Patrick Darcy, probably innocent of the IRA's charge of informing, reportedly told his killers: 'I forgive ye boys. Ye are shooting me in the wrong.'[11] In Cork, Major Geoffrey Compton Smith not only shook hands with his IRA captors, but wrote that 'I have been treated with great kindness and during my short captivity, have learned to regard Sinn Feiners rather as mistaken idealists than as a "Murder Gang".'[12] The tradition continued into independent Ireland. When IRA veteran George Plant was sentenced to death in 1942 following trial by a military tribunal composed of former comrades, one of the judges – J.V. Joyce, another one-time UCD medical student who had been 'out' on Bloody Sunday – observed that he 'took it well & clicked his heels'. Joyce later noted that Plant, faced with a military firing squad, 'died, as I thought he would, without flinching'.[13] In Northern Ireland, a priest described how 19-year-old Volunteer Thomas Williams was 'praying all the time' as he walked calmly to the gallows in 1942, and even ordinary criminals such as murderer Samuel Cushnan, who according to a clergyman died 'with great Christian courage and charity' in 1930, and Eddie Cullens, whose rabbi said he 'went to the scaffold' calmly, were reported as meeting their end with heads held high after prayer and reflection.[14] In Texas in December 1917, a white soldier described how thirteen African American troops sentenced to death after the most cursory of courts martial for alleged mutiny during the Houston Riot 'were shivering a little, but I think this was due more to the cold rather than to fear'. As the ropes were being fastened around the men's necks, 'big Johnson's voice suddenly broke into a hymn: "Lord, I'm comin' home". And the others joined him. The eyes of even the hardest of us were wet.'[15]

It can be difficult, reading sources such as BMH witness statements or cryptic notes in the Ernie O'Malley papers, to know whether such frequent reports of the graciousness and fortitude of condemned men and women emanating from judges, guards or executioners were partly a means of smoothing the edges of their own recollections of how they had contributed to the ceremonious termination of human life.

Accounts of Kevin's death follow that pattern. Dublin Castle official Mark Sturgis noted on 31 October that 'I hear Barry is quite calm and unrepentant, not at all like a boy driven into a deed by others.'[16] Canon Waters, the prison chaplain whom Kitby knew was hostile to the independence movement, told a journalist immediately after the hanging that he had never before encountered such a combination of fortitude and piety. In a letter to Mrs Barry, he spoke of how Kevin 'went between Father MacMahon and myself to his death with the most perfect bravery, without the slightest faltering, repeating his little ejaculations and the Sacred Name till the very last moment of his life'. Such comments unfortunately resonated around the world, providing a pious and virtuous and Catholic aura to Kevin in death, which was at odds with his roguishness, effervescence and cheerful impiety in life. General Winter was hardly fair in his remark that Kevin 'willingly accepted a martyr's crown ... Just before his execution he was informed that in a few hours he would be in the arms of the Virgin Mary, and that in 100 years he would be revered as a Saint. He went to his death with a smile on his lips, [and] he was proclaimed a martyr.'[17] Martyrdom was not something he craved. The family would probably have much preferred the account of his death offered to a railwayman at Holyhead port by a detective escorting the hangman Ellis back to his home from the mail boat. Ellis and his unnamed assistant had been paid their fees in cash on the spot, and left Mountjoy that afternoon:

> On his return from Dublin he [Ellis] was met on arrival
> by the same Irish detective (O'Leary) who escorted him

to the train. He was travelling to Rochdale where he carried on the business of a barber. He thanked O'Leary for looking after him so well and added 'Well Mr O'Leary I hanged that boy this morning and they are not going to answer the Irish question by hanging people – that boy did not give a damn.'[18]

Waters later told a fellow priest that 'Kevin was extraordinarily brave and never once faltered but died most heroically,' although one letter to the press reported 'hearsay' that he was 'crying'.[19] As recently as January 2020 I overheard the same claim in a barber's shop in Meath Street. Other accounts of Kevin's last hours indicate that he bore his fate lightly. Kitby, Michael and their mother found him in good, unforced spirits, although he struck somewhat more sombre notes in letters to his friends Gerry McAleer and Kathleen Carney. On 30 October he thanked Gerry for visiting with two friends:

> Now Gerry I can't indulge in heroics nor I can't curse so this is a very tame letter – not at all like the ones you used to get from me but you will make allowances ... There are several people in the College I would like to write to but I have neither the time nor the energy. But when the 2nd Meds are assembled tell the boys and girls that I wish them every success and ask them to say a prayer for me when I go over the top on Monday ... Remember me to Barney and all at home, also to all the boys in the College and to such of the girls whose acquaintance you can claim.
>
> Now good bye and the best of luck.
>
> Yours till I'm qualified.[20]

The following evening he wrote to Kathleen, evidently after his last visitors had departed:

I have just received your letter and thank you for it from my heart. I've had all sorts of letters during the last few days and I know the ones to be thankful for.

I had quite a busy day today. I had a visit from a most effusive young lady whom I didn't know from Adam. She knew all about me however. She wept, but she meant well. Then I had two Sisters of Charity, then three more visits. Then the chaplain followed by Father Albert. I then interviewed two Bon Secour Sisters and finished up with the Chaplain. The boys from the College were up outside the gate and they said the Rosary. They also sang 'The Soldier's Song' which did me more good than you can imagine.

Everybody has been very decent. I have just finished my hallow eve rations of apples and grapes but I missed the nuts. However, there is no rose without a thorn. I want you to thank Eily O'Neill[21] for me for her letter and also for all she has done for Mother. And I want you to thank all the people you know who have had masses said etc. Of course it is unnecessary to tell you how grateful I am.

Yes K as you remark we have seen some good times but not as good as we might have seen. I want you to keep up acquaintance with Jerry [probably a slip of the pen for 'Gerry' McAleer] and the boys. I believe the usual thing done in my case is to make a speech from the dock or something but I couldn't be serious long enough to do it. Besides anyone who ever knew me would never believe that I wrote it.

Now I'll shut up. I wish you every success in love and business. Give my adieux to Des [her brother] and your mother and say a little prayer when I cash in.

Your pal
Kevin[22]

One of his guards provided a whimsical account of Kevin's final hours. After the last of his visitors had gone, his

> conversation was mainly on sporting subjects such as football and hurling. He had never been out of Ireland and had very strange ideas about England. He appeared to think of it as all one vast industrial area … He considered himself unlucky to have been caught
>
> Towards the end he lost all hope of a reprieve and remarked somewhat cynically that these were only known in the cinema world. He went to his death with callous composure.[23]

Within hours of the hanging, a court of inquiry in lieu of inquest was convened in Mountjoy, chaired by another officer with close links to Lord French. This was Major John Linton Shore DSO, no stranger to death because as a mere captain he had had to assume command of the shattered 1st Battalion Cheshire Regiment when it suffered 770 casualties during the Battle of Mons in August 1914. Captured that October, he was held as a prisoner of war until 1919.[24] The court inspected the remains and heard from just two witnesses, Governor Monro and the prison medical officer Dr Hackett, who said that death was 'instantaneous and due to fracture of the cervical vertebrae'.[25] Kevin's remains were then buried with proper ceremony in 'a nice coffin' in the grounds of the prison, where they remained until October 2001.[26] A few months later, Mary Barry received 'a very courteous letter' from Monro, inviting her and family members to visit Kevin's grave. She did so. Kitby also heard that soldiers planted flowers on his grave and 'kept it in spotless order' until Mountjoy was handed over to the new state.[27]

Being inside the prison walls, the graves of Kevin and the other nine Volunteers executed in 1920–21 were in practice inaccessible to their families for seven decades. In 1948 General Seán MacEoin, a pro-Treatyite and Fine Gael minister in government with Seán MacBride's Clann na Poblachta, who had himself awaited the executioner in Mountjoy in 1921 until the Truce saved him, secured Mary Barry a pass to allow her to visit Kevin's grave at any time. This presumably was after the family had, on grounds of the still-unconsummated republic, rejected the state's offer to exhume his remains for reburial.[28] In 1924 the venerable Fenian and Clan na Gael man John Devoy celebrated his eighty-second birthday and last trip to Ireland by visiting prisons in which he had been held including Mountjoy, where he saw 'the graves of Kevin Barry and others'.[29] Presumably the plots continued to receive some attention, but generally speaking the families did not have access.

There is both a parallel and a fascinating coincidence in accounts of Kevin's last days and those of another man condemned by a British tribunal. It fell to the Chief Secretary for Ireland Sir Hamar Greenwood to defend Kevin's execution, as well as the many excesses of Crown forces in Ireland in 1920 and 1921, to the House of Commons. Greenwood, a plodding Canadian, often appeared somewhat out of his depth. Although he stoutly defended the actions of Crown forces, he did so without much force, conviction or ingenuity. In December 1921 Macready described him as 'that double-distilled ass Hamar', a judgement doubly cruel because Greenwood was a teetotaller.[30]

Yet a quarter of a century later Greenwood went through something not unlike what the Barrys and the families of other Irish rebels sentenced to death had experienced: the trial for treason and execution by hanging of his nephew, John ('Jack') Amery (1912–1945). Jack was the errant son of Leo Amery, a long-time Churchill loyalist in the 1930s, and from 1940 to 1945 Secretary of State for India in Churchill's wartime coalition. During years of erratic living in Europe in the 1930s Jack embraced anti-Semitism – perhaps not realising that he had Jewish blood – became obsessively anti-communist, fought for Franco in Spain and took up with the Axis powers. In 1942 he began making propaganda broadcasts from Italy. When Leo steeled himself to listen to one of these, he at first disbelieved that the voice was Jack's, but was quietly dissuaded from stating this in public by his cabinet colleague Minister for Information Brendan Bracken (who, as we have seen, had briefly overlapped with Kevin in the O'Connell School and with Paddy Moloney in Mungret in the course of 1915).[31] Jack also attempted to recruit British prisoners-of-war to join the Legion of St George, like Casement's Irish Brigade a dismal exercise, which attracted only a handful of volunteers lured by the offer of better conditions.[32]

Captured early in 1945 as he attempted to reach Switzerland, Jack was repatriated to Britain. Despite access to the most eminent lawyers, he insisted upon pleading guilty to treason under the same 1351 act last used against Casement, and with similar results. Sentenced to death in November 1945, his father, out of office following Churchill's general election defeat in July, and his younger brother Julian (1919–1996), who had led guerrilla bands behind German lines in Albania while Jack was extolling the virtues of Nazism, made frantic efforts to save him. Leo Amery suspected that the dyspeptic Labour home secretary Chuter Ede (who once told his private secretary that he despised all his cabinet colleagues) 'wishes to dispose of J[ack]' before 'Lord Haw'. This was William Joyce (1900–1946), who had arguably a stronger defence of not being of British nationality: the British passport he had used to travel to Germany in 1939 had been fraudulently obtained, as he was not a British but an American citizen. Joyce was, nevertheless, inevitably condemned to the gallows (he too, of course, had Irish links, growing up in Galway where he was said to have acted as a tout for the Black and Tans). He was eventually reinterred in Ireland in 1976.[33]

Jack Amery made recompense to his family by the manner of his death. He expressed relief that efforts to impugn his sanity had failed, and sorrow for the trouble he had caused. In their final meeting in Wandsworth prison, Leo 'said that this had been our happiest hour. He [Jack] said he was not worried about anything except the trouble he had caused me. I said "You have been very brave." He drew himself up and said "I am your son" ... It was all happy and quite unforced, just a natural parting on the eve of a long voyage'. Jack 'thanked the warders and chaplain for their courtesy and then walked unassisted to his end'.[34] 'He never was quite normal until in the face of death he rose to a super-normal height that anyone could envy and admire ...'[35] It is not recorded if his uncle Hamar, who had assured Leo of Churchill's deep affection for him after Jack's first broadcast in November 1942, noted any parallels with Kevin's fate.

One further minor coincidence connects Kevin's family with his executioners. Kitby's only son Patrick (Paddy) Barry Moloney (1927–1989), who bore the names of his two uncles killed during the War of Independence,[36] spent most of his adult life in Britain working for Mobil Oil. He provided his employers with a full written account of his family background. From 1975 to 1985 the Mobil chairman was Sir Nevil Macready, 3rd baronet and grandson of General Macready. Paddy told me that the chairman never alluded to his grandfather's Irish experiences, and he in turn never mentioned his slain rebel uncles. When Paddy retired, Macready wrote that 'I have appreciated your tactful & considerate help & advice & we shall miss you', in stark contrast to how his grandfather had signed off on Paddy's uncle Kevin's life in 1920.

Governor Monro, whose courtesy throughout was appreciated by the family, who had accompanied Kevin to the gallows, and who identified his remains at the inquest, retired in January 1923 under Article 10 of the Treaty, which gave preferential pension treatment to officials who did not wish to serve under the new Irish state. But he found himself in 'pecuniary embarrassment' in his Portstewart, Co. Derry home. Before he could receive his General Prisons Board pension, information was needed concerning the twelve years he

had spent in service in Burma prior to coming to Mountjoy in
1902. The matter was eventually somehow addressed. Four years
later, however, there remained some uncertainty about his precise
Indian entitlements. The India Office calculated his Indian pension
at 25 rupees 3 annas a month, or £26 9s. 0d. a year. But after
four months they had to write once more, because of an arithmetic
error. In actuality, his Indian pension was 1d. less than he had been
told.[37]

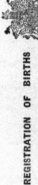

REGISTRATION OF BIRTHS AND DEATHS IN IRELAND.

Certified Copy of Entry in the Register Book of Births deposited in the Superintendent Registrar's Office.—(See Endorsement.)

1902. BIRTHS Registered in the District of 2 South City in the Union of South Dublin in the County of Dublin.

No. (1.)	Date and Place of Birth. (2.)	Name (if any) (3.)	Sex. (4.)	Name and Surname and Dwelling-place of Father. (5.)	Name and Surname and Maiden Surname of Mother (6.)	Rank or Profession of Father. (7.)	Signature, Qualification, and Residence of Informant. (8.)	When Registered. (9.)	Signature of Registrar. (10.)	Baptismal Name, if added after Registration of Birth, and Date. (11.)
174	1902. Twentieth January 8 Fleet St.	Kevin Gerard	m	Thomas Barry 8 Fleet St.	Mary Barry Formerly Dowling	Dairy owner	The mark of Twentieth Catherine Kinsella February present at birth 1902. 8 Fleet St.		J.F. Carter 2nd Registrar.	

I hereby Certify that the foregoing is a true Copy of the Entry No. 174 in the Register Book of Births of the above District deposited in my Office.

Office James's Street Dublin

Date 26th October 1920

N. Condon

Act. Superintendent Registrar of Births, Deaths and Marriages,

for the District of Dublin

A copy of Kevin's birth certificate, issued just five days before his death. Note that his birth was registered by housekeeper Catherine (Kate) Kinsella, who made her mark in lieu of a signature. (UCDA P93/1. Reproduced by kind permission of UCD Archives.)

Taken from the *Belvederian* annual, this picture shows Kevin Barry (middle row, third from left) as a senior student with the Belvedere hurling team, 1919. (UCDA P93/14. Reproduced by kind permission of UCD Archives.)

Detail of Kevin, taken from Father McGrath's 'Men of the House' photograph of 1918–19. (Reproduced by kind permission of the Jesuit Archive.)

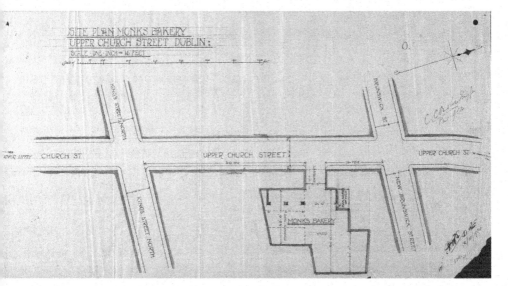

...cale map of Upper Church Street, Dublin, presented in evidence at Kevin's court martial, ...0 October 1920 (TNA, WO71/360).

The scene after the capture of Kevin Barry in Upper Church Street, 20 September 1920. (Reproduced by kind permission of RTÉ.)

Army Form W. 3996.

INSTRUCTIONS FOR THE GUIDANCE OF COURTS MARTIAL WHERE A SENTENCE OF DEATH HAS BEEN PASSED.

To _Kevin Berry, otherwise Barry_

The Court have found you guilty of the following charges _namely_

the charge of murdering no. 4603625 Private Matthew Whitehead on 20th September 1920.

~~but not guilty of the following charges,~~

The Court have passed a sentence of death upon you.

The Court have made _a_ _{no} recommendation to mercy in the following terms.

You should clearly understand :—

(i) That the finding or findings and sentence are not valid until confirmed by the proper authority.

(ii) That the authority having power to confirm the finding or findings and sentence may withhold confirmation of the finding or findings, or may withhold confirmation of the sentence, or may mitigate, commute or remit the sentence, or may send the finding or findings and sentence back to the Court for revision.

If you do not clearly understand the foregoing you should request to see an officer, who will fully explain the matter to you.

C.C. Oz Slow. Brigadier. President.

General Court Martial.

Marlborough Barracks, Dublin Place.

20th. October 1920 Date.

The original court martial verdict signed by Brigadier Onslow and delivered to Kevin by Captain Barrett. (Reproduced by kind permission of Ruth Sweetman.)

I want you to keep up the acquaintance with Jerry and the boys. I believe the usual thing done in my case is to make a speech from the dock or something but I couldn't be serious long enough to do it. Besides anyone who ever knew me would never believe that I wrote it.

Now I'll shut up I wish you every success in love and business. Give my adieux to Des and your mother and say a little prayer when I cash in.

your pal

Kevin

I'd write to Eily but I'm not sure of the address.

The final page of Kevin's farewell letter to Kathleen Carney. Dated Sunday, 30 October 1920, it appears to have been written on the evening of 31 October, the night before his execution. (Reproduced by kind permission of Ruth Sweetman.)

This photograph of women praying outside Mountjoy jail on the morning of Kevin's execution was carried in foreign as well as in Irish and British newspapers. This news-cutting featured in *The Sheffield Independent*, dated 3 November 1920. (UCDA P93/25. Reproduced by kind permission of UCD Archives.)

Front cover of the *Our Martyr Boy* pamphlet which was published in Buenos Aires in 1921. It carries the subtitle *Kevin Barry, Victim of Britonism in Ireland* and is just one example of the many publications across the world in which Kevin's execution was covered. (Reproduced by kind permission of Michael O'Rahilly.)

Kitby with grandchildren Dara, Eunan and Helen O'Halpin, Howth, summer 1955. (Image courtesy of the author.)

Sheila (O'Donovan) Hanna, Monty (Barry) O'Donovan and Mick Barry at the O'Donovans' golden wedding celebration, Dalkey, 28 April 1976. In the background from left are Jim O'Donovan, Jim Moloney and Moss Twomey. (Reproduced by kind permission of Louise O'Donovan.)

Contemporary interpretation of the iconic photograph of Kevin Barry by Dublin street artist, Canvaz. This is from the artist's popular The Rebels series of outdoor works, and is a good example of Kevin's legacy within popular culture. (Reproduced by kind permission of Canvaz, 2016.)

CHAPTER EIGHT

The Immediate Impact of Kevin's Execution

It is difficult to separate the impact of Kevin's execution from the broader press of events in Ireland. His death seemed to many, coming so soon after MacSwiney's and amidst a growing litany of unofficial reprisals and dubious killings by Crown forces, as confirmation that policy in Ireland was being conducted on entirely the wrong lines: that was certainly the view of Henry Wilson, who warned ministers that the only way to contain and justify reprisals was for the government to take responsibility for them and to set out a clear schedule of when, why and against whom they would be directed, as Macready demanded.

Further horrors shortly to come, including the IRA's 21 November Bloody Sunday morning killings, the RIC's shooting that afternoon of fourteen people at Croke Park and the spectacular success of Tom Barry's men at Kilmichael in West Cork on 28 November, deepened the gloom without changing most people's minds one way or the other.

What can definitely be said, however, is that Canon Waters' account of Kevin's last hours turned him from being solely a republican into an Irish Catholic martyr. Waters' version of Kevin was amplified particularly by the Irish Catholic clerical diaspora. It also resonated in Ireland itself.

In asking Cardinal Bourne of Westminster, the leader of Catholicism in England and Wales, to intercede with the British government to abandon their policy of coercion, a Kilkenny solicitor who described himself as an unrepentant Redmondite referenced 'the manly and religious death of Kevin Barry'.[1] The public conjoining of Kevin's Catholicism with his Irishness caused difficulties for other Catholics. Bourne found himself in a delicate position in addressing the Irish issue in 1920–1. Amongst his papers are various intemperate attacks upon him for not speaking out in support of Irish Catholics. One anonymous letter from Colorado termed him 'a dog posing as a Catholic ... a damned thief and murder[er]'. A Monaghan parish priest wrote in only slightly more measured terms to observe that 'Lloyd George the Baptist ... sent you greetings on your jubilee' and complained that when the Archbishop of Melbourne Dr Mannix, who four years later would introduce Kitby to an expectant audience as sister of 'one of Ireland's honoured martyrs', was prevented from landing in Ireland, 'you sang dumb' whereas other Catholic prelates across the empire had spoken in protest.[2] Catholic bishops – at any rate those of Irish extraction – were indeed more forthright on alleged British misdeeds in Ireland. In New Zealand Bishop Joseph Liston (1881–1976) was, in 1922, farcically tried for sedition for his St Patrick's Day utterances.[3] But Cardinal Bourne, though Irish on his mother's side, was an English prelate presiding over a body of Catholics who, though a small minority in Britain, undoubtedly outnumbered the Irish Catholic population. The point was indirectly made by Prime Minister Lloyd George, who had all the Welsh nonconformist suspicion of popery although not averse to sins of the flesh himself (his personal secretary Frances Stephenson had been his more-or-less openly acknowledged mistress since 1913). His letter of thanks to Bourne for leading the service 'in your beautiful Cathedral' for the three English Catholic officers killed in Dublin on Bloody Sunday stressed that 'the manner of their deaths has filled the hearts of Catholics no less than Protestants, with horror'.[4]

Curiously, the Archbishop of Canterbury, ecclesiastical head of the Anglican church, found it less problematic to speak out against government policy towards Ireland than did his Catholic counterpart. Although he did not mention Kevin by name, on the day following the execution Randall Davidson gave a powerful denunciation in the House of Lords of the conduct of British forces in Ireland. The Archbishop was not simply the Anglican church's most senior divine: he was also a pillar of the British constitution, and he did nothing in the public sphere on a whim or without first reflecting on its implications for the state and particularly for the Crown (with which he was in constant touch through the King's private secretary Lord Stamfordham). Davidson later noted how 'the speech attracted wide attention on account of its criticism of the Government's reprisal action'. The Liverpool Irish Party MP and father of the House of Commons T.P O'Connor hailed it two days later: he did not

> know of any ecclesiastic who has held that great and dignified position who has a higher reputation for caution and discretion ... the language of His Grace the Archbishop of Canterbury shows that he accepts one of the fundamental criticisms which I have offered ... namely, that this policy of frightfulness is doing great, if not irreparable damage to the good faith and the good name of England.[5]

When Davidson contemplated returning to the Irish issue in February 1921 to show 'that we do not tamely accept the responsibility for what is being done in Ireland', Stamfordham 'at first was against another public pronouncement ... but as we talked, he came around to my view'.[6]

J.H. Thomas (1874–1949), a leading trade unionist and the Labour MP for Derby, read Kevin's affidavit in its entirety to the Commons on 4 November. He stated that 'I condemn him as emphatically as anybody for the murder of that policeman [sic]. Remember, he went to the scaffold not as a coward: he was a studious boy, loved by everyone who knew him, brave and educated.' Why, he asked, should someone facing death swear a false oath? Hamar Greenwood, pompous and floundering as ever, responded that 'that affidavit alleges that he was tortured by two officers of the Lancashire Fusiliers. That is a question of veracity as to whether that man swore the truth or whether the officers, who deny it, told the truth.' He accepted their word over Kevin's sworn statement. This provoked an interjection from the Tipperary-born Labour MP John Jones (1873–1941): 'He was a Catholic going to face his death. I am not going to stand quietly and hear my faith insulted.' When Greenwood reiterated that 'I accept the word of the officers of the regiment,' Jones retorted: 'I accept the word of the man who was executed.' After further exchanges, Greenwood stated that 'if it is the torturing of anybody, whatever the crime is, then it is a damnable thing', but he attempted to discredit the affidavit: 'the last terms ... are couched in legal language, do not read like the words of a medical student, and they go to convince me that the affidavit was prepared for him'. Yet what is most striking about Kevin's statement is its matter-of-fact, deadpan tone.

Thomas's Irish sympathies were not of unlimited duration. Twelve years later, as dominions secretary in the National Government, he found himself at the epicentre of Anglo-Irish tensions during the most acute stage of the 'Economic War' of 1932–8. He proved quite unable to match de Valera's wiles, and was reduced to ineffectual huffiness well before he was obliged to resign from office in 1936 for his indiscretion in giving hints about the forthcoming budget to newly acquired wealthy friends.[7]

Mary Barry and her family were inundated with messages, Mass cards, telegrams and letters of condolence, admiration and condemnation of the British action in executing her son.

She reportedly took the view that 'she needed no sympathy, she felt proud', while Kitby was quoted as saying 'He is gone to a greater and nobler reward than any of us can expect. We feel, but we do not regret, his death.'[8] Commiseration came from within and beyond Ireland, and not all were from people and groups sympathetic to Irish republicanism. Some of these communications, and wider general sympathy, were prompted by Kevin's perceived youth: a Cork loyalist wrote to a friend of his outrage that the government should hang 'that boy'.[9] But in that respect indignation and compassion did Kevin a disservice. Whatever his hopes for a reprieve, he certainly did not want one on the basis of his age and imputed inability to act like an adult. He clearly saw himself not as a gormless teenager in thrall to older men whose orders he was afraid to disobey, but as a young man and soldier who had made his own choices and who was willing to fight and, if needs be, to die for his country.

Amidst all the sorrows and piety, perhaps a little levity may be permitted. A letter addressed 'To The Commissioner, Sinn Fein Headquarters, Galway, County Cork' found its way to the small propaganda unit based in Dublin Castle. Dated 2 November, it came from a Mrs J.A. Holloway, a medium, of Salford. She had 'heard a voice call out from the Heavens as I was in my kitchen'. It was Kevin, who had been reproved by God for killing nine victims: he was to 'mend those bodies and they will be your friends in Eternity … You have been a good lad but drawn into sin by those who stood at a distance while you were committing the deeds you have done.' According to Mrs Holloway, Kevin continued: 'For Christ's sake will you send a message to the people and friends of mine in Ireland. Tell them stop their wicked deeds that is sending so many people to their doom … they pray for the soul of an executed man but they don't call on their God when they are sending men to eternity.' He sent 'My sweet love to my dear mother & relatives also my fellow students tell them to leave off secret societies,' and gave news of Terence MacSwiney, who 'is far happier than he would be in Ireland. He sends his sweet love to his dear wife and family and all friends.'[10]

Eccentric though this letter was, the idea of psychic communication between the dead and the living was very much a part of post-Great War life across Europe as people attempted to come to terms with their losses. During the stressful months of the civil war Kitby, already a firm believer in the Tombeagh ghost and in the supernatural generally, frequently mentioned 'Kev' as her protector and guide in her letters to her fiancé Jim Moloney. She and Jim also experimented with mental telepathy and automatic writing, apparently without much success.[11] What she would have made of Mrs Holloway's report we cannot know, but it might have been, in a very dark hour, a welcome distraction for the Barry family.

Avenging Kevin

One of the many reasons why Kevin's execution was notable was because of what failed to happen in the immediate aftermath. Given the strength of feeling within the Dublin IRA about Kevin, this omission is rather surprising. There was some talk within the leadership of assassinating both Lloyd George and Bonar Law in revenge for Kevin, but this wild scheme did not materialise.[12] There was no immediate wave of IRA retaliation. In fact, Dublin was rather quiet for the following twenty days: this, it transpired, was because of preparations for the huge operation planned for 21 November, what became known as 'Bloody Sunday'. British officials were unsure of whether that action was 'a reprisal for Kevin Barry', although in point of fact it had been months in the making.[13]

The impact of Kevin's death upon young people, particularly UCD students, was immediate. In an often quoted diary entry, Celia Shaw recorded how 'we lost all our humanitarian feelings and actually rejoiced' when they heard of Crown forces deaths.[14]

In December the Labour party commission of inquiry visiting Ireland heard that Kevin's death had caused 'hundreds' of students to volunteer for the IRA, a claim which still needs to be tested. Todd Andrews doubted 'whether even Terence MacSwiney's death ... aroused such bitter anti-British emotions ... As rank and file IRA men we could not visualise ourselves cast in the same heroic mould [as MacSwiney] but it was easy to imagine ourselves sharing the plight of Kevin Barry.'[15]

Just a few days after Derry's 'Bloody Sunday' in 1972, P.G.B. Wills of Wadhurst, Sussex, attempted to explain matters on the letters page of *The Times*:

> The English are not great brooders on martyrdom. Ask any hundred people in London who was Nurse Cavell and it is doubtful if 10 could answer. Ask any hundred people in Dublin who was Kevin Barry, and it is doubtful if fewer than 90 would tell you, and at great length.[16]

After his trial, and in death, Kevin was called many different things in different places. The *Newcastle Chronicle, The Yorkshire Herald* and *The Sheffield Independent* spoke with typical northern bluntness of the 'Sinn Fein Murderer' and the 'condemned man', whereas the *Daily Dispatch* of Manchester discussed the 'boy student ... the 19-year-old' Kevin Barry. The day after his death, the *Freeman's Journal* reported one speaker who declaimed against the killing of a 'school-boy', and carried a picture of 'the school-boy who died'. *The Evening Standard* of London was unusual though accurate in pointing out that 'many of the young soldiers who have been cruelly done to death' in Ireland 'were but youths too. Barry was old enough to be a corporal [in the IRA]'. The *Edinburgh Evening Dispatch* advanced the same argument, saying of the soldiers killed that 'these poor youths were deprived of life without a moment for preparation. What sympathy there may be should be for them and their friends, not for deliberate murderers.'[17] Kevin was often a 'medical student', in Germany a *'Student der Medizin'*, in Spain *'estudiante de medicina'*, in Australia a '17-year-old Sinn Fein student', in a Lyon newspaper *'un jeune enfant de 13 ans, Nevan Barry'*, sometimes a plain 'student'.[18] In South Carolina, *The Dillon Herald* reported him as 'the only child of his widowed mother'.[19] An Alaskan newspaper inelegantly described him as a 'rioter', although acknowledging that he was executed for killing a soldier.[20] In Nottingham he was 'the boy Sinn Feiner'. He was occasionally a 'killer', frequently 'young', sometimes 'a boy', once 'an Irish Hero [who] Spurns Bribe', a 'youthful murderer' and in British military memory in 1921, 'notorious', although the former Auxiliary commander General Crozier wrote of 'the young student boy'.[21] *The Halifax Guardian* reported Kevin's fate under the headline 'The Penalty Paid: Youth who killed Halifax Soldier' (Marshall Whitehead was from Halifax).[22] *Dziennik Chicagoski*, a Polish émigré newspaper, reported the death of the '18-year-old Sinn Feiner' on the front page.[23] A Californian weekly stated that the 'calm and unflinching ... 18-year old Sinn Feiner ... told the prison chaplain that he forgave his enemies'.[24] In New Zealand, the *Matuara Ensign* stated 'Murderer Gets His Deserts', the *Fielding Star* 'Murderer [is] to be hanged', the *Marlborough Express* 'Boy Sentenced to Death'; all the detailed reportage in such newspapers, derived from one or another press agency, was however relatively sympathetic and subdued.[25] A Catholic newspaper in Perth, Australia, described his death under the heading: '"I'm off on Monday morning." A Graphic Narrative of Kevin Barry's Extraordinary Courage and Fortitude in Suffering Extreme Torture, and his inspiring Faith and Resignation.'[26] The *Times of India* simply noted 'Medical Student Executed'. In Buenos Aires in 1921, people could read *Our Martyr Boy, Kevin Barry, Victim of Britonism in Ireland*, which told of how 'the Englishmen trampled him on the ground, broke his ribs', wrenched his arms 'from their sockets', 'gouged' him with bayonets, kicked out his teeth, till eventually he 'finally succumbed to death', his body 'horribly mutilated'. He was convicted by 'a fake court martial', and 'his mutilated remains were then strung on the gallows'.[27]

Canadian newspapers in Newfoundland and Manitoba noted the sentencing and execution of this 'student', as well as his affidavit about 'torture'.[28] A French news agency reported on '*Exécution du jeune Sinn Feiner*', publishing a photograph of '*Femmes priant dans une rue*' as the execution took place. During the sedition trial of the republican monk Father Dominic in 1921, it emerged that in a captured letter he had written of 'poor little Kevin Barry', an epithet which would surely have embarrassed its subject as much as would have his becoming 'another martyr for old Ireland' in the hugely influential commemorative ballad 'Kevin Barry'.[29]

Kevin's background and age were often communicated together: he was the 'eighteen-year-old medical student' whose talismanic sports photograph the *Albuquerque Morning Journal* carried.[30] Two images of Kevin, copied from Belvedere team photographs, quickly circulated around the world. One was of him amongst the 1918–19 hurling team, aged sixteen, where his head is inclined and he is holding a hurley; a detail cut from that larger image appeared in the *Daily Sketch* of London on the morning of his execution. In the second image, which shows him aged seventeen in the Old Belvedere Rugby Club Second XI of 1919, his head is upright.[31]

Kevin's name and image were deployed for other purposes. As early as 1922, a detail from the 1919 'Pillars of the House' photograph was used on a memorial card printed as 'a means of raising money for the St Vincent de Paul Society'.[32] Kevin's status as a 'student' and as a 'medical student' had a distinct register, signalling a certain social status; just as the ordeal and death of the hunger-striking Terence MacSwiney in Brixton prison a week before Kevin's execution had captured the world's attention. This had been partly – if incongruously, given its British monarchical derivation – because he held the august title of 'Lord Mayor' of Cork rather than because when arrested he had been the officer commanding the IRA's Cork No. 1 Brigade. Kevin's association with the middle-class and largely Protestant secondary-school game of rugby was held against him by one sour monsignor. When Sarsfield Hogan, once president of the Irish Rugby Football Union, mentioned that he had played rugby alongside Kevin in Belvedere, the cleric remarked that Kevin would have been a better Irishman had he played only Gaelic games. Kevin's Catholic middle-class status, so similar to many of the 1916 leaders, may, as M.A. Doherty argues, have been one reason why the army were so determined to hang him.[33]

Perhaps the main problem with commemoration and invocation of his passing was how quickly Catholicised it became. It may be unfair solely to blame Canon Waters for this, but whatever the reason, allusions to his death quickly acquired an acutely Catholic character. For all Kitby's social and economic radicalism, and her fierce resentment of the Irish Catholic bishops for their denunciation of the anti-Treaty side in the civil war, she seems to have been comfortable enough with the very Catholic Kevin commemorated in the years after his death. In 1932 she was quick to tell an American priest how observant Kevin had been: '"Aye, yes, of course," Mrs Moloney answers readily, almost cheerfully. "Went to his duties, to Mass, said his prayers, was obedient and good around the house, and all that. But, of course, he was not studying for the Church".' Perhaps, of course, she was just being diplomatic.[34]

MacSwiney's death had the greater initial international impact, especially in India. Asked to name books that had made an impression during his student days, a leading nationalist could recall only 'Yes, one, a small pamphlet ... on MacSwiney, the Irish leader.'[35] Yet over the decades it is Kevin who has had the longer shelf life as an international icon of the independence struggle. One reason may be that, as was certainly the case in India, MacSwiney was understood as a political figure, an elected civic leader rather than as an IRA commander. Many leading Indian advocates of non-violent resistance to British rule, including Gandhi and Nehru, saw hunger-striking as a legitimate form of protest against coercive British authority, an alternative rather than an adjunct to physical force.[36] Internationally, MacSwiney was interpreted essentially as a political thinker and a pioneer of peaceful protest and heroic self-sacrifice, a Gandhian figure rather than a physical-force nationalist.

By contrast Kevin became an immediately recognisable and long-lasting youthful icon of armed struggle, his memory refreshed and amplified through his Belvedere photographs. In terms of the use of his image for contemporary political iconography, he resembles the 21-year-old Indian freedom fighter or *shaheed* (martyr) Bhagat Singh, executed in 1931 for killing a British officer, like himself just 21 years of age, in error for a more senior man. Bhagat Singh's dashing, moustached, slouch-hatted image is continuously rendered across India on posters, wall paintings, T-shirts and websites. He was a Sikh and an agnostic socialist revolutionary, yet his image and memory are now invoked not only by left-wing groups and progressive protest movements, but by right-wing factions including the Shaheed Bhagat Singh Brigade, an extreme Hindu nationalist organisation. Hindu nationalists often portray him wearing not his slouch hat, but a saffron turban, linking his Sikh identity with the colour sacred to Hinduism.[37]

Kevin's picture is, along with Nelson Mandela's, the only immediately recognisable image on Sinn Féin's 2020 calendar.[38] Contemporary Irish republicans fairly point to Kevin's youth not to argue that he was acting under orders and was barely old enough to take a decision, but to demonstrate that the young are well capable of fighting and dying for Ireland.[39]

CHAPTER NINE

Not Forgotten

The dramatic deaths, in quick succession, of MacSwiney and of Kevin resonated across nationalist Ireland and around the world. Sympathy for their fates generally transcended the chasm between the ascendant separatist movement and the waning, though still deeply embedded, Redmondite constitutional nationalist movement.

The very act of remembering Kevin may have led other young men to their doom. Patrick Kennedy, an 18-year-old plasterer from Corporation Street, was searched by Auxiliaries when leaving the cinema on the night of 9 February 1921. The only suspicious thing found on him was a poem about Kevin. He and James Murphy, a young grocer's assistant, were taken to Dublin Castle for interrogation. The Auxiliaries said that the two were later released; in fact they were murdered. A witness told the IRA he saw a car containing seven men arrive at Clonturk Park, heard shots, and then saw five men re-enter the vehicle and leave. At 11.10 p.m. a policeman on duty heard moans from Clonturk Park and found Kennedy dead, shot twice in the back and once in the head. Murphy, also shot in the head and body, died at 5 a.m. Three Auxiliaries – Captain H. L. King, Cadet H. Hinchcliffe and Cadet Welch – were tried for Murphy's murder but acquitted on 15 April 1921. The only surprise was that Dublin Castle had put them to the trouble of defending themselves.[1] Three months later 19-year-old Stephen O'Reilly of Wellesley Place was shot dead by Auxiliaries during the Custom House raid, a disaster alike for the Dublin IRA and for posterity as most records covering the development and administration of Irish local government were destroyed. As well as being assistant adjutant of the 2nd Battalion, Dublin Brigade Stephen wrote as 'Banba' in the *Meath Chronicle*, his last piece being a eulogy of Kevin.[2]

Not remembering Kevin appropriately could also be fatal. Antagonists of Sinn Féin and the IRA remained visible and unapologetic actors in local politics not only in Redmond's personal bailiwick of Waterford but in the Ulster counties, where the AOH provided comradeship, muscle and a considerable counterweight to local republicans. Such fraternal resilience was not enough to save 47-year-old Arthur Treanor of Emyvale, district president of the AOH and an elected member of the Monaghan Board of Guardians and Monaghan Rural District Council. According to his widow, at a council meeting in November he disassociated himself from a resolution of sympathy on the deaths of MacSwiney and of Kevin. This demonstration of moral courage set in train a series of events, which decades later still troubled the consciences of some Monaghan republicans. In December 1921 a large party of Volunteers visited Treanor's home, 'called him to account for having refused to associate himself with the resolutions of sympathy, and told him he must pay a £10 fine for spying'.[3] After two further such visitations when he happened to be away, Treanor left his farm, wife and six children for England, remaining there for some months. IRA veteran Patrick McGrory maintained that Treanor, who 'was too intensely Irish to betray a fellow Irishman', eventually returned in mid-May because he had received an IRA safe conduct. On 21 June at 10 p.m. his daughter Kathleen was on her way to 'close the fowl house door' when she 'heard boys coming down the lane'. Her father slipped away out the back door just before three armed men entered and demanded the fine. Mary Treanor paid them the money and they assured her that they would 'do their best to get her husband out of further trouble', and left. Treanor returned home early the following morning, believing he was now safe. But the three Volunteers soon came back, tied his hands and led him away. They took him some distance to his other farm – suggesting that a grievance about land might have underpinned the accusations against him – and there shot him in the head. A paper attached to his body stated: 'Spies and informers Beware, Tried and Convicted by IRA'. His remains were brought home to 'scenes of indescribable grief ... one of the little children went over to the body, caught one of the cold hands, and attempted to raise its daddy'. *The Anglo-Celt* reported that 'though the time fixed for the funeral was not widely known', presumably for fear of republican intimidation, 'thousands assembled ... for the interment at Carrickroe'. The AOH later erected a large Celtic cross over Treanor's grave, as they did over those of two other members killed by the Monaghan IRA. A military court of inquiry pinned responsibility on 'Owen Duffy', the local IRA commander later to become first a pioneering Garda commissioner, and from 1933 the first president of the newly formed Fine Gael party as well as the preening leader of the short-lived quasi-Fascist Blueshirt movement.[4]

In October 1921 Lady Augusta Gregory was 'so glad to give' permission to Kevin Barry's 'own Company' to perform her play *The Rising of the Moon* in the Queen's Theatre, Dublin, in a fundraiser for 'war-stricken Volunteers'. On St Stephen's Day that year, local Wren Boys who called to her home at Coole entertained her and guests including her near neighbours the Bagot family. Just seven months earlier the Galway IRA had killed the heavily pregnant Eliza Blake, her RIC husband and two army officers at the front gate of the Bagots' house as they left a tennis party. The singers, 'knowing but few lines about the wren', instead 'gave a song about Kevin Barry being hanged in Mountjoy gaol "for Ireland's sake"'.[5] We may wonder if the Bagots sang along.

Namesakes

Over the years Kevin's first name and surname were given to generations of Irish boys, and boys of Irish extraction, in a wide range of places and communities. An Internet survey in 2018 threw up some surprises. The first is the sheer power of the names. This seems partly a function of the fact that conjoined they are balanced in four syllables, and also perhaps that Kevin Barry reads and sounds as natural as two Christian names as it does as a Christian name and surname.

Of births in Britain during the 1920s and 1930s, ten boys had the name 'Kevin Barry', most of these in the north of England. In Ireland there were many more. Amongst early such christenings were the historian and fearless conservation champion Kevin B. Nowlan (1921–2012), born a year to the day after Kevin's execution, who made little of his middle name. Another early exercise in naming caused some controversy in New Zealand, at the time a loyal and Protestant-dominated dominion where there was precious little sympathy for Irish separatism. In October 1921 the Otago Trotting Association refused to accept an entry named 'Kevin Barry', prompting one newspaper to observe that 'You can call a horse after a dead Turk or a living actress, but it will not do to call it after a dead Celt.' The animal had already run in the 'Geraldine Handicap Trot of 120 sov[ereign]s' and was entered for other races, apparently without much success: perhaps the Otago trotting authorities were not prejudiced imperialists after all, but just better judges of horseflesh.[6]

Another horse reared a commemorative head in 1951, when Ballyneety became the first Irish-ridden showjumper in decades to win the prestigious King George V Gold Cup at Hickstead. If any English observers realised that the horse was named to commemorate the feat of Galloping Hogan, who had helped Patrick Sarsfield to destroy King William's siege train during the Siege of

Limerick in 1690, and that its Irish army rider Captain Kevin Barry
bore the name of an executed Irish rebel, they smarted in silence.[7]

No one passed comment in Britain in 1963 when Kevin Barry
(1936–2014), son of an Irishman and named after our Kevin, toured
England and Wales with Wilson Whineray's powerful All Blacks
New Zealand rugby union squad. Nor was there any fuss when his
son Kevin (b. 1959) won a bronze medal in the light heavyweight
boxing division at the Commonwealth Games in Brisbane in 1982.
The boxer Barry recalls the occasion as 'one of the best memories
… My father loved this.' Barry went on to greater glory two years
later in the Los Angeles Olympics, when he won a silver medal
at light heavyweight. Yugoslavia's Anton Josipovic – later to be
seriously wounded by a would-be assassin in Bosnia – secured the
gold medal without having to throw a single punch: safety protocols
prevented Kevin from fighting because he had been knocked out in
the semi-final by an illegal blow. His opponent Evander Holyfield,
soon to become a giant of the professional game, and in time
himself the victim of a gross breach of fight rules when part of his
ear was bitten off by Mike Tyson, was disqualified for punching
after the bell, a verdict most observers (including the New Zealand
team) thought harsh. Kevin had hoped to call his own first born
son Kevin, but 'when I found out I was having twins I couldn't do
it': the boys were instead christened Michael and Joseph.[8]

Bearing a celebrated name is no guarantee of virtue. Newspapers
record a variety of Kevin Barry criminals of varying degrees of
delinquency. There were a medley of drunk drivers, street brawlers
and petty thieves. In 1977 22-year-old Kevin Barry received a
suspended sentence for stealing two piano accordions and a tape
recorder from the Presentation Convent in Carrick-on-Suir, and two
bottles of wine from a shop, shaming not one but two icons of the
revolutionary era as he lived in Pearse Square.[9] Other namesakes
carried out far more horrible crimes. In 1959 21-year-old Kevin
Barry O'Connor of Sunderland mortally injured a disabled woman

with whom he had been drinking, after she refused his sexual advances: on appeal his life conviction for murder was reduced to five years for manslaughter.[10] Kevin Barry McKenna of Leeds, leader of a gang that preyed upon elderly people across Britain, was convicted of the manslaughter of an 80-year-old woman they tied up while robbing her of £20 (they missed over £300 hidden in a cupboard). In 2003 18-year-old Kevin Barry Moyna was charged with attempted murder using a hammer during a burglary in Belfast.[11]

The conjoined name also lives in the public sphere. Prominent twenty-first century bearers include the American playwright Kevin Barry (b. 1951), whose *Rebel County* was performed in Cincinnati in 2010; Limerick author Kevin Barry (b. 1969), who won the 2013 International Impac Dublin Literary Award, worth £100,000, for *City of Bohane*; and the former head (2003–5) of the powerful British GMB (General, Municipal, Boiler-makers') union, Kevin Barry Curran, son of a Carlow man who named him for our Kevin. Curran wrote that 'my name sometimes got me into a few tight spots specially ... in Scotland in the mid to late 70s', which suggests it had a continuing register not only for proponents but for opponents of Irish republicanism.[12] Why the Kildare singer-songwriter Luka Bloom forsook his given name of Kevin Barry Moore is unclear: his celebrated brother Christy has given voice to many an Irish republican ballad.

Despite his strong association with rugby – the playing of which would have seen him disbarred from Gaelic sports until the 1970s – there are some GAA clubs named after him. In Carlow, the Kevin Barry club drawing on Rathvilly, Grange and Tullow were in 1989 reportedly 'keeping hurling alive in football country'; a quick scan also disclosed clubs in Tyrone, the United States and Australia.[13] The appropriateness of clubs of what is notionally a non-partisan apolitical organisation being named after republican heroes has sometimes been questioned, but it seems unlikely that any change

of policy will emerge.[14] No rugby club followed suit, although the
Old Belvedere clubhouse in Dublin still displays Kevin's portrait,
and awards an annual Kevin Barry Trophy for the winners of a
game between the club's under-20s and Belvedere College's senior
cup team. In Hartford, Connecticut, a Kevin Barry basketball club
was doing well in local leagues in the early 1930s.[15]

What did not endure were the 'Kevin Barry clubs' set up in
Carlow and elsewhere under Catholic auspices in the 1940s
as a vehicle for pious youth recreation: these never caught the
imagination of the public, and they petered out fairly quickly. Given
Kevin's unblemished record of mild dissolution in the matters both
of girls and of drink, this was no great shame. The Kevin Barry
Chess Club was a significant force in Leinster chess for over half a
century.[16] The Irish army veterans' association established a Kevin
Barry branch, which is still in existence.[17] In Duchess County, New
York, a Kevin Barry Club was established in the early 1970s to
provide holiday breaks for Northern Irish children 'of both religious
faiths and of both sexes'.[18] One way and another, his name became
a synonym for the Irish revolution: the Glaswegian Catholic John
Reid MP (b. 1947, now Lord Reid), successively Secretary of State
for Defence and for Northern Ireland and home secretary in Tony
Blair's Labour governments between 1997 and 2007, 'learned
stories of Irish rebels such as Kevin Barry in the playground'.[19]

Soldiering On

So many men with Kevin Barry as all or part of their name are
listed as having served in the British armed services that it is
not feasible to check them all. Eleven Australian soldiers named
Kevin Barry born in 1921 or later appear in the official database
of Second World War veterans. Amongst them was the 21-year-
old Christian Brothers-educated Private Kevin James Barry, son of
a stationmaster from Brisbane, who was killed in action fighting

the Japanese in Papua New Guinea on 29 August 1942.[20] Dublin-born Gunner Kevin Barry Williams, who died in Borneo just as the war in the South Pacific ended, was born in 1918 and so was probably not named for our Kevin, unless he added Barry at his confirmation.[21]

The Australian data suggests a generational effect: most of the men with Kevin Barry within their names, whom I identified through military records, were born in the years immediately after Kevin's execution to parents with an Irish surname. There is no Kevin among the seven Barrys listed as serving in the Korean War, and only one Kevin amongst the twenty-four Australian Barrys who fought in Vietnam (the database does not allow searches by Christian names only). But Private Barry Kevin Bartsch of Brisbane, who on 21 March 1967 rallied his section in fierce combat with Viet Cong forces in Vietnam and was decorated in the field, was named for our Kevin.[22] Records of Canadians' Second World War service and fatalities yielded just six Barry fatalities, none of them a Kevin.[23]

In Northern Ireland Kevin Barry is most likely to be found within republican families: in 1938 Kevin Barry Hughes was charged with illegal drilling, in 1940 18-year-old Kevin Barry McNulty was charged with possession of explosives, and the following year Kevin Barry McQuillan was convicted of possession of firearms.[24] During the more recent Northern Ireland Troubles 21-year-old agriculture student Kevin Barry O'Donnell came to prominence. He twice secured acquittals in trials in London and in Belfast on arms charges, and then suffered a violent death: he was one of a group of Provisional IRA Volunteers killed after a poorly executed operation in Coalisland, Co. Tyrone, in 1992. In an echo of the disastrous Brookeborough raid at the start of the IRA's 'border campaign' of 1956–62, the IRA party drove into the town in a lorry upon which was fixed a heavy machine gun and shot up an unoccupied police station in a show of force and bravado. When their lorry reached a church car park where they had planned to disperse, they were ambushed by British special forces. Four young Volunteers were killed.

Kevin Barry Artt was more fortunate. Jailed for the murder of a prison official – a crime which he still denies – he was one of the thirty-eight IRA prisoners who escaped from the high-security Maze prison in 1983. In 1992 he was arrested in California and held for six years on immigration charges: in 1994 *The Times of India* noted how the four grand marshals, including Artt, 'could not make it' to San Francisco's St Patrick's Day parade 'as they were in prison', whereas gays and lesbians 'make their debuts'.[25]

It is perhaps surprising that the most recent Kevin Barry confirmed to have died in conflict was a Royal Air Force pilot. Flight Lieutenant Kevin Barry Main and his navigator were killed over Iraq in 2003 while returning from a bombing raid, when their Tornado aircraft was shot down by an American anti-aircraft battery, which had mistaken it for an Iraqi plane. The chairman of the United States Joint Chiefs of Staff said there was 'simply no excuse for his force to make such fatal mistakes'. The irony of a man carrying the name of an Irish freedom fighter being killed by a Patriot missile drew no comment.[26]

Kevin in Song and Story

Whereas his image, bravery and status as the first Irish republican to be executed since 1916 do much to explain Kevin's continued celebrity, songs bearing his name have copper-fastened it. Within a couple of years of his death, 'Kevin Barry' was a recognised republican anthem, easy to remember and easy to sing. From its opening lines 'In Mountjoy Jail / One Monday morning' to its culminating 'Lads like Barry will free Ireland / For her sake / They'll live and die,' the song has become a staple of Irish nationalist commemorative culture. An American journalist wrote in January

1922 that 'no one knows who wrote it or who fitted the words to it. But from lip to lip that song has passed until, through all the length and breadth of Ireland, there was scarcely one boy or girl who didn't sing it. You heard their clear treble voices.'[27] On 3 July 1926 'a party of tramps invaded Enniskillen', 'sang songs about Kevin Barry' and 'were caught by the police begging'.[28] The song was performed more decorously across the world at Irish functions such as that at the Irish Club in Wellington, New Zealand in 1940, where a reception in honour of the visiting Archbishop Mannix, an old friend of the Barry family, heard Miss Eva Higgins sing 'Fairie Tales of Ireland' and 'Kevin Barry'.[29] It featured constantly in medleys of Irish patriotic ballads: in 1966 the Limerick band The Monarchs, republican in spirit if not in name, released it as a single just before their first American tour, during which the group's John Frawley 'hit the headlines ... when a priceless rosary beads owned by his mother was stolen in New York and later recovered'.[30]

If not universally popular – Kevin's siblings generally disliked it, and his sister Monty regarded it as 'maudlin' and forbade it from her home – by the 1960s the ballad had also become part of the repertoire of the international folk music movement energised by the threat of nuclear war and realisation of the evils of colonialism. Inevitably, details became a little blurred. In 1964 a well-known Swedish folk group, the Hootenanny Singers, tried their hand with 'Have You Heard of Kevin Barry', a reworking which placed Kevin's death in an international setting.[31]

The ballad's adapter, Bjorn Ulvaeus, had rather greater success in co-writing a song about another inveterate enemy of cruel Britannia, Napoleon Bonaparte: in 1974 'Waterloo' won the Eurovision Song Contest, catapulting the group Abba to lasting fame. They later sang a political folk ballad based vaguely on Mexican revolutionaries, *Fernando*, but never tried their hand with any Irish-related anthems. Lonnie Donegan (1931–2002), the Glaswegian king of skiffle and singer of the improbable number-one hit 'My Old Man's a Dustman' in 1960, released a cover. Pete Seeger (1919–2014), a founding father of the international folk music movement, sang the song in concert and on *Strangers and Cousins* (1964). Leonard Cohen offered another rendition in 1972, although he thought the song was about the 1916 Rising.[32] The great African American singer and progressive Paul Robeson issued a powerful recording of the original ballad in 1957, with 'Ol' Man River' on the B-side.[33] 'Seán South of Garryowen', the singalong ballad that came to represent the IRA's shambolic 1956–62 border campaign (outdoing Dominic Behan's far superior 'The Patriot Game'), borrowed the line 'another martyr for old Ireland'. Perhaps as a consequence South, a prim reactionary who regarded cinemas as places of sin where 'the American tentacle of the Communist octopus' corrupted Irish youth 'by glorifying the passions', has eclipsed the rather more appealing young sportsman O'Hanlon in republican propaganda and memory.[34]

'Kevin Barry' still resonates in popular culture, although more recently created anthems such as 'The Fields of Athenry' (1979) and 'Grace' (1985) now have a far wider register, particularly with sports followers. 'Grace', a melodic dirge commemorating Joseph Plunkett, is now a staple of Glasgow Celtic supporters, and was covered in 2018 by the club's most famous fan, Rod Stewart, on his album *Blood Red Roses*. It at least makes a change from 'The Merry Ploughboy', 'Sean South of Garryowen' and other ballads favoured by Celtic supporters. As recently as July 2018, Boy George (George O'Dowd), who achieved worldwide success as lead singer of Culture Club, broke into 'Kevin Barry' on air during the filming of an episode of the BBC's *Who Do You Think You Are?* This was after he was revealed to be a grand-nephew of the young Volunteer Thomas Bryan, executed in Mountjoy on 14 March 1921. Three of Bryan's comrades died with him that day, including Kevin's friend UCD engineering student Frank Flood, who had commanded the party of Volunteers captured after the Drumcondra ambush in January 1921.[35]

In his 1989 study Donal O'Donovan reproduced twenty-six poems, songs and ballads focussing on Kevin, his death and his memory. Some were intensely pious and Catholic, such as Constance Markievicz's 1922 poem 'Kevin' which ends:

And Christ, who died for love of us,
Tortured and bruised and shamed,
Gives courage to such hero souls
Unbending and untamed.

Others, including Thomas Furlong's 'The Grave of a Rebel' published the very day Kevin died, were republican and entirely secular musings. In total, twelve of Donal's selection have clear religious overtones. Perhaps more surprisingly, fourteen do not, including a number that appeared in 1920 and 1921, and those in *Goodbye, Twilight: Songs of the Struggle in Ireland*, an anthology edited by Leslie Daiken, a Jewish progressive, published in London in 1936 by the Communist publishers Lawrence and Wishart. Síofra's father, and my own, each wrote poems about Kevin. Paidín O'Halpin's rather elliptical one ends:

Make a little pile truck driving, look sometimes at the sky:
He gave not to you or I, we do not own him
Yet do you think the streets fail to see him
Or the tree roots in vain feel for his bones?

Donal's 'A Crowded Year' (1989) essays a more straightforward exploration of Kevin's life and his resonance in death, blowing away any whiff of incense and martyrdom with suitable irreverence. It begins:

Are you the nephew of?
Who tried to inveigle the elegant tart
In the train from Rathvilly?[36]

CHAPTER TEN

Writing About Kevin

Kevin's Biographers

Kevin was a natural subject for hagiography if not for biography. Jim O'Donovan's efforts, initially commended by Kitby as those of a 'leading republican', never found a publisher. Both as husband of Kevin's sister Monty, and as a leading republican militant whose mutilated right hand bore testimony to his own activities – he lost a couple of fingers in April 1922 while demonstrating a new type of grenade – he had good access to records and to people. But he had a lot on his plate in the 1930s what with his day job, and with his sideline as editor and publisher of *Ireland Today*, a journal of political, economic and social comment. He was also the strategic planner of the IRA's 'S-Plan' British bombing campaign of 1938–9, and consolidator of the IRA's relationship with Nazi Germany. Given those links, he might have been better employed producing a study of John Amery.

Much of the material he collected now lies in his papers in the National Library. Kitby wrote in October 1948, 'I formally record my joy that you have undertaken this book on Kevin, my admiration for the manner in which you have handled the matter' and her respect for his 'monumental amount of work ... to make it the fine thing it is' (although she then gave a considerable list of factual corrections). She went on to describe how she had just seen General Richard Mulcahy and given him extracts from

O'Donovan's work, and how General Hugo MacNeill 'has some men digging up whatever they can in various sections of Military Records and Archives'. In a subsequent document she refers to them as 'Dick' and 'Hugo' – this from the woman who, following the termination of the Emergency in May 1945, had refused to let her daughter Mary attend a ball held to honour the defence forces! As is clear from her witness statement, Kitby had forgiven Mulcahy his role as the military leader of the pro-Treaty forces whose men had executed at least seventy-seven civil war prisoners and murdered many more. This was because he had ousted de Valera from power in the 1948 general election, and gone into government with her friend Seán MacBride.[1]

It was not against 'Bloody Dick' Mulcahy but against true-blue republican Jim O'Donovan that Kitby later turned. In a ferocious and lengthy letter sent in 1964 commenting on his manuscript *Ireland's Kevin Barry* she reproved him for factual errors, for ignoring key evidence in her BMH statement which she had lent him, and above all for his portrayal of Kevin as 'a prosy [sic], foolish youth of no particular importance to anybody', who had generally been well treated by his captors and his judges. She also took exception to two articles he had published in *The Irish Press*: 'It is surely peculiar to create a quite distorted image ... of a boy you never knew and are obviously unable to understand and unwilling to learn about.'[2]

Seán Cronin, who twice served as IRA chief of staff in the late 1950s, eventually produced what might be termed a booklet, *Kevin Barry*. It was first published in 1965, though judging by his correspondence with Kitby the project had been in the making for over three decades after the family agreed he could undertake it. In December 1933 Kitby wrote to him to put off a meeting with Kevin's mother, as she was caught up in 'all the Christmas fuss' (Kitby and her daughter Mary always put enormous effort into Christmas no matter how parlous their finances) and there is correspondence from 1936 and 1937 to the Department of Justice requesting help in tracing warders who served in Mountjoy in 1920, and seeking access to Kevin's grave in order to take a photograph. Largely based on Kitby's heartfelt and detailed recollections, Cronin's booklet bears considerable similarities to her BMH statement released in 2003.[3] She probably gave him sight of her copy, of which there is no trace among the cache of personal papers donated to UCD Archives in 1990. Cronin's own working papers have not been found, there is nothing of relevance in the small collection under his name in New York University's Tamiment Library.[4]

Cronin's booklet, respectful rather than reverential in tone, tells Kevin's story almost entirely from Kitby's perspective. Originally published by the Anvil Press (owned by *The Kerryman* newspaper in Tralee) it was reprinted in what appears the original format and cover by the 'Irish Freedom Press' in 2001. Copies are often offered for sale online. As ever, confusion can arise: the 2001 edition is presented on some sites as 'The Story of Kevin Barry' despite carrying the original cover and title, while in 2019 one copy was advertised as 'Cronin, Seán – Kevin Barry – Paperback Booklet 1st Ed 1965 Cork War Independence', although Kevin had no contact whatsoever with Cork in those years.[5]

Donal's own book, launched in the Kevin Barry Room in UCD in Earlsfort Terrace on 5 October 1989 by Taoiseach Charles Haughey, was altogether more satisfactory.[6] Far from being an exercise in familial pietas, this dispassionate, humorous and well-grounded study rescued Kevin once and for all from pious martyrdom. Had Donal lived a little longer he might have produced a revised version. His own *Irish Times* obituary was captioned 'Journalist, PR executive and freelance spy for East Germany' but it should also have headlined his study of Kevin. Donal supported and greatly helped research for an important if disturbing study of his father Jim's Nazi connections, *The Devil's Deal*, by David O'Donoghue.[7] Jim O'Donovan, of course, was not alone in his support for Germany's war against Britain. Kitby and Jim Moloney were, their leftist outlook notwithstanding, also cheering for Hitler until very late in the day, and their friend Dan Breen was left in the depths of despair by the Führer's death: on 5 May 1945 he sadly wrote 'Heil Hitler. May he rest in peace' in his diary.[8] When I asked my grandfather about his and Kitby's enthusiasm for Hitler's war, he replied that it grew out of nationalists' experience in the early years of the Great War: everyone had believed British and Belgian stories of German atrocities, which turned out to be largely false (in fact recent scholarship indicates that the British, French and Belgians may have exaggerated the scale of such atrocities, but did not fabricate the most serious accusations). Consequently, he maintained, it was natural for Irish people who had also heard blatant British lies and seen the excesses of British forces during the War of Independence to discount Allied claims about Hitler's conduct of his war. Coming from a man who, as Michael Gorman noticed in the 1940s, had 'behind his chair ... a row of orange coloured books, a comprehensive selection of volumes from the Victor Gollancz Left Book Club ... he had socialist leanings', this illustrates how direct and bitter experience can distort a broader moral picture.[9] Whether his friend and family connection Jim O'Donovan ever had qualms about his links with Nazi Germany is not known, but O'Donovan would probably have rationalised his actions in much the same terms.

Kevin has been the subject of a number of plays, whose authors could not resist portraying him as a high-minded, spiritual martyr. None of these, suffused with religiosity, attracted any sustained interest. Of one Donal wrote that it was better not read: the same is true of a more recent effort.[10]

A few films borrowed elements of Kevin's story. I have only been able to track down a couple. In 1962 Kitby told a Liverpool production company enquiring about Kevin's character traits – Was he 'a wild or studious child'? Did he have a 'romantic interest in his life'? Was he 'responsible for the death of anybody'? 'How soon after his death did the song "Kevin Barry" appear?' – that 'we have been much distressed by the showing of a small film made by an amateur which contained gross inaccuracies – some of them historical and some of them giving an entirely false picture of my mother'.[11] The film to which she objected, and some others said to have been planned or perhaps even to have been produced, have not been found, but in February 1941 a German studio released *Mein Leben für Irland* (*My Life for Ireland*). Its young protagonist, Patrick O'Brien, son of an Irish rebel executed for killing a bailiff, is sent to a British-style public school intended to inculcate British values, where the boys wear formal dress and top hats and play rugby – alas, not in Belvedere-style hooped shirts – before he and others join in a successful rebellion against British rule.[12] There is nothing to suggest that either of two Irish republicans who made their ways to Berlin in 1939–40, Kevin's UCD contemporary Frank Ryan (1902–1944) and the writer Francis Stuart (1902–2000), each of whom have generally been dealt with sympathetically and uncritically despite their conscious decisions to base themselves in Hitler's capital and to aid the German war effort, had any hand in the production of this exercise.

Michael Anderson's *Shake Hands with the Devil* (1959), starring James Cagney and Don Murray, was shot in the newly built Ardmore Studios in Bray, a facility which so impressed producer Walter Seltzer that he told New York journalists that 'Dublin may one day rival Hollywood.' It includes themes which echo aspects of Kevin's story. In the film, the War of Independence is seen through the eyes of young Irish-American medical student Kerry O'Shea (Murray), who is accidentally drawn into the conflict, and then discovers that one of his professors (Cagney), a chemistry expert and republican fanatic not at all unlike Jim O'Donovan, is a key figure. But Murray survives the movie, whereas the extremist Cagney, whom critics singled out for particular praise, dies rather than accept that with the Truce the war is over. Although the eponymous book upon which the film was based had been banned in Ireland in the 1930s, possibly because one of the female characters was a prostitute, the author Rearden Conner, the Cork-born son of an RIC man, bore no grudges and attended the world premiere in the Savoy cinema. The film was temporarily banned in Belfast city on police advice during the 1959 summer marching season, although it was seen elsewhere in Northern Ireland without incident, and the ban was lifted that August.[13] It would be interesting to know if Jim O'Donovan saw it and identified anything of himself in Cagney's character.

Physical Commemoration in Bricks, Mortar and Institutions

In the centenary year of 2016 the Irish Pubs Global Federation declared the Kevin Barry Bar in Savannah, Georgia to be the 'most authentic Irish pub in the world'. This accolade may have come as a surprise to the thousands of publicans and millions of drinkers on the island of Ireland. The Savannah pub was also a shrine to American military service of all kinds, housing a 'Hall of Heroes', a name 'reflecting the portraits of men and women who have laid down their lives that we might remain free'. This is slightly ironic in an era where the mainstream Irish republican movement espouses leftist, anti-colonial internationalist rhetoric in which the armed forces of the United States are objects of excoriation rather than of veneration. The pub closed in December 2019 when the lease expired, and its owner retired.[14]

Closer to home, the republican premises at 44 Parnell Square, now controlled by the Sinn Féin party, has long borne his name. So too does a block of 1940s-era city council flats on Coleraine Street, adjacent to Church Street where Kevin was captured, as do Kevin Barry Villas in Tralee, Co. Kerry. He is commemorated in other towns across the country including Carlow and Ennis. A plaque that used to be on a wall on Church Street has disappeared along with the building to which it was attached, but there are many other memorials. These include a remarkable likeness sculpted on a spandrel in St Catherine's Church, Meath Street, executed in the 1920s. In 1958 a bust mounted on a pillar was unveiled at Rathvilly by Mrs Kathleen Clarke, widow of the executed 1916 leader, before a crowd estimated at 10,000.[15] An admirer later commissioned a metal statuette of Kevin in a trench coat, based on the 1919 'Pillars of the House' photograph, which was presented to the Barry family and is now in Tombeagh.

Within a year of Kevin's execution, there was talk of a student-funded memorial in UCD. Some money was collected and placed with trustees, but the initiative ran into the sands under the pressure of other events, not least the Treaty split and the question of how to commemorate all UCD students killed during the civil war. Donal noted in 1989 that the initial idea amongst students was for a joint memorial to Kevin and his friend and fellow student Frank Flood, since he too had been executed. After intermittent pressure from the student body, and the election to UCD's governing body of Mac O'Rahilly in 1931, the project was revived, though not without difficulty in raising the requisite funds, and not without some controversy.[16] Early in 1934 UCD's Fine Gael *Caoimhín Ó hUiginn* (Kevin O'Higgins) *cumann* (branch) was exercised by reports that 'a political party' proposed to make a donation to the fund, and deplored 'any attempt to make party capital by auctioning the name of Kevin Barry ... an opportunity should be given to all to forget their politics and unite in respecting the memory of one of Ireland's dead'. Although itself named after 'one of Ireland's dead', the Kevin O'Higgins *cumann* perhaps assumed, rightly, that no anti-treaty UCD students would ever wish to commemorate the acidulous and divisive Kevin (1892–1927), assassinated by republicans, whose name they carried. It was presumably open to them to make a donation themselves.[17]

The memorial eventually produced is often cited, yet seldom seen. A large stained-glass window divided into eight painted panels depicting Irish figures and events from different historical periods up to 1920, it locates Kevin's story within long centuries of Irish struggle against foreign oppressors. The sixth panel and the eighth, directly below it, physically link Kevin with Robert Emmet by placing Kevin's head on Emmet's shoulders (although Emmet was a Trinity man), thereby embodying him as a student patriot. In the long historical context within which it locates Kevin's story the window is, as Jay Winter observed, far from being an Irish Catholic anomaly and very much of a piece with visual memorial culture in France and Germany in the post-Great War era, where both Catholic and Protestant churches carried windows using mythological and medieval historical references to commemorate the recently fallen.[18] We might also note that almost every Commonwealth war grave cemetery across the world, designed to provide 'the link between the fallen and Christian sacrifice with its hope of resurrection', has an explicitly Christian 'Cross of Sacrifice' as an integral element.[19]

The committee established to bring the project to completion toiled long and hard before the tribute was finally unveiled. Mary Barry and some of her children were present. Republicans grumbled that the ceremony was superintended by the president of UCD, Michael Tierney, whose Blueshirt associations and general hostility towards republicanism were well known (although he was on close terms with Jim O'Donovan, which may in part have reflected a shared intellectual arrogance and disdain for conventional democratic politics).[20] Others felt that not many people would get to see the glass, tucked away in the student recreation room on the first floor of UCD's main building in Earlsfort Terrace. While saving the memorial from an explicitly confessional existence and clerical supervision, in terms of public access its location was indeed somewhat unfortunate. So too, of course, was the eventual omission of Frank Flood from the finished project.

The former student recreation room is now the 'Kevin Barry Recital Room' of the National Concert Hall. The window was removed to UCD's Belfield Campus in 2011. There it can be seen, again upstairs and in an out of the way location, in a poorly lit setting in a space overlooking a car park and linking the Charles Institute, a dermatology centre, with a biomedical research building. The issue of easy access persists, as very few UCD students or anyone else not involved in specialised medical research, or perhaps suffering from exotic skin ailments, are likely ever to pass it. Public art is supposed to be displayed in places where the public can see it.[21]

The UCD Commerce Society (now the Commerce and Economics Society) established a 'Kevin Barry Memorial Medal for impromptu speaking', although there is nothing to suggest Kevin had been a debater in school or university. Kitby would surely have preferred the Literary & Historical Society (L&H), which has always had a broader cross-faculty appeal, superior oratory and rather greater prestige. Amongst its auditors have been various scions of Jesuit schools, including medical students Anthony Clare (Gonzaga, 1963–4) and Michael Moloney (Belvedere, 1975–6).[22]

When UCD opened its restaurant block in Belfield in 1971, the downstairs restaurant carried Kevin's name and the upstairs that of Thomas MacDonagh, executed in 1916, although when the building was reconfigured some years ago both names disappeared. Kevin's memory in Belfield is preserved through the Fianna Fáil Kevin Barry student *cumann*, although that party had no particular claim to his name. Nevertheless, he would surely have felt at home: 'Beyond politics altogether, the K[evin] B[arry] C[*umann*] and its members are renowned for partying and holding some of UCD's legendary drinks receptions, the first of which is our annual Hot Whiskey Session on the Thursday of Freshers' Week ... it is worth being a member ... if only for the sessions, craic and above all the friends you will make during the year.'[23] Sinn Féin's north-west inner city *cumann* couples Kevin's name with that of Frank Stagg (1941–1976), who died fifty-six years after Kevin in Wakefield prison after undertaking three hunger strikes in two years. The Glasgow-based Volunteer Kevin Barry pipe and drum band played a significant role in the centenary commemoration of 1916 at the GPO, proof positive that his name lives on within the diaspora.

Persisting the Most: Kevin in British Political Discourse

In 1956 John Anderson, by then ennobled as Viscount Waverley, spoke during a debate on the abolition of capital punishment in the House of Lords of 'the argument that was addressed to me many years ago by the aged Archbishop of Dublin when he was carried up to my room in Dublin Castle to plead for clemency for young Kevin Barry ... I had to tell him, to my sorrow, that to do what he asked would be to proclaim the helplessness of the law.' Waverley also reminded the House that when home secretary in 1940 – shortly after moving from public service into politics – he had had to turn down pleas for clemency for two other Irishmen, Peter Barnes and James Richards (also known as McCormack), who were convicted of causing an explosion in Coventry, which killed five people, the final fruits of Jim O'Donovan's much vaunted 'S-Plan'.[24] As with generals Macready, Crozier and Winter, all of whom discussed him in their memoirs, Kevin's was not a name to be forgotten.

In 1974, just three weeks after the Provisional IRA's Birmingham pub bombings which killed twenty-one people, MPs again debated the question of capital punishment for terrorist killings. The Labour MP Phillip Whitehead observed that 'There is not a single pub in Ireland where one cannot hear every verse of "Kevin Barry" sung. Who now remembers, who can tell us the name of, the young soldier, also 19, who was shot by Kevin Barry? We do not remember the victims.' If Whitehead realised that he shared

his surname with the forgotten victim for whose killing Kevin
was convicted, Marshall Whitehead, he kept that detail to himself
and no one else noticed. In the same debate the Tory MP Sir Peter
Rawlinson, who as attorney general in Edward Heath's 1970–4
government had been a terrorist target, also warned against the
death penalty: 'those who fought openly and courageously in 1916
could not be compared with people who would plant bombs to kill
civilians and then slink away unnoticed'.[25] No one pointed out that
Kevin had done his fighting in civilian garb, indistinguishable from
the general public on a Dublin street.

Opposing further calls for imposition of the death penalty for
terrorist killings in 1982, Roy Hattersley, a senior Labour figure
who as a Birmingham MP had particular knowledge both of the
Irish diaspora and of IRA bombing, agreed that Kevin's name lived
on: 'It exists and has become a symbol, for right or for wrong,
in a way that ... would not have been the case had he not been
executed.'[26] In October 2009, in a discussion of the desirability
of a global ban on the death penalty, the Labour MP Stephen
Pound remarked that 'when I went to Mountjoy prison, I was
one of the last people to visit what was called the "hang house",
where not only Kevin Barry but twenty-seven other people were
put to death'.[27] Other MPs referenced the Guildford Four and the
Birmingham Six as people who would have been wrongly executed
had capital punishment not been abolished, although in Kevin's
case no serious question of wrongful conviction arose.

Kevin in the Oireachtas

Kevin's name and memory have been invoked on many occasions
in both Dáil and Seanad. Amongst the more surprising usages was
the moment during a discussion of the government's intention to
propose the removal of the six university seats from Dáil Éireann,
when a Fianna Fáil deputy very reasonably argued that, while 'I

believe in the National University and the type of people such as Kevin Barry which that university produced,' it was 'an extraordinary thing that the 7,000 voters in the two Universities should have six Deputies while a rural constituency has only one'. The failure to reform the university Seanad franchise to include degree-holders of all other Irish third level institutions – for which preparation was made through a constitutional amendment over forty years ago – should long since have punctured the self-satisfaction of the senators from the existing universities represented in the Seanad, i.e. the National University of Ireland and the University of Dublin (aka Trinity College). These are routinely lauded as a uniquely public-spirited, high-minded, wise and fearless cohort who stand above the common herd of displaced TDs and ambitious county councillors in the Seanad chamber, having only the national interest in mind. Yet they and their universities have studiously ignored the one obvious injustice in the Irish political system which is uniquely within their power to fix.[28]

In 1967 the dynamic Minister for Education Donogh O'Malley (1921–1968), in defending his proposal for a merger between UCD and Trinity College, waxed lyrical on UCD's tradition of scholarship. The college 'can claim ... the name of Kevin Barry, which is graven in the hearts of the Irish people, and many others who played a valiant part in the struggle for independence'.[29] In recent decades, the song's status, rather than the man himself, was invoked: in 1992 Brendan McGahon TD observed that 'people tell us daily that they have rights ... they, too, have their duties. They have a duty to vote and it is not enough to sing "Kevin Barry" in a pub through an alcoholic haze and feel that they are being patriotic.' People should 'give five minutes of their time every four or five years to vote, be it for Fine Gael, Fianna Fáil or the loony-Left'.[30] In 2006 Willie Penrose TD argued for improved pension terms for people who had emigrated when young and had returned missing pensionable years: 'we sent them out to make their living elsewhere and then said to make sure to send home a few bob to the old sod and sing "Kevin Barry" on a Friday or Saturday night in the Crown'.[31]

The Jesuits and Kevin's Memory

Professor Fred Halliday (1946–2010), a world-renowned scholar of international relations (and who, educated by the Marists in Drogheda and the Benedictines in Ampleforth, knew a thing or two about Catholic religious institutions), once described to me how he had visited various South American universities on behalf of the London School of Economics. He had one particularly awkward meeting with a bleak monsignor, head of a university run by the conservative Opus Dei movement. Running out of things to say, he ventured to ask the gloomy cleric a political science question: 'Who are your enemies?'. Fred waited to hear 'the Communists'; to his astonishment, the monsignor's eyes blazed as he spat out 'the Jesuits!'

In Ireland, the order certainly displayed a knack for producing revolutionary leaders, albeit on both sides of a conflict. Their embrace of Kevin's memory is not surprising: he was a Belvederian, the Jesuit scholastic Tom Counihan had offered him solace in his last hours, the most iconic images are those of him in Belvedere sports colours, and his case aroused immediate and longer-term interest both at home and abroad. Because he died during the War of Independence, furthermore, he was never a divisive figure in Irish public memory or political discourse (although Kitby, citing remarks he made to her when he was seventeen, maintained that he would never have accepted the Treaty).

Jesuit investment in his memory, however, rather contrasts with that of at least four other young Volunteers killed during the War of Independence, whose Jesuit connections seem never to have become part of Irish Jesuit culture – indeed, a recent article on the

Jesuits and the War of Independence makes no mention of them whatsoever.[32] Yet their photographs were carried as a frontispiece in *The Mungret Annual 1921*. Two of them died in the same month as did Kevin: Christy Lucey, in an exchange of fire near Ballingeary, Cork; and Alf Rogers, shot by Auxiliaries after capture and sustained mistreatment, along with three other 'Scariff martyrs', on a bridge at Killaloo.[33] Another of these Mungret four was my grandfather's brother Paddy Moloney, killed in an engagement outside Tipperary town on May Day 1921. Unusually for an IRA man in action, and unlike Kevin, he was wearing his Volunteer uniform (most likely because he had sat on a court martial the previous day, which had sentenced a local labourer, a father of ten, to death for spying, a verdict suspended on reflection until higher authority could be consulted). *The Mungret Annual* entry for 1 November 1920 recorded how news of Kevin's death 'wired' by his mother cast a pall over the school: 'We thought of him as one of ourselves – a schoolboy. Shall not his hero's death be always an inspiration to Irish boys?' The response to Paddy's death was altogether more routine: it was 'a great shock ... all, both masters and boys, knew him as a generous and manly boy'.[34]

Why the Mungret old boys have not registered in the collective memory of the Jesuit order in Ireland is surely due essentially to the kind of school it was; a remote bucolic outpost catering not for the sons of the Catholic elite, as did Belvedere and Clongowes, but merely for the progeny of Munster shopkeepers and middling farmers.[35] Like the two hunger-striking Volunteers whose agonised deaths in Cork jail in October 1920 passed largely unremarked as the world waited breathlessly for Terence MacSwiney to expire, it is not simply the person and the sacrifice, but social standing and how that is relayed and amplified, which garners attention and enduring commemoration.

Olivia Frehill's significant study of the Irish Jesuit province and the civil war focuses on how the order dextrously managed the varying political viewpoints and allegiances among its members.[36] What the Jesuits never dwelt on were the significant roles in the Treaty split and in the civil war of 1922–3 played by former pupils. An example is George Gavan Duffy (1882–1951), a negotiator of and signatory to the Treaty, though he was courageously critical of Free State abuses during the civil war and was ultimately appointed to the High Court by a Fianna Fáil government (in 1917 his sister Louise (1884–1969) established Scoil Bhríde, the socially and politically select Dublin *gaelscoil* to which Kitby sent her children in the 1930s). The Clongownian Kevin O'Higgins came to prominence as a government minister during and after the civil war as much for his scarifying, sometimes near hysterical counter-revolutionary language and oratory as for his competence (his bitterness against the 'Irregulars' was understandably compounded by the murder of his father, a respected doctor, in his Stradbally home in February 1923). He was joined by fellow Clongownian Patrick McGilligan (1889–1979), who as Minister for Industry and Commerce notoriously told the Dáil in 1924 that in prevailing economic circumstances people might have to die of hunger; Seamus Burke (1893–1967), Minister for Local Government and Public Health from 1924 to 1927; and John Marcus O'Sullivan (1879–1948), Minister for Education from 1926 to 1932. They formed a conservative, privileged Jesuit and UCD elite within the Cosgrave government, at odds with the Christian Brothers-educated W.T. Cosgrave, born and raised in an inner-city pub.

What has been generally overlooked is that on the other side of the civil war split, by far the two strongest candidates for the title of Robespierre of the Irish revolution, pushing for an ever-more radical approach in opposing the Treaty settlement, were both Jesuit educated. Just as the rebel bastions of the 1916 Rising (in the midst of the most densely populated and poorest part of the city) were chosen by Joseph Plunkett, a military dilettante and alumnus of not one but two Jesuit schools, Belvedere and

Stonyhurst (the latter as a pre-university student, and where the school Officer Training Corps records give no indication that he was ever a member), so the almost nihilistic drive for confronting the pro-Treaty majority in 1922 by force of arms came principally from Cathal Brugha (a Belvederian) and Rory O'Connor (a Clongownian).[37] In the autumn of 1921, Brugha sent O'Connor to make arrangements for a widespread bombing offensive in Britain should the Anglo-Irish negotiations fail. O'Connor was commander of the anti-Treaty forces which occupied the Four Courts in April 1922. That action, followed by the kidnapping in June of Major General 'Ginger' O'Connell (another Clongownian) and compounded by the assassination in London on 22 June 1922 of Sir Henry Wilson by the Jesuit-educated Great War veteran Reginald Dunne, ultimately triggered the civil war.[38] Within the anti-Treaty military leadership, my great-uncle Con Moloney (1898–1951) – successively Adjutant General (July 1922 to February 1923) and Deputy Chief of Staff thereafter until his capture on 7 March 1923 – and his brother Jim, then Kitby's fiancé and director of communications on Liam Lynch's GHQ staff, were Mungret old boys.[39] Kitby's future brother-in-law Jim O'Donovan, as pure a republican hardliner as ever breathed, and the last of the pre-split IRA Executive to die in 1979, was educated at St Aloysius' College SJ, Glasgow, Scotland's only private Jesuit school: 'Give me the boy ... and I will give you the man' indeed.[40] To this list of Irish Jesuit-educated radicals of consequence we might add William Joyce, 'Lord Haw-Haw', once of St Ignatius College SJ, Galway (now Coláiste Iognáid SJ). He was, like Jim O'Donovan, an academically talented young man who took his admiration for Nazi Germany to its logical conclusion, becoming the Reich's most notorious English-language propaganda broadcaster and taking German citizenship during the Second World War. This was, as we have seen, insufficient to save him from the hangman in January 1946.[41]

The Reinterment of 'The Forgotten Ten'

As misnomers go, 'The Forgotten Ten' deserves a prize. No single Volunteer who died in the War of Independence has been so continuously remembered as Kevin. 'Kevin Barry and the Forgotten Nine' would have been a more accurate if clumsier slogan under which to campaign for reinterment of the ten executed Volunteers buried in Mountjoy jail. The other nine families had neither enjoyed nor endured remotely the same degree of association with their executed relatives as had anyone related to Kevin Barry who cared to let the fact be known. Donal O'Donovan's line from 'A Crowded Year' – 'Are you the nephew of?' – still resonates.

There had been talk for many years of petitioning the state to allow the disinterment and reburial of the executed Volunteers lying in Mountjoy. As well as Kevin, these were his UCD friend Frank Foley, hanged on 14 March 1921 with Bernard Ryan, Patrick Doyle and Thomas Bryan following the disastrous Drumcondra ambush of 21 January 1921; Thomas Whelan and Patrick Moran, also on 14 March, hanged for the killing of British officers on Bloody Sunday; Thomas Traynor, a father of ten and, like Kevin, a Carlow man, executed on 25 April for possession of a gun following an ambush on Brunswick Street; and Edmund Foley and Patrick Maher, hanged on 7 June 1921 for murder at Knocklong railway station in May 1919 (Maher being entirely innocent).

The Barrys had declined suggestions in 1922, 1932 and 1948 that Kevin's remains might be exhumed and appropriately reinterred, on the Robert Emmet-like argument that this should not happen until 'the Republic was established'.[42] But in the theology of purist republicanism, an Irish republic already existed – created by the IRB in 1859, reiterated by the 1916 Proclamation (which held out that the republic was already in being), and by Dáil Éireann in 1919. Furthermore, in 1949 the Barrys' friend Seán MacBride took pains as Minister for External Affairs to sign the foundation document of the Council of Europe as the representative of 'the Irish Republic'.[43] Yet for whatever reason, there was no movement on the reinterment question for decades.

Opinions probably varied between and within the extended families of the 'Forgotten Ten'. Tess Carney, a stalwart of the strongly republican National Graves Association until her death in 2000, wrote in 1996 of how a request by the surviving eldest daughter of Thomas Traynor for his exhumation and reburial in the Republican Plot in Glasnevin was refused by both 'the present government & the previous government'.[44] Many relatives were reluctant to support a collective exhumation and reburial for a variety of reasons, some perhaps because they felt that, just as Emmet wanted no epitaph until 'my nation takes its place upon the nations of the earth', so the executed should remain where they were until an all-island republic was achieved; others, including Kitby's surviving children Mary and Helen, were wary of reinterment for fear the process would be hijacked by the Provisional IRA, still conducting its war, and with its ruling army council still claiming to be simultaneously the legitimate army, legislature and government of the Irish Republic.

What changed minds was the Northern Ireland peace process, culminating in the Good Friday Agreement of 1998, which involved mainstream republican recognition of the right of the majority in Northern Ireland to determine their own future, the foreswearing of any further violence to achieve Irish unity, and unequivocal recognition of the existing Irish state. Bertie Ahern's coalition government, conscious not only of the past but of the present and the future, and of the political desirability of reasserting the legitimacy of the War of Independence while sending a positive signal to contemporary republicanism, took the lead.

Those preparing the way for exhumation and reinterment had to address a range of issues. In addition to the many relatives of the ten executed men who had to be consulted, there were sectional, bureaucratic and political interests to be considered. Seán Sherwin, briefly a youthful Fianna Fáil TD before leaving to join Kevin Boland's ill-starred republican party Aontacht Éireann in 1971, was an unflappable intermediary between state authorities, families, Glasnevin cemetery and the National Graves Association, whose representative was common sense personified.

When the detailed arrangements were unveiled Dublin's easily outraged newspaper commentariat huffed and puffed at what was deemed a cynical sop to Sinn Féin and the Provisionals (still refusing to decommission), and a celebration of the murderous forebears of the Enniskillen and Omagh bombers. That the Dublin ceremonies would coincide with the Fianna Fáil Ard Fheis was also noted: opposition leaders were reportedly furious at this obvious exercise in stroke politics, although they would 'with great reluctance' attend proceedings.[45] In the *Sunday Independent* Ronan Fanning declared that 'Bertie rattles the bones of the dead'; Alan Ruddock's headline was that 'sectarian thugs deserve no honour or legitimacy, here or abroad'. Under the headline 'the fools commemorate our Fenian dead', an echo of Pearse's famous declamation at the IRB-orchestrated funeral of the erratic Fenian bomber O'Donovan Rossa in 1915, Declan Lynch maintained 'we need to say, loudly, clearly and repeatedly, that the IRA had then, and has now no legitimacy'. One-time Labour Party éminence grise Fergus Finlay described Kevin somewhat condescendingly in the *Irish Examiner* as 'a young lad ... whose mother would have been furious if she had known he was out', deplored the provision of 'military honours', deprecated the 'cheap party politics involved' and said he would have counselled holding a 'respectful, quiet and dignified reburial'.[46] A more thoughtful Fintan O'Toole, who had taken the trouble to read Donal's biography, decried 'an act of denial, deliberately designed to sanitise the ambiguities of people like Kevin Barry whose idealistic certainties makes them careless of other people's lives', an argument which laid down a fair challenge to those who maintain that the violence of 1916 and the War of Independence was legitimate whereas later republican violence was not. An essay in 'An Irishman's Diary' lamented the fact that Donal's careful book had not dispelled 'the cult of Barryism' as might have been expected.[47]

Todd Andrews' son David, a former Minister for Foreign Affairs, espoused a contrary view, arguing that 'there is nothing wrong with mourning those who fought and died for Ireland'. I took a similar line: 'it is surely right to remember all the dead of the War of Independence, and these funerals should be seen as a part of that process rather than as an exercise in atavistic republicanism'. I maintained that the state should assert the legitimacy of the War of Independence, however reprehensible much of the violence on all sides – separatist as well as Crown and loyalist – and to distinguish that era from later republican violence against the state itself, against the United Kingdom and against the general public of all persuasions and beliefs in Northern Ireland.[48] One Newry correspondent reproved me for achieving 'a particular low' by comparing a recent hunger-strike commemorative march of white-shirted, black-gloved and beret-sporting republicans through Dublin to the Mosleyites of the 1930s. But, shirt colour apart, that is exactly what they looked like as they passed me by, more or less in step, on Nassau Street.[49]

Rumours abounded that the correct remains would never be identified. It was said that the corpse of Dublin-born William Mitchell, the only Black and Tan executed for murder during the War of Independence, lay amongst the republican dead. But the plots were identified without much difficulty from a contemporary sketch made by a British NCO. Kevin's grave was number one on the left-hand side. Exhumation apparently yielded a few bone parts, coins, strands of fabric and a pen, which had probably been in his jacket pocket. Everything recovered was sealed in his coffin together with surrounding earth.

Officials and warders in Mountjoy took an intense interest in the exhumations, as apparently did prisoners, and invested proceedings with due dignity. Male relatives – in Kevin's case grand-nephews from each of his six siblings' families – were summonsed for one practice lift and carry of empty coffins from trestles beside the graves to waiting hearses. The task seemed simple enough. On the day of the reinterment, things were rather different. Light rain had rendered the plastic pathway matting slippery underfoot. The bearers also received an unpleasant shock when they lifted the coffins because these were extremely heavy, filled with the soil surrounding the few remains of each dead man. I found the lift and brief carry of Kevin's coffin along the pathway to the first hearse, under the eyes of relatives and television cameras, nerve-racking. It must have been more difficult for the parties bearing the subsequent coffins, as they had equally heavy burdens to carry and farther to walk. Solemnity was not marred by any mishaps.

The most powerful element of the Mountjoy ceremony was the tolling of the bell customarily rung to mark an execution as the cortège paused inside the gate. The coffins were then brought to the Pro-Cathedral via O'Connell Street. At Glasnevin nine were borne to the gravesides by members of the Defence Forces. A striking and moving aspect of the reinterment was how much it meant to families because it recalled relatives who had carried grief for the fallen with them through their lives but who had not lived to see the problem resolved. All proceedings were well and respectfully received by the general public in Dublin and in Ballylanders, where Patrick Maher was buried. His grand-niece Geraldine Quinlan later spoke with particular eloquence and feeling of the enduring impact, which his unfair conviction and execution, and his dismal resting place, had had upon her family. Kevin's nephew and namesake observed that the funerals would 'bring tears to a stone'.[50]

The funerals did something, at least temporarily, to dilute the solitary celebrity attached to Kevin's name, which was probably quietly resented by other families whose relatives had died on the Mountjoy gallows in 1921. Frank Flood was often mentioned in that connection as unfairly forgotten. Yet neither his nor Kevin's stories can remotely compare in tragedy with that of Thomas Traynor, a bootmaker and father of ten. Traynor had already risked his life for Ireland in 1916: what on earth possessed him to return to the front line, his youngest child only a year old? And what possessed his commanding officer to let him? Kevin's siblings sometimes struggled to avoid being identified simply by reference to him, whereas Traynor's widow and ten children had no such weight of celebrity to cope with. They were left to struggle to survive in obscurity, it proving impossible, despite President Cosgrave's personal intervention, to increase the allowance payable to his family under the first army pensions legislation. Yet Elizabeth Traynor, who wrote that her husband 'always spoke about the good education he would give his children', managed to keep most of them in school or training until adulthood.[51] We might also think of Louisa Doyle, widow of Patrick, executed on 14 March 1921. That was the very day that Louisa Patricia, one of his infant twin girls, was buried, two days after their father saw his children for the last time.[52] Perhaps we focus too much on youthful sacrifice, and should spend more time wondering how it was that men with such family responsibilities were willing to risk their lives in the independence movement, and how their widows, left with young families, found the strength to cope.

The only untoward notes were struck at Glasnevin by some self-styled republicans who jeered the Gardai and Defence Forces personnel with 'you're not a real army' and similar comments.[53] But Sinn Féin leader Gerry Adams attended the funeral mass along with Martin McGuinness and the veteran Joe Cahill (1920–2004). They were greeted with raucous cheers at Glasnevin. Cahill – and, of course, quite possibly other republicans present who had overseen the 'courts martial' of alleged informers – knew what it was like to hear the death penalty imposed. He had been sentenced to death, along with five others, under the doctrine of common purpose, for the killing of an RUC constable, Patrick Murphy, a father of nine, on Easter Sunday April 1942. Murphy died after a poorly planned attack on a police car, which ended with the surrender of the six-man IRA party in an upstairs room of a house into which they had foolishly fled. Cahill's death sentence had been commuted, unlike that of the group's leader, 19-year-old Tom Williams, who had met his hangman with appropriate courage in Crumlin Road prison on 2 September 1942. Hundreds of people, mainly women and children, gathered nearby, and sang 'The Soldier's Song' and, inevitably, 'Kevin Barry'. There were scuffles when women from the adjoining 'Unionist quarters came out and jeered', and 'sang Orange songs'. Joe Cahill attended Williams' reinterment in 2000 in Milltown cemetery. Did anyone present reflect that this was also where lay the remains of Patrick Murphy?[54]

Adams deemed the 'state funerals ... a fitting tribute' – a remarkable observation from the head of a movement which, until three years previously, had adamantly denied the state's very legitimacy. Belfast republican Jim Gibney described how he was torn between applauding the general public's response as the coffins passed and denouncing the speeches of Cardinal Daly and Taoiseach Bertie Ahern. These had drawn a distinction between the IRA campaign of 1919–21 (fought under the authority of the democratically elected Dáil Éireann) and later phases of republican violence. Their speeches 'marred a perfect day ... a subtle form of revisionism to complement the more brutal form from [Kevin] Myers, [Fintan] O'Toole and John A. Murphy'.[55]

Press denunciations continued afterwards: a columnist who had stood to watch the cortège pass declared, under the headline 'Dallas Meets our Fenian dead', that the event was 'beyond farce and beneath tragic/comedy', of benefit only to 'the funeral directors', vendors of 'tacky tricolours' and 'contemporary terrorists'.[56]

Thousands of people of all ages and political allegiances evidently thought otherwise, lining the streets in respectful silence.

In 2001 it was contemporary republicans who read Kevin most accurately. Although young, he already had a good fighting record by the standards of the time in Dublin and in Carlow. He was clearly a Volunteer of nerve and initiative rather than a hapless youth; and while he had no martyr complex he was willing to die for his cause. This has, however, not prevented the routine use of the misleading term 'martyr' to describe him and others, notably the H-Block hunger strikers who died in 1981 and who continue to be commemorated as 'martyrs'.[57]

There has been one further state commemoration of Kevin, an exercise inexplicably scrambled together in haste by the state only days in advance. It took place in Glasnevin cemetery on a sunny though chilly Saturday, 1 November 2014. Unfortunately, just a handful of relatives were notified in time. The attendance consisted of Kevin's niece Ruth O'Rahilly, her husband Roger Sweetman and me, together with junior minister Aodhán O'Riordan TD, Senator Mary White of Lir chocolate fame and her husband, an army piper and flag party, a Glasnevin cemetery representative and a couple of officials. After some uncertain shuffling, it occurred to someone to ask Ruth to lay the state's wreath on her uncle's grave, which she did with accustomed grace. Kevin would surely have been amused by this ill-prepared, underpopulated and mildly comic event in his honour.[58]

CHAPTER ELEVEN

A Martyr in the Family

K evin's death was a huge burden upon his mother, his siblings and in due course their own families. Donal O'Donovan's 'A Crowded Year' nicely captures the phenomenon. It is clear too that his closest relatives dealt with Kevin's memory in different ways.

Mary Barry

Apart from extraordinary telegrams of condolence and congratulations to the families of other Volunteers executed in 1921, Kevin's mother Mary bore her loss in private and in silence. She also coped with the stress of seeing her firstborn son Michael (Mick) arrested in December 1920, charged with possession of two bullets, one of them apparently cut down to act as a 'dum-dum'. The death penalty could easily have been imposed; in fact he was sentenced to two years. Shortly afterwards she wrote to her cousin Mary Dowling in California about Kevin: 'Thank God for his glorious death, and that he died for Ireland.' She expressed her pride in both her sons, who 'grew up to be men although boys in years'. She had survived 'the awful time' thanks to 'Kathy … She is really wonderful. The girls are indeed splendid … They are all grit.'[1]

Donal O'Donovan cites one family letter to the incarcerated Mick just after the Truce, which shows not only Mary's own grit but her sense of humour: describing the arrest of Kevin's UCD friends Gerry McAleer and Charlie O'Neill, who had come down to help with the farm after their examinations, she wrote that 'Every old fogey in the country was taken for a few hours, even your uncles.' The girls added their own high-spirited greetings and news. Further letters from Mary and her daughters promised Mick a cake, kept him up to date on how neighbours were helping with the threshing, on how the oats were coming on and the turnips had been dug, about the price achieved by a local farmer for two pigs, about a new fence running up from the river, about harrowing the ground for next season's potatoes, about a sturdy foal, a calving cow, their dog Darkie's six puppies and a new kitten that had died. Monty told him about her Lenten commitment to be at school by nine every morning. Kitby wrote about both the family and the conflict. The Barry family hold many such letters, which show that Mick shared his brother's and mother's laconic wit, and that his sisters wrote with fluency, irreverence and affection.[2]

Such entirely prosaic, good-humoured correspondence must have been balm for the souls of Mick and of his correspondents and speaks volumes for Mary's and the girls' humanity and balance in the midst of grief. While in prison in June 1921, Mick bought out Kathy's and Shel's interests in Tombeagh for £50 each. Following the Truce, most likely in September 1921, Kitby and Elgin made their way across England to visit him in Lincoln jail, an expedition of which Elgin told her daughter Ruth she had no memory whatsoever other than of their arrival back in Dublin: let us hope that when they saw Mick they talked about Tombeagh, the family and the future rather than only of Kevin and the past.

Mary evidently managed quite well on the proceeds of the Carlow farm and Dublin dairy for years. In November 1937, however, she wrote to Frank Aiken, the Minister for Defence: 'I wonder if I am too late to apply for a pension in respect of my son ... I did not apply sooner because I could manage without it but I find myself compelled to now if it is not too late.' Her reason was that 8 Fleet Street, which she leased from the Corporation at £50 per annum, was in very poor condition and would soon have either to be rebuilt at a cost perhaps of £2,000 or £3,000, or demolished: 'I am sorry if my application is inconvenient at this late date but it is only now that it has become necessary.' She explained to an official that in 1920 she was 'living comfortably and supporting herself and seven children on the income derived from farm and shop', but that had now changed. The children were all gone, her son Michael was running the farm and the dairy had closed. Her net income in 1938, generated by subletting most of the building, was estimated at £70 6s.1d. But there was an obvious and fatal flaw in Mary's application: she had plainly not been dependent on Kevin at the time of his death.

Mary inherited some of the £7,209 3s. 5d. estate of her prosperous grocer brother Patrick Dowling after his death in November 1941 but continued to live in Dublin in spartan circumstances.[3] The question of providing her with some kind of pension was reopened in 1950. The chief inspector in the Department of Social Welfare, a Mr Healy, reported that special legislation would be needed, as her case was not covered by the relevant acts. He had interviewed both Mary and Kitby. Mary was now living in a flat at 3 Molesworth Street, paying rent of £1 a week. Her only income was, apparently, £60 interest on £1,200 in 5 per cent Dublin Corporation stock. When Healy suggested she could increase her income by selling the stock and buying an annuity, Kitby explained that her mother 'wished to preserve her stock intact and to arrange for its distribution on her death between her children'.[4]

It may be that the pensions issue played some part in the family's collective shunning of de Valera, then Taoiseach, when he attended Mary's funeral in August 1953, ignoring him as he stood outside the church. Kitby obviously felt bad about that action. She drafted – and may have sent – an apology saying she had not realised what was happening at the time, and regretted it: 'We feel it was nice of you to come to Mother's Mass.'[5]

As Mary lay dying she clasped rosary beads, which Kitby had placed in her hands. This occasioned a spat between Kitby and her youngest sister Peggy, whom she overheard saying, in a whisper, 'of course you know what she [Kitby] will have wrapped around her hand when she is dying [a telephone cord]'. But for the most part the five sisters were very close, and Shel, Elgin, Monty and Peggy met regularly on Fridays for coffee in Bewley's. Kitby's surviving letters to her son Paddy from the late 1950s and early 1960s are full of news of her siblings and their various children, interspersed with comments on contemporary politics.[6]

Mick

Mick was arrested in Tombeagh in December 1920, hiding in a small attic room. He might have escaped discovery had there not been a clean shirt hanging in the kitchen to wear to Mass as it was a Sunday. He was charged with possession of two bullets found on the farm, one of which had been cut down 'so as to make a more serious wound'. A carload of grenades was, apparently, also seized. Held initially in Baltinglass, where Mary and Shel could visit him, he was moved to the Curragh and eventually on to Lincoln jail. Convicted by court martial on 24 January 1921, he was fortunate: other Volunteers were executed for offences of the same order. The Carlow Brigade nominal rolls list him as 3rd Battalion adjutant at the time of his arrest (he apparently made a military service pension application in 1935, but if so his records are among many thousands of files yet to be readied for release).[7]

When Mick was arrested the British military seized a full plait of brownish hair tied with string, which they found when they searched Tombeagh: they impounded it, presumably on the assumption that it had been shorn from a woman in an IRA punishment attack. Mick maintained that it came from a relative who had supposedly cut it off when she took her vows as a nun and sent it home. This explanation was aired in the House of Commons in a parliamentary question about his arrest.[8]

The parliamentary question may have prompted the military to return the plait, as it was posted from the Curragh to Mary Barry in Tombeagh in March 1921 with a request to acknowledge receipt. In reality, according to a recent newspaper report, the plait was the product of a punishment inflicted upon a local woman.[9] 'Bobbing', frequently used both by Crown forces and by the IRA, was a gendered form of violence more or less regarded as a minor inconvenience, yet it marked young women out for communal shame. Cumann na mBan's Peg Broderick from Galway was on the receiving end of such an attack, describing how her hair was cut 'to the scalp with very blunt scissors' by Crown forces. What else might young women have feared, surrounded and overpowered by armed men, whether Crown forces or IRA?[10]

With Mick imprisoned until the general release of prisoners after the signing of the Treaty, the family had to hire a labourer to manage the farm. Even then they were hard pressed to cope. On release, he resumed his IRA activities as well as his farm work. He is listed as Vice OC, 3rd Battalion, Carlow Brigade on 1 July 1922, just after the outbreak of the civil war.[11] He stood as a republican candidate in the Carlow/Kilkenny constituency in August 1923, securing 4,355 first preferences and finishing sixth in a five-seat constituency dominated by W.T. Cosgrave, whose massive vote of 17,709 brought in a running mate who had garnered only 615 first preferences.[12] He stood again in a by-election in March 1925, losing to a Cosgrave supporter in a straight fight. But the farm had to take priority and it became his life. His son, born in 1974, was named Kevin, and his first grandson was christened Kevin Gerard, the second name being a fluke. Young Kevin's mother Evelyn had long promised to use that second name in honour of St Gerard if ever she had a son, not knowing then she would end up marrying a Barry.[13]

Tombeagh had been a safe house for de Valera on occasion during the civil war, hospitality which 'the Chief' apparently took as no more than his due, offering not a word of thanks to the family for the risk they ran in sheltering him.[14] Mick brought him and other notables including Frank Aiken and Austin Stack across the mountains to the Bartons' house at Annamoe. One day there was mild consternation in Tombeagh when a lanky, buck-toothed young man with 'a long nose' came down the lane, as initially it was thought this gawky stranger was Kitby's new love interest, Jim Moloney. In fact it was Todd Andrews, a man who never made any bones about his awkward appearance.[15] The family had to wait until the more regularly featured Jim's release from internment in July 1924 to survey and approve him.

The Barrys all felt that de Valera betrayed the republican cause. It is hard to determine when this view crystallised. His outlawing of the IRA in 1936 after their murders of Admiral Somerville and John Egan were a turning point for Mick in Tombeagh. The government's robust treatment of the IRA from June 1940 onwards, after evidence of its German connections emerged, solidified Mick in his antagonism towards de Valera. In particular, the lengths to which the state went to secure the conviction and execution for murder in 1942 of Wexford man George Plant (a popular IRA veteran well-known to most Fianna Fáil ministers) was considered outrageous, although Plant and his co-accused had undoubtedly been involved in the crime, the killing of a suspected informer. We have already noted the sangfroid with which Plant, like Kevin, accepted his verdict and faced his executioners. The same penalty was imposed on two other IRA men alongside him, but their sentences were later commuted. A fourth, as one of the judges laconically noted, 'got [the] benefit of [the] doubt & was acquitted'.[16]

Although he did not court attention, Mick was ready to defend his brother's name and the cause for which he died. In 1962 he intervened in a dispute in the letters page of *The Irish Times* about calls for a reappraisal of the role and motivations of the RIC during the War of Independence. Mick stated his case succinctly: 'My brother ... was fighting for Irish freedom against the occupying forces. There were those who took that stand, and there were those who backed the enemy.'[17]

Kitby

Kitby threw herself heart and soul into the independence struggle after Kevin's execution. She apparently acted for some time as a republican judge in Dublin, worked for Austin Stack in the Dáil Department of Home Affairs and joined Cumann na mBan. An *Irish Press* obituary stated that she was a member of its Executive during the civil war, although other sources do not confirm this.[18]

Kitby visited the United States in April and May 1922, in company with Countess Markievicz, Austin Stack and J.J. Kelly (*Sceilg*). Accounts of aspects of the trip vary. In the 1960s she assured Markievicz's biographer Anne Marecco that she and the Countess got on very well throughout. Yet her daughters Mary and Helen and son Paddy all said that the Countess was high-handed and ungrateful for all Kitby's work, which included writing her speeches. Kitby also felt she went unthanked for engineering a reconciliatory meeting between the Countess and her estranged daughter. Kitby did some fundraising on her own, arriving in Butte, Montana, in May to considerable fanfare amongst the Irish Catholic community. She was presented with an illuminated scroll, which is now amongst her papers. She also accompanied the Countess and J.J. Kelly to San Francisco, where they addressed an audience at the Dreamland rink.[19] The entire delegation left New York on the Cunard liner *Berengaria* in a rush ahead of time due to news of the 'Collins–Griffith–de Valera peace' – the pact by which pro- and anti-Treatyites agreed on how they would contest the coming general election. They received 'a rousing send-off' from about 2,000 people as they sailed for Liverpool.[20]

In the first week of the civil war Kitby, Elgin and about thirty other Cumann na mBan women were in the ill-chosen anti-Treaty headquarters in the Hammam Hotel on Sackville Street. Also there were nurse Linda Kearns and Terence MacSwiney's widow Muriel. As fighting intensified along Sackville Street, the women were ordered to leave. De Valera found Elgin hiding in a barrel, and evicted her along with most of the others. After de Valera tried and failed to carry Kitby out, she, Muriel MacSwiney and Linda Kearns hid out of sight overnight. A few months later, she wrote to Jim of how some of the fighters welcomed their presence, in contrast to Cathal Brugha's absurdly gendered attitude: 'he approved of me making tea and Bovril but not of me filling sandbags ... how I love those three days at the end because I felt I was nearly as useful as a man and you don't know how helpless a feeling it is to be a woman when you feel you ought to be a man'. [21] In the 1960s she portrayed herself in more conventional feminine guise in an interview with Brugha's nephew: 'I gave Cathal, who was sitting on the stairs ... Bovril and biscuits ... I sat down beside him.' They chatted as the flames grew closer. For a time firing intensified, and he seemed to think that their comrades outside were coming to rescue them, but that hope evaporated. Eventually he said '"Now I need you to leave." [Kitby] began to cry ... Muriel and I left. The two of us were crying.' They were indignant at newspaper reports that they had immediately been released by government forces. Kitby said they had been prisoners for a time, and she had feared that if searched £800 of Dublin Brigade funds 'concealed under my clothes', would have been seized. As soon as she was released she entrusted the money to the ever-faithful Kate Kinsella in 8 Fleet Street, who hid it 'in her bosom' and acted as a brigade treasurer thereafter.[22]

From 22 July to 26 November 1922, when the anti-Treaty military leader Liam Lynch ordered her back to Dublin to be general secretary of the Irish Republican Prisoners Dependents' Fund (IRPDF), Kitby exploited her gender in doing what was far more important work than engaging in street fighting, when she acted as the main link between the itinerant de Valera and Lynch, moving constantly between the two men and other key figures. Although arrested more than once – she appeared alongside Muriel MacSwiney, Margaret Pearse (mother of Patrick and Willie), Sinéad de Valera and 'the mother of Joe Plunkett' in a list captioned 'Who is the enemy' of women persecuted by 'Free State' Forces – she told her grandchildren that she was never held for long and that she was always well treated, being brought boxes of chocolates and jellies by Free State officers. When detained in February 1923 she told Monty that things were not too bad: 'I'm fed from the Officers' Mess', but 'the first day I get home I want roast apples.'[23] In 1936 she gave an invaluable account of her own activities between early July and 26 November 1922, moving between Dublin, Tipperary and Cork, on occasion cycling long distances between Munster towns.[24] While visiting Lynch in his rather grandly titled 'Field General Headquarters' at Rossadrehid in the Glen of Aherlow in early autumn 1922, she was treated brusquely by his director of communications, Jim Moloney, of whom a comrade wrote that he 'at the time had a rather acerbic temper'.[25] She was furious, and to make matters worse her head and face were covered in watery pink streaks, as rain had washed the paint from imitation berries on her hat. It was inevitable that they should fall madly in love.

Kitby combined activism with style. Not long before Lynch was shot in April 1923, he was staying in a farmhouse near the Cork–Kerry border. His adjutant Todd Andrews described how they were surprised to see

> a young woman fashionably dressed in city clothes. As she approached she paused ... to apply lipstick. In the wilderness of West Cork to be faced with such an exotic

figure was as if we were seeing an apparition ... lipstick was not commonly used even in the cities, certainly not by the women of the Republican movement. This was an exceptional young woman ... a sister of Kevin Barry, a woman very prominent in Republican circles, working close to de Valera. It was as an emissary from him that she had come down from Dublin to discuss details of the coming meeting of the Executive.[26]

Her various arrests, releases and escapes were routinely reported in news-agency stories across the world. When Lynch was killed, *The San Francisco Chronicle* carried an inaccurate report from Belfast that 'Countess Markievicz, Dan Breen, Mary MacSwiney, and Miss Barry' had been with him in conference just beforehand.[27] In 1954 Kitby told Lynch's biographer Florence O'Donoghue how she 'recalled vividly' her final talk with him in Kilcash in Tipperary. Lynch had identified three courses of action, 'to fight on, to surrender, or a third that he would not name, but did not like – which was in fact a dumping of arms ... Even then he had an optimistic faith in the ability of the western divisions to continue the fight.' Her old friend Moss Twomey told O'Donoghue that 'she is full of praise. She asked me to let you know ... And she said to be sure and tell you that she is very proud that she and Jim are the only married couple in the Index! Katty is a good sort.'[28]

In 1933 a priest wrote to Elgin from Notre Dame, the Jesuit-run Indiana university and bastion of Irish-American Catholic learning. He enclosed an issue of the magazine *America*, in which he had just published 'Kevin Barry's Secret'. The piece was based largely on talks with Mary Barry and on what he learned during 'my wonderful short visit to your sister, Mrs Moloney ... Mrs Moloney may flare up over the "upturned chin" and "tilted nose". But I really meant all as [a] compliment ... she is a sweet, charming, wistful Irish young mother.'[29]

Kitby married Jim in October 1924, just three months after
his release from internment on 7 July. She then set off by ship for
Australia: far from being a romantic honeymoon, she did not bring
her new husband along on her mission to raise money. She had told
him: 'I hate the thought of deserting you immediately when married
... do you think it would be better if we waited till I come back?'
but he had obviously said no. Her task was to raise money for the
IRPDF of which she had been general secretary.[30] Accompanied by
1916 veteran Linda Kearns, they were accorded a good deal of
press attention and enjoyed considerable success. Kitby (although
she used her maiden name in public) wore her wedding ring, made
from a gold sovereign, which Jim had beaten into shape in jail.
Dianne Hall argues that the £8,000 they raised in four months
compared very favourably with the £15,000 raised in a ten-month
tour by John and William Redmond in 1883. In 1923 J.J. O'Kelly
and Father Michael O'Flanagan had exacerbated tensions in Irish-
Australian circles by their rigid espousal of the anti-Treaty cause,
and had clashed with Irish-Australian bishops, before they were
peremptorily deported for collecting funds essentially to support
the anti-Treaty side in the civil war. Hall also maintains that Kitby
and Linda Kearns deliberately 'shaped their public appeals ... to fit
in within the prevailing ideologies of non-violent Irish nationalist
women's roles and a femininity enhanced by images of women as
grieving mothers, sisters and widows, who fed and cared for Irish
male soldiers'. Thus, 'the history of the women's own activism with
the anti-Treaty forces was referred to only incidentally'.[31]

The latter argument hardly holds up. A Queensland newspaper
reported that Miss Barry, sister of the '18-year-old boy ... executed
in Mountjoy jail ... for refusing to divulge certain secrets in
connection with the trouble in Ireland', though

> quite a young girl ... has held important military posts and
> been entrusted with 'responsible missions' in the Republican

Government. Miss Barry was appointed secretary of the first Dáil Relief Bureau in 1921. On the signing of the Treaty, she was chosen [as] one of the Republican Delegation to America. With passionate energy she devoted herself to the task of avoiding civil conflict between Republicans and Free Staters until the attack on the Four Courts into which building she dramatically gained admission in the height of the fighting. Later she joined the Headquarters Staff at the Hammam Hotel, being one of the last to leave ... Released a short time after her capture, she remained part of Headquarters staff until December 1922, when she was transferred from the Military wing and placed at the head of the Relief organisation Irish Republican Dependants' Fund. In February 1923 she was arrested [in Cork] but released after a brief hunger strike. A County Carlow girl, Miss Barry's devoted work has brought her into contact with all parts of Ireland and its national figures anent whom she is a virtual encyclopedia.

The Catholic Press of Sydney was even better informed: Kitby 'first came into the "public eye" at the execution of her brother Kevin ... from then on it was generally known' that she 'had the same beautiful spirit as her brother of finding nothing too difficult to do if done for Ireland. In May 1922 she made her first public speech on the election platform of Michael Collins in Armagh.' Linda Kearns was similarly recognised: an active worker in the Red Cross 'during the Easter week fighting', she was 'arrested with a flying column in 1920', sentenced to ten years in prison and escaped from Mountjoy by 'climbing an 18 foot wall' during the Truce. After the civil war broke out, she 'tended to Cathal Brugha when he fell mortally wounded'. Another paper noted that 'she attended to Cathal Brugha ... within 200 yards of where she had seen The O'Rahilly die for the same cause six years before'.[32]

That kind of coverage scarcely suggests undue sensitivity towards conservative Australian gender stereotypes, or that the women 'presented themselves … in the context of traditional female patriotic roles, as nurturers of men fighting for Irish freedom'; serving on flying columns, acting as judges, running large relief organisations, were scarcely conventional female roles.[33] Neither Kitby nor Linda Kearns dwelt on their own exploits in their speeches. They were not there to bolster their reputations but to raise money for a genuine cause – destitute republican activists and their families – and, unlike the irascible duo J.J. Kelly and Father Flanagan the previous year, they did not ask for cash to keep the civil war going.

Kitby, who was clearly a fluent public speaker and not averse to celebrity, addressed large crowds. In Melbourne Archbishop Mannix introduced her as 'the sister of Kevin Barry, one of Ireland's honoured martyrs', and in Sydney she was 'the sister of the immortal Kevin Barry', but her words were her own and concerned not his or her actions, but the needs of thousands of recently released republican prisoners and their families.[34] During the trip she met various dignitaries including the Queensland Secretary for Mines, Alfred Jones. She and Linda Kearns displayed finesse in avoiding involvement in disputes within Irish communities, and were so diplomatic in their public pronouncements that the Australian government could find no grounds for deporting them as they had J.J. Kelly and Father O'Flanagan.[35] Both women emphasised 'the distressful state of Ireland, ravaged by war and famine', in stark contrast to the upbeat image the Free State government sought to project abroad.

The Worker of Brisbane carried a notably confused interview with Kitby, 'who by the way is a sister of the remarkable youth of 18 … a medical student, who, holding republican sympathies, was shot for refusing to divulge information to the Free Staters shortly after the signing of the Treaty'. Kitby spoke of 'the industrial, economic, and political chaos in Ireland', where 'much distress prevailed' because of 'the economic and industrial depression following on the instability of the form of Government'. She predicted that the next election would see victory for 'a "cut the painter" republican form of government through a representative franchise'.[36]

Most of Kitby's surviving photographs of the visit are blurred shots of unnamed muddy, rain-soaked Australian towns. An exception is one taken in Atherton, Queensland, on 29 January 1925.

A couple of others, unfortunately somewhat out of focus, include disconsolate Indigenous Australians, one carrying a boomerang. Photographs taken on the liner capture more conventional scenes of sunlit decks and groups of smiling passengers.

Never one to waste time, within a year of her return to Ireland Kitby gave birth to twin girls, Mary and Helen, in January 1926, Paddy a year later, Katherine in 1928 and Judy in 1930. Notably liberal and forthright about sexual matters – she offered advice to Paidín O'Halpin, her future son-in-law, on how women liked to make love – it seems likely that thereafter she and Jim, a pharmacist, secured suitable means of avoiding further pregnancies. From first to last her notes and letters to Jim brimmed with affection: by now bed-bound, on his birthday on 1 January 1968 she wrote 'All my love and thanks for all the good years since the Glen in 1923 ... Thank you for everything. Love always.'[37]

Kitby secured a curious post as 'Publicity Sales Advisor' in the recently created Electricity Supply Board (ESB) in 1930, apparently by the simple means of browbeating the managing director Dr T.A. McLoughlin, whom she knew from revolutionary days, into giving her a job (this presumably entailed her at least temporarily forgiving him his pro-Treaty views). He employed the Moloneys' friend and fellow anti-Treatyite Todd Andrews around the same time, on that occasion taking the initiative.[38] The demands of full-time work in the ESB from 1930 onwards, combined with vigorous trade union activities, while also supervising a family of five small children and servants, pulled Kitby away from the front lines of republican politics and commemoration. But she maintained her network of radical and also some not-so-radical friends – Mary MacSwiney, Máire Comerford, Seamus Robinson, Ernie O'Malley – who became familiar figures to her children. Though her days of foreign campaigns were over, her papers show that she also continued to promote and to protect Kevin's name and to assist her mother in doing the same. Alone of the five Barry girls, she coupled her maiden with her married name lest anyone forget who she was.

Kitby resolutely ignored the Free State and all its works, save when it suited her to demand some favour or other (her son Paddy's friend Michael Gorman recently wrote of how in the 1940s 'I had to keep my ... efforts in job seeking to myself, to prevent her interfering on my behalf'). When her daughter Judy's marriage plans fell through at the last minute in San Francisco in 1960 – unlike her mother, she had given up her job 'and I won't work again, oh goody goody' – Kitby wrote to her suggesting that she ask the Irish consul Kevin Rush to help her find employment. Joan Barrett, her daughter Mary's housekeeper, was one of the few people who would take no direction from Kitby, in person or by telephone.[39]

Jim's attempt to run a pharmacy in inner-city Dublin failed, leaving him bankrupt for some years. It was not until 1934 – and then presumably through Fianna Fáil patronage – that he secured a prosaic job in purchasing in the Irish Sugar Company in Carlow. Despite an acute shortage of money, the Moloney children were raised, with the help of one and sometimes two servants, in enormous houses in Wilton Terrace, in Carrickmines and from the mid-1930s, in 3 Palmerstown Road. These were rented from genteel Protestant landlords who asked for very little payment and who sometimes, along with sundry butchers and grocers, had to

wait a while for that. In 1960, with help from their well-off son
Paddy and son-in-law Paidín O'Halpin, the Moloneys finally got
their own home – a handsome Victorian villa on Winton Avenue,
Rathgar. For an elderly couple with mobility problems, it was an
impractical though highly respectable residence. Kitby's lower
limbs may have weakened, but her social sensibilities were as acute
as ever. When she heard that the newly married daughter of her
old Cumann na mBan friend Nora Bulfin had finally identified
an affordable house, she issued a stern interdict: '<u>Nobody</u> lives in
Kimmage!'[40]

Despite her metropolitan glamour, Kitby never lost her love of
Tombeagh. When she was close to death she told her nephew Kevin
that he would surely meet her ghost on the stairs there from time to
time. With the exception of her son Paddy, who adored Tombeagh
and who built a retirement home there, her children turned out to
be very much city people.

Elgin's son Michael O'Rahilly summed her up thus: 'Kitby was
a very dominant figure. Jim Moloney [her husband] was a kindly
soul … When she retired she took to her bed, summoning people
to her room – it was like the Royal Command.' Ruth recalled Kitby
in similarly imperious mien, Jim waiting upon her like a devoted
and dutiful butler. Michael Gorman, who spent a lot of time in
the Moloneys' Palmerston Road home, is particularly interesting
because he was an outside observer of the dynamics of the family.
Kitby dominated the house and 'expressed her views strongly at
all times' on everything, whereas Jim 'was a reserved man who
said nothing much … just looked on benignly'. In later years Jim's
daughters found him rather distant – he and my mother Mary never
seemed to have anything to say to each other, while his daughter
Judy marvelled at the news that her sister Katherine had moved in
with him following the death of her husband Patrick Kavanagh. His
surviving daughter Helen was astonished by the depth of feeling
shown in Jim's letters to her mother during the fraught months

of their engagement in the midst of the civil war.[41] But, of course, children don't know as much about their parents' inner lives and relationships as they may think.

Kitby's younger children carried Kevin's memory with them through life. Her son was christened Patrick Barry in honour of his two slain uncles; her third daughter styled herself Katherine B. (or sometimes Barry) Moloney; and Judy, her youngest, also was sometimes B. and sometimes Barry Moloney. As Kitby's eldest grandson, I assume that the names Kevin Barry would have fallen to me, were it not that my father's youngest brother Eunan had died in Letterkenny at the age of eleven the year before my birth. Instead of being named after someone hanged for Ireland, as a small boy I worried for years that I might not outlast my own namesake by reaching my twelfth birthday. My brother, born in 1961, was christened Kevin Barry, but within weeks we were told to call him Barry.

Although Paddy Moloney's fate was known to Kitby's family, her curation of memory meant that his family's role, loss and suffering never got a mention. When she occasionally advised a grandchild to be 'a brave Republican soldier' on foot of some minor cut or impending ordeal, it was clearly Uncle Kevin, not the obscure, unmentioned slain Uncle Paddy, who was being invoked. Although a true blue anti-partitionist, she never alluded to her son-in-law Paidín's Co. Down republican family, or to their narrative of enforced exile, hardship and premature death from prison-related illness. (Seamus Woods, once OC of the Belfast Brigade, described Paidín's father, who was only fifty-two when he died in 1943, as 'the pioneer of the Sinn Féin and Volunteer movement in Co. Down'.)[42] Nor did Kitby ever acknowledge the existence, still less the achievement of Paidín's Letterkenny-based mother Annie, widowed at thirty-eight, who raised and educated a family on her own, virtually penniless. A few days after Hugh Halpenny's death in April 1943, confirmation of the award of his military service pension arrived. Annie wrote a diffident, almost apologetic letter to the Department of Defence explaining that he had just died, 'leaving 13 children behind him, none of whom are earning anything. The youngest was born three weeks before his death.' Fortunately someone in the department heeded her, as she received the £150 16s. 8d. back money due only a few months later, and £36 a year thereafter.[43] When Jim and Mick each applied for military service pensions in 1935, Kitby promptly secured a personal interview with her former comrade Minister for Defence Frank Aiken to ask him to expedite matters (which, as a note on Jim's file shows, he immediately duly did).[44] It was, of course, only right that Annie Halpenny should occasionally make respectful allusion to Kevin to her visiting O'Halpin grandchildren.

Kitby's capacity to vary her fatwas to suit circumstances continued into old age. By and large it appears that civil war differences did not mean all that much to her. On a rare visit to town in 1964 she arranged to meet 'Jo[sephine] MacNeill' (1895–1969), with whom she had served on the executive of Cumann na mBan in 1921 before the split, for coffee in Brown Thomas's. Josephine had gone on to marry James MacNeill, the second governor general of the Irish Free State (1928–32) and the last to take that office seriously, who was regarded by republicans as a toxic symbol of the limitations of the Treaty. Widowed, she had been parachuted into the Irish diplomatic corps in 1950 by Kitby's friend Seán MacBride when he was Minister for External Affairs, being appointed Irish Minister at the Hague – the first Irish woman to hold what would now be ambassadorial rank. Kitby and Jo 'covered a lot of ground – Dublin, Fermoy, London, Dublin, the Hague, Vienna, Switzerland ...' While waiting for Kitby's taxi they encountered Anna McGilligan, 'Paddy's wife of whom I am really fond' (Paddy McGilligan having been a minister in W.T. Cosgrave's cabinet from 1923 to 1932). Old comradeships and friendships easily bridged the civil war divide when it suited her.[45]

Kitby's attitude towards those Irish who continued to serve in British colours was also somewhat nuanced. In 1963, irritated by a piece in *The Irish Times* by her nephew Donal O'Donovan about the Royal Irish Fusiliers in West Germany that 'Daddy & a lot of other people found disgustingly like a recruiting campaign,' she thought the paper 'should have been more choosy in its representative', sending somebody 'with a more suitable background'. Kitby told her son that 'while I yield to nobody in my prejudice against the British Army ... so many young Irishmen that I knew & liked went off to die for the Freedom of Small Nations ... I've always had a feeling for the PBI (poor bloody infantry) but preferably without Irishmen in it.' (Her husband's older half-brother William Hannon (1888–1943) had enlisted in the Royal Irish Regiment in 1914 before qualifying as a Royal Flying Corps pilot in 1916, ultimately leaving to join the new Free State air corps in December 1922.)[46] She also exempted Kevin's old Belvedere and UCD friend Gerry McAleer from her general abhorrence of British militarism. So far from damning McAleer as an apostate for joining the Royal Air Force as a medical officer, she practically purred when she mentioned him in her BMH statement: 'He is now Group [Wing] Commander ... and I read lately in *The Irish Times* that he is very close to the top. We see him very often when he is in Dublin' (in April 1957, by which time he was an air commodore and principal medical officer 'to the Far East', *The Irish Times* carried news of his appointment as honorary physician to Queen Elizabeth. In the 1960 Birthday Honours List he received a CBE).[47]

By the time I was old enough to take anything in, Kitby was largely bed-bound due to the consequences of a stroke in 1949, which badly affected her right foot and caused her to retire early from the ESB. She also had trouble with the circulation in her hands. She gradually grew less mobile, though her family letters show she was still able to leave the house occasionally in the 1960s, and she was evidently more agile than her grandchildren realised: in 1966 she told Paddy how 'I got up immediately after breakfast ... and I've been ... pottering.'[48] She generally received visitors in state, in bed, in the first-floor front room of 4 Winton Avenue. On her bedside table were books, a cream-coloured telephone in constant use, cigarettes, an ashtray, bags of expensive coloured cotton-wool balls from Brown Thomas, eau de cologne, powder compacts, perfume, nail varnish, pillboxes, *The Irish Times* and, when available, *The United Irishman*. On the other side of the bed was a sturdy leather-padded wooden seat, in fact a commode. There was always a vase of fresh flowers, and the room was always clean and tidy, and smelt of cigarettes, polish and talcum powder. She took meals on a polished wooden bed tray, covered in a linen cloth, with a napkin and silver ring. In the early-1960s a television was hired, which she watched assiduously. Ironically, in view of the ghastly vendetta he later pursued against Kitby's daughter Katherine, Peter Kavanagh – brother of the poet Patrick, whom Katherine married in 1967 – ingeniously fitted a switch and cable so that she could turn the set on and off from her bed. This must have eased things for her husband Jim, who waited on her every whim quietly and uncomplainingly following his retirement in 1961 from the Irish Sugar Company.

Her letters to her son Paddy were far from melancholy and indicate that she was constantly in touch with her sisters and with her own children. In February 1962 she was intrigued by what she judged an indirect olive branch from de Valera. 'The old schemer' asked Dr Joe Brennan for his recollections of Cathal Brugha's last days, as Brennan had been with the anti-Treaty party in the Hammam Hotel, and had tended Brugha after he was mortally wounded as he left the Gresham Hotel. Brennan said he had only limited memories. De Valera then said that he had heard from Máire Brugha that Kitby 'had the best information' and he asked Brennan 'to approach me'. Brennan said de Valera had 'gathered

... that I might not be prepared to collaborate direct with him!!! I said, "How right he is," and I feel that my life as a Republican was crowned with success. In his devious way he has talked so many decent people ... into speaking to him ...' There was 'joy in my heart to know that KBM is still a thorn in his conscience'. She told Joe Brennan to say that 'I was in no way collaborating with the Viceregal [Lodge, now Áras an Uachtaráin].' Yet her 'old brain worked Jesuitically', and she came up with the idea of suggesting that Brennan track down a recorded interview she had given some years before to Brugha's nephew and biographer Tomás Ó Dochartaigh. She did not wish to appear 'a dog in the manger' if her 'memories of the last stand' would help in vindicating 'Cathal's honour': 'It is gorgeous to refuse a Command Performance ... still more gorgeous to know that the person hasn't the guts to get in touch with me himself.' She told Cathal's son Rory that she could never assist 'the Person in the Park who had betrayed everything, national & social, in which he had professed to believe'.[49]

Kitby was wary of the Common Market, writing in 1962 that she hoped Britain 'may escape by some miracle becoming the western-most post of the German Reich' – this from a woman who had cheered for Hitler, and who never looked askance at her brother-in-law Jim O'Donovan, at the centre of IRA/Nazi intrigue.[50] In the run-up to the fiftieth anniversary of the Rising, she expressed some optimism about Ireland, detecting 'a new spring coming ... I feel like an old Fenian in 1916'. But she feared the perpetuation of 'Maynooth Rule' despite 'Pope John & his [Vatican] Council ... our 26 Popes [bishops] are getting back into their stride. But ... they can't live for ever & all the indications are that the young priests are more Christian.' She was pleased to receive an invitation to a High Mass in the Pro-Cathedral on Easter Monday 1966, relieved that her assigned seat was close to the altar rails so 'at least I would not have been beneath the salt'. She sent a polite 'regrets', but was annoyed that Jim, 'a [War of Independence] medallist', had not yet been contacted about any official events – 'there would be no excuse ... since they send his pension ... Anyway we'll see, and he probably would not go anyway.'[51]

When Kitby died quite suddenly following a further stroke in January 1969, the Áras rang Jim to ascertain if President de Valera would be welcome at her funeral. Jim said of course. Kitby would undoubtedly have been furious had the state's first citizen failed to attend her obsequies in his elegant old Rolls-Royce. Other prominent old revolutionaries present at her funeral included her civil war foes Min and Dick Mulcahy. There were also old anti-Treaty comrades such as Todd Andrews, Frank Aiken, Eileen McCarville and Seán MacBride, true blue republicans Máire Comerford, Joe Clarke, Seán Dowling and Moss Twomey, Sinn Féin president Tómas MacGiolla, and the serving IRA chief of staff Cathal Goulding. General M.J. Costello, who had made his name humiliating the anti-Treaty IRA during the civil war, attended, as did many people from well-got Fianna Fáil families – Ryans, MacEntees, Ruttledges and Brughas – and some such as Joe McCullough from old Sinn Féin pro-Treaty families. Dr Honora Aughney, once one of Kevin's dance partners, was there, together with an eclectic mix of artists, writers and musicians including Luke Kelly of The Dubliners, reflecting the bohemian friendships of her daughters Helen and Katherine. Also there was Melville 'Sandy' Miller, once her son Paddy's boss in *The Irish Times* advertising department. It may well have been he who ensured that her death and funeral were duly reported in her favourite newspaper. Her burial was entrusted to the National Graves Association, and the graveside prayers were led by Kevin's old mentor Father Tom Counihan SJ.[52]

Jim outlived Kitby by twelve years. Todd Andrews told me he had several times tried and failed to get him to come out to talk about old times with old comrades, without success. But when Andrews' memoir *Dublin Made Me* was published in 1979, Jim telephoned to thank Todd for what he had written about Kitby

and himself (Andrews described him as 'one of the finest characters
I had met in the Movement', who 'never appreciated his [own]
worth').[53] In April 1973 Paddy drove Jim and me down to the
fiftieth anniversary commemoration for Liam Lynch, organised
by Provisional Sinn Féin. Jim temporarily shed decades; chatting,
laughing, shaking hands and embracing, practically running from
one old comrade to another across a windy mountainside, and
afterwards in a very crowded pub, where old IRA men mixed easily
with contemporary republicans and sundry Fianna Fáilers including
TDs David Andrews and Rory Brugha. I was solemnly introduced
to Seán Keenan (1921–1993) from Derry, a man who had spent
fifteen years in detention without trial over various periods from
1940 to 1972, as 'a grand-nephew of Kevin Barry'.[54]

Jim must also have attended many funerals of IRA veterans, at
least in Dublin (he did not have a car). In one letter Kitby recorded
how he had just about made it in time by train to Tipperary in
August 1963 for the funeral of his 3rd Tipperary Brigade comrade
Artie Barlow. Yet so far as I know the only old comrade he saw
frequently was Jim O'Donovan, once Ireland's self-appointed
Gauleiter-in-waiting, who brooded on the past just a few hundred
yards away from Jim and Kitby on Rathgar Road. In 1966 Kitby
lamented that 'James L unloads all his woes on him … the problems
there have got him down … It is really a tragic situation but I often
wish we lived farther away from it.'[55]

Whenever I had an opportunity in the 1970s, I asked Jim
Moloney a few questions. Why had he and Kitby supported Hitler's
Germany? How had Paddy died? Had he been sworn into the IRB?
Where had he stayed and trained while studying in Dublin? He
answered that he lodged in Kingstown in the house of two pleasant
Protestant ladies, one of whom stumbled upon his revolver and
holster hanging behind a door but said nothing. He took the tram
across the city to Jones's Road for Volunteer parades. When I asked if
he had ever shot anybody, he said he had shot two Free State soldiers

in a house in the Glen of Aherlow, before he escaped out a window: I did not like to ask whether they had died. He was proud of the fact that, while OC of prisoners in Newbridge internment camp in October/November 1923, he had only ceased a hunger strike after thirty-five days when ordered to do so. He recalled his hunger strike as not too difficult after the first week, and described how he and his comrades were given eggs beaten in brandy when their protest ended (he suffered thereafter from stomach problems). He approved of the ongoing IRA campaign of killing in Northern Ireland as regarded soldiers and policemen, though not civilians. He also once made a remark along the lines of 'if I had a penny for every request I had to write a letter saying So and So was in the IRA, I'd be a rich man'.

Jim was willing to answer specific questions but never to yarn, so conversations tended to dry up. It was only after his last child Helen died in 2011 that I came across a copy of the *Rubáiyát of Omar Khayyám*, with his name and 'March 1923 Limerick Prison' on the flyleaf. This indicates that it was in Jim's possession just after he, his brother Con and Tom Conway were captured on 7 March in the Glen of Aherlow, following a fierce gunfight during which Con and Conway were badly wounded.[56] On 8 December 1923 Jim used the volume to collect the autographs of fellow prisoners, mainly from Tipperary and Kerry, presumably men who shared a hut with him. He probably did this expecting that many would be released before Christmas. On a back page, he wrote: 'The man who will venture something in a big cause, even if he utterly fails, is a man who rises above ordinary human stature, and surely the difficult failure is more honourable than the facile success.' The quotation comes from *Our American Adventure*, a book detailing Arthur Conan Doyle's American lecture tour of 1922, during which he preached the virtues of spiritualism, which was much in vogue amongst the bereaved of the Great War and which particularly interested Kitby because of Kevin.[57]

Kitby's children received appropriately republican upbringings, all being sent to Miss Gavan Duffy's Scoil Bhríde, where they were taught through the medium of Irish. All bar Mary and Judy seem quickly to have forgotten the language thereafter. The girls were enrolled in Cumann na gCáilíni, a kind of republican girl guides, which they did not much enjoy, and took Irish dancing lessons in Madam Cogley's. Three of the girls attended the Loreto Convent secondary school in St Stephen's Green, while Paddy left Scoil Bhríde at the age of eight for Belvedere. Money could be found for university only for Paddy. My mother Mary, who had always done well in school, was instead sent off to Belgium for a year to teach English in a convent school while improving her French. Kitby, in her customary fashion, then prevailed upon the Irish minister in Paris Seán Murphy, whom she knew from pre-civil war days, to fix her daughter up with a secretarial job in the OEEC (Organisation for European Economic Cooperation, now the OECD) in Paris, which Mary adored. Helen, who had left Scoil Bhríde before her fourteenth birthday, by her own account without a word of Irish and barely able to read, was somehow permitted to start attending the National College of Art, again through Kitby's exercise of influence. Katherine had no academic interests and drifted into office work, her world thereafter defined by books and conversation in Dublin and in London. In 1954 she briefly returned home, 'ragged and penniless', at Kitby's behest, although she felt 'her lack of qualifications' militated against getting work in Dublin: her sisters 'are all clubbing together to get her outfitted', Mary 'getting my wedding coat dyed dark green for her' in order to enhance her employment prospects. Mary wrote that 'We have hinted to Ma to take her casually ... as Ma was getting all het up with zeal about finding her a job.'[58] But Katherine soon headed back to London's wider literary horizons. Judy trained as an architectural draughtsman.

Kitby's first four children eschewed radical politics. Helen was interested only in art, at first focusing uncertainly on painting until she discovered that stained glass was her true métier. For many years she was a part-time art teacher in Blackrock Technical College, although her stained-glass commissions enjoyed critical success and she was one of the first visual artists elected to Aosdána in 1983.[59] Her twin Mary, who inherited her mother's sense of style, accentuated by two years working in Paris as a young woman, became active in Fianna Fáil along with her engineer husband Paidín, with whom she worked in a successful industrial boiler import agency, initially based in their small flat in Rathmines, from 1954 onwards. Paidín (1923–1978), a Lemass protégé and ally of George Colley (1925–1983), was Fianna Fáil director of elections for Dublin city in 1965 and was for a time quite high in the counsels of the party. He rather feared Charles Haughey, whereas Mary was always a great fan.[60]

Kitby's son Paddy followed his famous uncle to Belvedere. Disbarred from field sports following a serious accident in which he fractured his skull, he became an enthusiastic cyclist, undertaking long excursions through Ireland with his friends Michael Gorman and Frank Winder. On one such trip in 1945 he called into Tipperary town to see his grandfather P.J. Moloney, whom he had never met because of a family rift shortly after his birth. P.J., who died two years later, gave him the handsome sum of ten shillings.[61] After UCD he worked in the advertising department of *The Irish Times* while he completed an MA in Economics in UCD on nineteenth-century Irish newspapers. His departure for the Vacuum Oil Company (which became Mobil Oil in 1966) was noted by the paper's legendary editor R.M. Smyllie (1893–1954), writing as 'Nichevo' in *An Irishman's Diary*: 'one of my little birds … whispers that his thesis is really brilliant … I was delighted to hear … that on the eve of his departure he was given a "knockdown" in the composing room – a very high honour indeed'.[62] As that suggests, Paddy had a marked talent for getting to know and of getting on with everyone, for staying in touch with family and friends, whatever rows and rifts there had been, and for hearing people out. His friend Tony Cronin (1928–2016), himself no stranger to strong disagreements, particularly noted this trait in an impromptu address at Paddy's burial in Glasnevin cemetery in July 1989.

Katherine moved in smoke-shrouded literary and artistic circles in Dublin and London pubs, republican and anti-capitalist in thought though not in activism. Her mother did not seem to mind. When she returned home at about two in the morning, 'still pretty drunk' from the wedding reception on 13 August 1960 in the Shelbourne Hotel of Paddy's friend Frank Winder and Jeanne Bulfin – 'I'm very confused about the time ... we were in McDaids and Jammetts, but it is all a bit vague' – 'Mummie was awake and I gave her all the news. She was delighted that I was in that state, as she said she would not have got nearly as much news if I had been sober.'[63]

Katherine worked as an office factotum and bookkeeper in London and later in Dublin in order to live the bohemian life she wanted. I recall staying with my father in her pokey flat in Gibson Square in Islington for a couple of nights in 1964, when I was nine: it was the first time I saw a set of book proofs, which she explained she was checking on behalf of a publisher. She was one of a cosmopolitan Soho set, which included the American poet Elizabeth Smart, Tony Cronin and his wife Therese (who may have been married out of Kitby's Palmerston Road home), Patrick Swift, Robert MacBryde, Paul Potts, Colin McInnes, George Barker, her great friend Leland Bardwell, Dom Moraes, Martin Green and Tim O'Keefe, Patrick Kavanagh's publisher and later a disastrous literary agent for the Patrick Kavanagh estate whom it eventually fell to me to dismiss by letter after Katherine became seriously ill in the early 1980s.

It was in London that Katherine met Kavanagh, with whom she lived on and off and eventually married in March 1967. In his poem 'News Item' he writes of Gibson Square, where 'I have taken roots of love / ... I walk in Islington Green / Finest landscape you've ever seen / I'm as happy as I've ever been.' Poet James Liddy described how, after Katherine's and Patrick's nuptials in Rathgar church, he met Kitby in her elegant bedroom in 4 Winton Avenue: 'We were introduced to the mother lying a-bed, an older version of Mise Eire!' When Kavanagh, a far from blushing groom, was introduced to Mac O'Rahilly, he immediately brought up The O'Rahilly's death on Moore Lane in 1916: 'That must have been a terrible end, dying drop of blood by drop of blood and no-one could come to him for [fear of] the snipers' cross-fire.' Mac, a courteous man, 'paled'.[64] It was Kitby's last proper party, and how she must have loved it.

Judy, Kitby's youngest daughter, followed her mother into radical republican intrigue. She worked first in Dublin, then emigrated to the United States, returned to Ireland in the early 1960s and left again because the damp Irish climate accentuated circulation problems in her hands, a complaint which she had inherited from Kitby. Based in San Francisco when the Northern Ireland troubles broke out, she saw the crisis as her chance to make a contribution to Irish republicanism as her parents had done. She wrote to Helen expressing some bewilderment at fissures within the republican movement in Ireland and abroad, and outlined what she and others were doing to raise awareness of Irish issues. Her mother's daughter, she called regularly at the Irish consulate to read the Irish newspapers, although she suspected the consul sometimes kept them on his desk an extra day to spite her because of her politics. Amongst her group's activities was a weekly slot on a radio station, 'which gives time to all ethnic groups to do their own programmes'. They experimented with Irish language lessons, and for the fiftieth anniversary of Kevin's execution, 1 November 1970, planned to present

> the full programme on Uncle Kevin, so I have a lot of work to do, not only writing what I will say but also

making out the questions the others will ask me, and trying to get hold of some good records.

I am, as always, very involved in Irish politics, in fact am now the Sinn Féin representative on the West Coast, a real honour, as all who join the Republican Clubs which are being started here will have to write an application which will go through me to Dublin and then Dublin decides who is 'in' or not, needless to say I am very happy not to have this responsibility, as there are spys [sic] in literally everything.[65]

She hosted kingpins of the leftist 'Official' arm of the now split republican movement: Seán Garland (1934–2018), 'a really great person', had been out to organise networks the previous November, and 'Thomas MacGiolla [1924–2010] will be out late Jan or early Feb and will also stay with me.'

She continued: 'How much poor Mother would have loved all this, as it is I know it bores the hell out of the rest of you, but as it is so much a part of me, I have trouble writing about anything else, but try not to be a fanatic. It is just that it is all so very important.'[66]

Amongst her tasks was to collect *The United Irishman* from the airport and arrange for its distribution. It was while driving back from the airport with the latest edition of the newspaper in February 1971 that she experienced the car crash in which she was mortally injured. Her sisters Mary and Helen were with her for her last four days, as she struggled for life on a respirator: Helen wrote that 'at least she died without the terror of knowing that she was going to die'. Unable to speak, there was 'delight on her face' when Helen asked her if she had left anything in her will to Sinn Féin.[67]

Helen and Mary were disconcerted on their arrival in San Francisco to find that the bulk of Judy's papers, and memorabilia relating to Kevin, had been removed by fellow republicans and was never recovered. Her father Jim nevertheless donated her entire estate, consisting mainly of the $8,000 proceeds of an insurance policy, to the Sinn Féin (Gardiner Place) party.

Judy had her dearest wish of a republican funeral, complete with a black beret colour party who carried her coffin from the hearse to her mother's grave in Glasnevin Cemetery (*The Irish Times* carried a photograph of the event).[68] IRA Chief of Staff Cathal Goulding gave an oration, and came back to the Moloney home in Winton Avenue where he and I, then sixteen, talked for some time at cross-purposes about the utility and the futility of political violence.

Elgin

Elgin became a determined activist. Not yet eighteen, when ordered out of the Hammam Hotel in early July 1922, she smuggled a weapon away under her coat. When she reached St Stephen's Green, she realised that pedestrians were being searched as they crossed the nearby canal bridges. She slipped into the basement of her alma mater, Loreto College, and hid the gun in the coat rack. It was, she told her daughter Ruth, the most useful thing the school had ever done for her. She once told me of how, on attempting to return to her civil service typing job days after the city centre fighting had died down, she was quizzed closely about her unexplained absences from duty before being turned away. She never forgot that the officious young man concerned was Leon O'Broin (1902–1990), destined as secretary of the Department of Posts and Telegraphs from 1957 to 1965 to be the midwife of Telefís Éireann, and also a notably thorough and productive scholar of Irish revolutionaries and of their Castle opponents from the eighteenth to the twentieth century.

Elgin was later arrested and jailed in Kilmainham and in the North Dublin Union, where female prisoners were badly treated. She took part in the women's hunger strike there in 1923 (at more or less the same time as Kitby's fiancé Jim Moloney was on hunger strike in Newbridge). A year later, she wrote to Kitby of her horror at how Dubliners had observed Armistice Day: 'If you didn't know how to count past ten, you could count the people [who were not wearing poppies].' 'Really, I think we are rather wonderful to have the cheek to think that we could ever have made a republic out of this country.'[69]

Like Kitby before her, Elgin visited the United States in 1928–9 to raise money for a republican cause, in this case Scoil Íde, the private school established by Mary and Annie MacSwiney in Cork in 1916 to educate children in a Gaelic, republican spirit. Despite her efforts, she was unable to raise anything approaching the ambitious target of $150,000 that had been set. Her daughter Ruth has a watch presented to 'Eileen M. Barry with Esteem from the St Ita's Committee New York August 1929' just a couple of months before the Wall Street crash, which probably brought Irish diaspora funding for republican activities temporarily to an end. In New York Elgin worked closely with veteran Cork republican Connie Neenan, who remained a great friend: her children used to tease her every Christmas when a pair of silk stockings would arrive from New York.[70] In the intervals of rearing four children after her marriage in 1935 to 'Mac' O'Rahilly, she remained involved behind the scenes in republican affairs. When Ireland became a republic in 1949, she and her close friend Sighle Humphries, Mac's cousin, transferred some hundreds of pounds from a Cumann na mBan account to an unspecified beneficiary, most likely the IRA.[71]

A dignified woman who never talked politics and who very seldom spoke of Kevin to her children as they were growing up, Elgin made sure each of them got a good grounding in Irish through being sent as boarders to Ring for a year, although she did not have a word of the language herself. She did not push them into republican activism, though she remained a quietly adamantine republican even when Mac, a close friend of Seán MacBride and the founding treasurer of the Clann na Poblachta party in 1946, began to question hallowed republican verities in the 1960s and 1970s.[72]

I know less of Kevin's other siblings, and of how they chose to honour his memory. Shel, who managed the house in Tombeagh, was active in Carlow in Cumann na mBan and in the support roles allocated to young women during the War of Independence and civil war. She settled on a farm outside Athy, marrying Kevin's friend Bapty Maher, a well-known publican, undertaker and all-round local character, a striking figure who customarily wore dark suits and a broad black hat (he was so dressed on the only occasion I met him, outside the mortuary at St Vincent's Hospital after the death of Jim Moloney in April 1981).[73] Absorbed in family life with five children to raise and an unsupportive husband, there were few opportunities for any kind of political activism in South Kildare. She was very attached to Tombeagh and had the resilience and resolution that characterised all the Barrys. Donal recalled her and her five children as 'good company'.[74] Her granddaughter Katherine Logan, whom I knew slightly, certainly possessed such qualities. Monty and Peggy were so young that events between 1920 and 1923 rather passed them by. Monty was, however, co-opted into radicalism through her marriage in 1926 to Jim/Seamus O'Donovan, a UCD chemistry graduate and, like Kevin, a Jesuit boy. Many years later she remarked to her son Donal that 'she had been foolish to marry' at twenty. Jim, nine years her senior, had been appointed to the IRA Executive as 'Director of Chemicals' during the Truce, and later took the anti-Treaty side in the civil war. He launched *Ireland Today* as a journal of ideas, politics and aesthetics in 1935. He combined intellectual activism with unrelenting devotion to the republican cause and was the architect of the 'S-Plan' for attacks on British transport infrastructure and manufacturing targets for the IRA's ill-conceived 1939 bombing campaign. Characteristically, he blamed others for its utter failure to achieve any of its objectives. O'Donovan also cemented the IRA's alliance with Nazi Germany, travelling to Europe several times in 1939 for discussions with German intelligence officials and other contacts, and to receive money and radio equipment. He twice brought Monty along as cover. The most significant German agent sent to Ireland, Hermann Goertz, was sheltered for a fortnight in O'Donovan's home in Shankill in June 1940, and befriended Jim's young son Donal.[75]

When Jim was, belatedly, interned in the Curragh in 1941, Monty rather came into her own, taking on paying guests and starting a cheese business with a friend in order to make ends meet with four children to feed, clothe and manage, a servant to supervise, and a house to keep. Jim was released in 1943 and, notwithstanding the nightmarish complications his machinations with Germany had created for the state as it strove to protect neutrality, he was allowed to resume his ESB employment as though nothing had happened (in captivity he had continued to receive his 50 per cent disability pension for his wounded right hand as well as his military service pension because he had not been convicted of any offence).[76] Old comrades later spoke of him as very clever but too conscious of that fact, and too self-absorbed for effective leadership. Todd Andrews once told me that O'Donovan had remarked to him that his own name would be remembered in Ireland when de Valera's was long forgotten.[77]

As a child in the 1960s I met Jim O'Donovan a few times in his Rathgar Road home. This was because my father, who as a young engineer had worked in the ESB in the late 1940s and early 1950s, was on good terms with him and used to call in to talk about the ESB and about state enterprise more generally. To my child's eye O'Donovan was notably well-dressed in a tweedy, almost country-house fashion. He wore a glove on his disfigured right hand. He was distantly civil towards children, whereas his wife Monty was very pleasant to me and my siblings in an unfussy, granny-ish fashion. Inquiries of others with childhood memories of the O'Donovans yielded the description of her as 'a lovely, kind person'.[78] Jim, and subsequently also Monty, moved to a nursing home in Bullock Harbour in the late 1960s. My mother Mary used to visit Monty there, and so she probably looked in to say hello to Jim. After Jim's death, Mary also acted as a trustee for Monty, by then severely ill, along with Mac O'Rahilly.

Donal O'Donovan has written extensively about his difficult relationship with his father Jim. In 1972 he brought his wife Jenny and stepson Julian to visit de Valera in Áras an Uachtaráin. As they were leaving, de Valera turned to Donal and asked: 'Would you say something to your father from me? Tell him I hope there is not bitterness in his heart towards me as there certainly is no bitterness in my heart towards him.' But Jim was furious when he heard of this tentative olive branch: how could the visionary architect of the IRA/Nazi alliance, which at one point in 1940 had threatened to drag Ireland into the war by provoking a British invasion, possibly lower himself to acknowledge that de Valera had felt he was acting for the best in repressing the republican movement? Jim O'Donovan was the last member of the pre-split 1922 IRA Executive when he died in 1979, and he features in Leo Whelan's famous unfinished group portrait, belonging to the Mulcahy family but hanging in the officers' mess in McKee Barracks.[79]

Not long after his marriage to Monty in 1926, Jim O'Donovan began assembling materials for a biography of Kevin. The task was, instead, eventually completed by Donal in 1989, more interestingly, humanely and engagingly than Jim's stilted, formulaic, unpublishable hagiography, *Ireland's Kevin Barry*.[80] Of Monty's and Jim's children, Donal, Gerry, Sheila and Aedeen, Donal was the one most caught up in political affairs and in Kevin's story. His courageous memoirs of a picaresque life as an *Irish Times* journalist and Bank of Ireland public relations executive disclose that, like his father before him, he became involved in German intrigues. For a time in the early 1960s he wrote economic and political assessments of Ireland for an East German intelligence agency who 'wanted me to be their eyes and ears in Ireland' in return for money. But unlike his father, he supported Fianna Fáil, and for some time up to June 1981 was the party's director of elections in the Wicklow constituency.[81] He was a strong supporter of Charles Haughey (Taoiseach from 1979 to 1981, in 1982, and from 1987 to 1992), for whom he wrote a short poem with a repeated line to the effect that 'the saviour [or rescuer?] of our people has come' on one of the occasions when Haughey became Taoiseach. I saw a finely lettered version framed on the wall of a downstairs back corridor in Haughey's Kinsealy home around 2002.[82]

Donal's younger brother Gerry, a Teilifís Éireann set designer, took an extraordinary photograph of Kitby in her Winton Avenue bedroom in October 1968, only a few months before her death. On her lap was *The Irish Times*, its headline 'Massive No to Government' announcing a crushing defeat for Fianna Fáil in their second attempt to persuade the electorate to dispense with proportional representation by amending the constitution. A previous referendum, held in 1959 on the same day as de Valera was first elected president, had narrowly failed. Kitby's introduction to political affairs had come when her employer Ernest Aston had made her the assistant secretary and effectively the administrative heart of the Proportional Representation Society of Ireland, before revolutionary nationalism swept her into a different channel. She surely relished this second kick in the teeth for Dev and Fianna Fáil.

Kevin's youngest sister Peggy Cronin appears least in this discussion of the Barry siblings. Her mother's 'consolation', we know that she too never forgot the day Kevin was captured. She wrote of how, then just twelve, she was sent out to scour his usual haunts nearby in hopes of finding him on the afternoon of 20 September 1920, and of her despair that she could not do so. Four decades later, 'I am totally unable to see the whole thing objectively – to me it is still a *very* close, terrible and personal matter.'[83]

The Barry Women at War and in Peace

The passing of Tom Barry in 1908 transformed the family from a highly patriarchal organism – to judge by the terms of his will – to a matriarchal one, in which first his sister Judith and then his eldest daughter Kitby dominated affairs. This probably lessened inhibitions upon active involvement in matters political as the Barry girls grew up. By 1916 Kitby was already immersed in the Proportional Representation Society of Ireland. Yet, although 1916 evidently turned her into a convinced separatist, supporting Kevin in his Irish Volunteers activities from 1917 onwards, neither she nor any of her sisters rushed to the colours by enrolling in Cumann na mBan. By her own account she felt she had too many family responsibilities in Dublin: she only joined the university branch of that organisation after Kevin's death, and then initially in the unaccustomed role of ordinary member although by the time of the Treaty split she appears to have been a member of the Executive.

This raises the wider question of what Irish female rebels were and were not allowed to do to further the fight for independence. One of the curiosities of the Irish struggle against British rule is the contrast with so deeply conservative a society as early twentieth-century India where girls and women irrespective of religion were subject to extraordinary social control. The Irish example helped to inspire a handful of young Indian women to take up arms.[84] Kamala Dasgupta, involved in the attempt in 1930 to assassinate Charles Tegart, the much-loathed Irish chief of police in Calcutta, had been radicalised through hearing of 'the Irish insurrections, the rising movement of Cavour in Italy and the Russian Revolution. Fights and resistance, small separately were converging towards a

full-scale revolution.' Once inducted into a secret group, she 'began
to read about Irish insurrections, the Russian Revolution, the lives
of the revolutionaries, their history etc.' Another young student,
Ajuna Sen, was mortally wounded when her grenade bounced
back off Tegart's car before exploding. The following year Kamala
supplied the revolver with which graduate Bina Das fired on the
governor of Calcutta, missing her target, at a conferring ceremony.
Another female student later arrested in Calcutta, when asked
by Tegart's successor Patrick Kelly why she had got involved in
revolutionary conspiracy, rejoined: 'You are an Irishman. What do
you feel about it? He kept mum.'[85]

Although they had far greater practical freedom, killing was
not an acceptable military role for Irish women. Neither Kitby, nor
Elgin, nor Mary MacSwiney ever got the chance to fight, although
in reality their value to the cause was far greater not only as symbols
and reminders of their dead brothers, but as formidable advocates
of the anti-Treaty causes. Despite Constance Markievicz's theatrical
brandishing of guns to emphasise that armed combat was not solely
a male preserve, and Margaret Skinnider's courageous engagement
in the fighting around St Stephen's Green in 1916, so far as is known
Irish women did not directly inflict violence upon their opponents
through the use of arms during the War of Independence, or during
the civil war, or during the sectarian violence, which claimed
hundreds of civilian lives in Belfast between 1920 and 1922, and
in Derry in 1920.[86] This is perhaps one of the ways in which the
societally conservative nature of the Irish revolution is apparent.
In the independence movement up to the Treaty, and on the anti-
Treaty side thereafter, the roles assigned to females were strictly
non-combatant. Many hundreds, whether formally members of
Cumann na mBan or not, supported the independence struggle
by gathering intelligence, moving and hiding weapons, identifying
and shadowing suspects, carrying communications, providing safe
houses and medical aid, and performing crucial administrative

tasks including record-keeping, typing, and preparing propaganda. In a conservative, male-dominated society there were practical advantages in using women in such roles: they were generally far less likely than young men to be suspected of subversive activities, and less likely to be searched or arrested.

Support work could be extremely dangerous and must have been very stressful. Hannah Hanley, Captain of the Eyries company of Cumann na mBan on the Beara peninsula, was questioned by the pensions board about her care of the hapless Bridget Noble, one of three women whom the IRA executed as spies. Hannah described how she looked after 'a lady prisoner': 'She was two nights in the area. She was moved on then and I got other girls to attend to her.'[87] Other women such as Thomasina Lynders identified alleged enemy agents who were subsequently killed, and were proud to let this be known.[88] Margaret Cromien (*née* Morris) joined Cumann na mBan after the Rising, in which her fiancé Jack Cromien was killed, but seemed anxious not to appear to have been seeking revenge: she told official interviewers that 'My boy was killed in 1916,' but felt she should not have stated this on the form, as 'It was a foolish thing to do ... It only led up to my joining. He was near me. He had his gun and all. I tried to get his rifle.' In the course of her activities to the end of the civil war, she shadowed 'Hoppy' Byrne, a disabled man shot as a spy in 1921 (he survived the initial shooting only for the IRA to carry him out of Jervis Street hospital and finish him off on his stretcher).[89] Others again, such as Seán Nathan's wife – identified only as 'Mrs Nathan ... a great help ... Her help and indeed her pram was of great use. That brave woman took great risks ... without fear or question' – moved guns, carried messages and hid people.[90] Females could do everything save kill (or exercise command over men).

In her witness statement Kitby mentioned and then brushed aside her own War of Independence activities, and by extension those of all other women who smuggled or hid weapons, carried despatches, collected information, spied, endured the repeated searching and thrashing of their homes and provided safe havens for Volunteers as essentially not worthy of discussion or commemoration. Yet anyone who consults the military service pensions archive will see that even the crustiest and most conservative IRA men generally had more than a few good words to say for Cumann na mBan and for individual women and girls who took risks during the fight. So why should Kitby be so dismissive? Did she really believe that men made better revolutionaries, simply because convention dictated that they alone could use lethal force against their opponents? Did she really believe that she or her sisters could have achieved more for the republic with guns in their hands?[91] Was Kevin's ghost whispering in her ear to do as he had done, to kill and perhaps then to be killed?

We might end with consideration of a woman who was alongside Kitby in the Hammam Hotel and the adjoining Gresham Hotel during the fighting, which culminated in the anti-Treatyite leadership's abandonment of the building on 5 July 1922, who like her served the anti-Treaty cause throughout the civil war, but who then took a more radical path – by her own account, joining the Irish communist party as early as 1923.[92] This was Muriel MacSwiney (1892–1982), who had endured the agony of seeing her husband starve himself to death in 1920, and who in 1924 chose to raise her daughter Máire outside Ireland. This accentuated what was already clearly a divide with MacSwiney's forceful sisters Mary and Annie. In Europe Muriel made another life. A radical in her attachment to a Moscow-centric brand of communism, she was also somewhat unconventional, bearing a daughter, Alex (1926–2014) in France by Pierre Kaan (1903–1945), a Jewish leftist who was to die from privation after two years in a concentration camp.[93] Kitby told her daughter Helen that Muriel, who remained her friend although she was also very close to Mary, was shattered by what happened in

1931. Her young daughter Máire, whom she had placed in the care of a German family, was taken from Germany to Ireland by her aunt Mary without Muriel's knowledge or permission. Ironically for a woman who refused to recognise the state, Mary's right to act as her niece's guardian was upheld by a decision of the High Court in 1933 in an action brought by Muriel in which she alleged Máire had been kidnapped. The court was told that Terence had, 'on his deathbed', appointed Mary as joint guardian of Máire (probably without Muriel's knowledge). This unusual measure was, as his daughter believed, probably an indication that he was already acutely concerned about his wife's mental health; it might also be further evidence of Mary's overpowering influence over him as he prepared for death.[94]

In old age Máire MacSwiney Brugha published a heartfelt memoir outlining her difficult and confusing early upbringing in Ireland and on the continent with and often without her mother, her sense of bewildered abandonment as Muriel repeatedly farmed her out, and her intense relief when she was finally provided with a stable home and upbringing in Cork in the care of her aunts. She recalled that the last occasion on which she encountered her mother was in Bewley's Café in the early 1960s, when she recognised her voice at another table and saw her deep in conversation with Kitby. Máire left unobtrusively.[95]

Muriel, who suffered from depression throughout her life, seems never quite to have got over what happened between 1920 and 1933, losing first her husband to the Irish revolution, and then her daughter to a court in independent Ireland. In 1950 special legislation was passed to award her a dependent's pension. Muriel explained that she accepted this only because her income from the Murphy family trust had diminished, and she needed money for medical treatment. She 'would gladly go without ... if our Irish children, [and] the Old IRA men, or the many people who need help would benefit but I know that it would only go to big capitalists lay

and clerical.'[96] Her letters to the leading British communist Rajani
Palme Dutt (1896–1974) in the 1960s indicate someone who became
not simply an ultramontane Stalinist applauding Soviet suppression
of unrest in Hungary and Czechoslovakia in the 1950s and 1960s,
but an eccentric obsessive fixated upon the Catholic church: she
detected Nazi influences underlying unrest in Nkrumah's Ghana,
maintained that the PCF (Parti Communiste Français) was being
manipulated by the Vatican, loathed the Common Market as 'a
Catholic stunt' and opposed the renaming of the Communist Party
of Great Britain's newspaper *The Daily Worker* as *The Morning
Star*, as she believed that the latter had Catholic resonances. She
survived in France on dividends on stocks held in a Murphy family
trust, paid annually through a bank in London. In 1975 Máire
sought news of her mother through Muriel's solicitor: 'as her
whereabouts are unknown, she is worried that this old lady may
become ill and even die' without Máire even being informed.[97]

Kevin and Family Memory

This book ends where it began, with Kevin at the centre. What has
puzzled me over the years is why Kevin stood not on the highest
but on the only plinth in the family pantheon as curated by Kitby.
In a revealing letter in 1953 to de Valera's Minister for Justice
Oscar Traynor (her commanding officer in 1922, her opponent in
1949 in the row over their conflicting accounts of the collapse of
the last plan to rescue Kevin, her sworn enemy as a Fianna Fáil
loyalist yet evidently her confidant when she so chose), Kitby
lamented not writing anything down about her own activities for
the benefit of her grandchildren: 'My part especially after the death
of Liam Lynch [reads] so like a resistance thriller.'[98] Even had she
done so, Jim, his slain brother Paddy and their father P.J. would
still have had to find their own historian, as would her own stoic
brother Mick, her dignified and humane mother Mary, her activist

sisters Shel and Elgin, her brother-in-law's father The O'Rahilly, and her daughter Mary's obscure Northern republican in-laws, the Halpennys and Rices. Enduring fame – not simply activism, allegiance and suffering – seem to be what really mattered.

This deference to the famous dead was not peculiar to Kitby. For decades after the War of Independence and civil war, the annual commemorative ceremony at the Tipperary graveside of Seán Treacy (1895–1920) was a major event. The presiding dignitary, year after year, was the chairman of the organising committee, P.J. Moloney. Was it that Treacy was to him somehow more worthy of a decade of the rosary and a stirring oration than his own dead son Paddy? (In 1940 he criticised 'the failure to give a decent livelihood to every Irish man and woman' despite 'the terms of the Constitution' and a year later repeated his prediction that economic prosperity would bring about a united Ireland.) Or was it just less painful to remember and laud a former comrade in public than his own slain flesh and blood? P.J. had made no mention of Paddy during his brief contribution to the fractious Dáil debates on the Treaty, whereas others had produced the rebel dead (including Kevin Barry) like snared rabbits out of a bloodied hat to bolster their arguments: Mary MacSwiney said of pro-Treaty TD Seán MacEoin, who had been saved from the Mountjoy gallows only by the Truce, that 'if he were my brother, I would rather he were with Kevin Barry'.[99] P.J.'s son Jim was similarly reticent about his dead brother: when he was asked by the pensions board in 1936 how he had become adjutant of the 4th Battalion, Third Tipperary Brigade in May 1921, in succession to Paddy, he simply replied 'the adjutant was killed, and I took his place'.[100]

In the manner of his dying and death Terence MacSwiney became an international icon not simply of the Irish independence movement but of peaceful civic protest (and who could be more civic than a lord mayor?) as the world watched, fascinated and moved by the remarkable duration of his hunger strike in Brixton prison between August and October 1920. Yet in his native city at the very same time two other Volunteer hunger-strikers languished unto death in relative obscurity, one denied even the privilege – extended to Joseph Plunkett in 1916 – of marrying his fiancée in his final days; the other, American-born and thereby surely worthy of some propaganda in the United States, surviving without food in the gloomy precincts of Cork jail for four days longer than did MacSwiney in Brixton. But it was MacSwiney whose suffering and end were broadcast around the world and who was venerated as 'enduring the most', surrounded by attentive doctors including an independent, titled physician of Irish extraction, and with a concerned British monarch fretting in the background. His emaciated corpse was displayed for all to gaze at in Cork city hall. Sir Henry Wilson noted sourly that 'the savages had dressed him up' in his Volunteer uniform.[101] Fitzgerald and Murphy went quietly to their graves with the lids firmly fixed on their coffins.

Conclusion

There is a limit to what can be written about the motivations, commitment and likely development of someone who died before his nineteenth birthday, who never wrote anything save school essays and breezy personal letters, whose student days, although busy, did not involve making speeches, organising marches or producing political tracts, and who eschewed the opportunity beloved of many Irish rebels of making a speech from the dock. This is particularly so when a good study already exists. Nevertheless, that a relative felt impelled to write about Kevin Barry a hundred years after his death emphasises the point that he has cast a long shadow within the family, just as his name has become synonymous with youthful republican sacrifice.

Kevin Barry seems to have been a well-balanced, humane young man, undoubtedly an observant Catholic but, as Donal O'Donovan demonstrated in 1989, also one with plenty of sins to confess. He did not seek martyrdom, and while he died a conventional Catholic, there is no evidence that he construed his fate in sacrificial religious terms (as could be said of Patrick Pearse in 1916, and of Terence MacSwiney in 1920). Kevin was not a hapless youth swept away in the maelstrom. By his mid-teens he had strong separatist leanings, was conscious of issues of race and inequality and was very critical of colonial rule across the world. Some of this may have come from his schooling, but much of it came from home. Like his older brother Mick in Carlow, he made an early and clear choice to fight and if needs be to kill and to die for independence because he thought that was the right thing to do for his cause and his country.

We should not be surprised that Kevin showed no regret about the soldier he killed. Would he have mobilised on Bloody Sunday morning and shot a defenceless man in his pyjamas as his wife screamed in the corner of the bedroom? Why not? Other UCD medical students did. Would he have been willing to pass sentence of death for spying upon a poverty-stricken labourer, as did Paddy Moloney on 30 April 1921? Certainly. Would he have hustled an ex-soldier down an alleyway, ignored his pleas for mercy, pushed him to the ground and shot him as a spy? Definitely, if ordered to do so. Would such acts have tormented him thereafter, his victims and their families haunting his dreams? Probably not. These are things young men did for Ireland because they believed it was their duty, and because this was how their war was fought. Some, like Mick McDonnell, Charlie Dalton and Ernie O'Malley, suffered terrible psychological damage from their experiences; others involved in close-up killing such as Seán Lemass – who had to deal with the memory not only of killing an unarmed man on Bloody Sunday and of the murder of his older brother Noel in 1923, but of accidentally shooting his infant brother dead in January 1916 – seem to have coped. As far as I know, so too did most of the policemen, British military, intelligence officers and loyalists who carried out targeted killings or shot prisoners out of hand – sometimes Volunteers, sometimes unlucky civilians – in 1920 and 1921.[1]

The immediate impact of Kevin's execution in Ireland was so considerable because of how he conducted himself once arrested, and of how he was portrayed to the press and public: exceptionally young (although in truth, almost nineteen), nonchalant and humorous in the face of death, a medical student (with an implied social status and long-term economic value) and a much-loved friend. It also helped that he was a photogenic Jesuit boy, radiating confidence as had so many young English officers lost in the Great War. His fate resonated in middle-class Ireland and Britain just as did that of Terence MacSwiney (as Lord Mayor of Cork rather than as a captured IRA commander). The deaths of Joseph Murphy and Michael O'Sullivan in Cork, and of James Daly in the far-off Punjab, had not remotely the same social register in either Britain or Ireland.

Kevin was most likely doomed from the moment of his arrest. The evidence was overwhelming. Like James Daly in India, the decision to confirm the death sentence was not taken on foot of moral outrage, or out of deference to the families of the young soldiers shot at Monk's Bakery. The key consideration was military discipline. General Macready believed that executing a man convicted of killing soldiers would encourage his troops to exercise restraint in the face of IRA provocation. In India, the commander in chief believed that if Daly were spared, he would never be able to execute any Indian soldier for a comparable offence. Using similar logic, Leo Amery believed that the Labour government's refusal to grant clemency to his errant son John was due to the home secretary's determination to make sure that William Joyce did not escape the noose.

Kevin's determination not to contest the charges against him, and GHQ's eventual acceptance of this, were nevertheless significant. His family's unconditional support for his position may have weighed upon them in later years.

Within Kitby's family, memory of Kevin precluded much mention of, let alone serious reflection on, anyone else's actions or bereavements. It was left to Patrick Kavanagh to break ranks, musing out loud at his wedding reception in Kitby's house about Mac O'Rahilly's father dying 'drop of blood by drop of blood' on Moore Lane in 1916. Uncouth poets have their uses.

Kevin's other siblings bore his loss in different ways, and without the same relish for public engagement that characterised Kitby. Mick, who had taken to arms in Carlow as early as 1917 despite having a farm to run and a Dublin dairy to supply, became involved in electoral politics out of duty immediately after the civil war, but Tombeagh, his widowed mother and his younger siblings were more than enough responsibility for a young man to have to bear. Elgin, who with Kitby and Mick had been most exposed to the overwhelming sadness of their brother's last weeks, remained a radical, yet she and her husband took care not to burden their children with expectations that they too should follow a militant republican path. Her sisters Shel, Monty and Peggy also protected their children from the pressures of what Donal O'Donovan encapsulated in his 'A Crowded Year'. None of Kevin's siblings raised their children in an atmosphere of anti-British or of civil-war rancour, and they were free to make friends and fall in love with whomever they chose. The one person the siblings collectively appear to have abhorred was de Valera, for abandoning the pure republican ideal in 1925–6 and for executing IRA men between 1940 and 1944 (all but one, let us remember, for killing people).

Kevin grew up, died and was remembered in a matriarchal family. The dominant female in his life and afterlife was his eldest sister Kitby rather than their mother Mary. It was through Kevin's imprisonment and death that Kitby became a public figure, and through him that her talents were recognised, accepted and for a time exploited in the separatist movement. The same held true for her great friend Mary MacSwiney. Each woman had unconditionally supported, even egged on, their courageous captive brothers when other relatives might have urged the choice of life over death, and in Terence MacSwiney's case the promise of a future with his wife and young daughter instead of an eternity of sterile martyrdom.

Kevin is remembered by contemporary Irish republicans as a young person ready to fight, to kill and to die for Ireland. That his name endures in the wider world is explained not only by the laconic courage with which he faced execution, but by the enduring power of a few photographs from 1918 of a wholesome young schoolboy and sportsman; by his status as a medical student; and by a song, which not everybody likes but which very many people still know.

Endnotes

Preface

1   David O'Donoghue, *The Devil's Deal: The IRA, Nazi Germany and the Double Life of Jim O'Donovan* (Dublin, 2010); Desmond G. Marnane, *The Third Brigade: A History of the Volunteers/IRA in South Tipperary, 1913–21* (Thurles, 2018), pp. 50, 180, 425–8; Marcus MacRuarí, *In the Heat of the Hurry: A History of Republicanism in County Down* (Castlewellan, 1997), pp. 71–3, 94; Public Record Office of Northern Ireland, HA5/2317 (Daniel Rice).

2   Donal O'Donovan, *Kevin Barry and His Time* (Dublin, 1989).

Introduction

1   Richard English, 'Devouring her children', *Books Ireland* (May 1990), pp. 95–6; *Armed Struggle: the History of the IRA* (London, 2003; Macmillan (ed.), 2004) pp. 19, 19–22; *Irish Freedom: The History of Nationalism in Ireland* (London, 2006), pp. 105, 317, 372.

2   *The Harrovian Supplement September 1918*, p. 13 (notice for 2nd Lieutenant John Ormonde Butler, Royal Air Force, d. 11 April 1918); *The Eton College Chronicle*, 31 Jan. 1918, p. 348, reviewing *Letters from an English Boy, being the letters of Richard Byrd Levett Kings Royal Rifle Corps* (London, 1918), reissued in 2014; '2nd Lieut. Reginald A. Jermy Gwyn', *The Stonyhurst Magazine 1916*, p. 1573.

3   Jessica Meyer, *Men of War: Masculinity and the First World War in Britain* (London, 1st ed., 2009; pbk, 2011), p. 83.

4   Aidan Beatty, *Masculinity and Power in Irish Nationalism, 1848–1938* (Palgrave, 2015), pp. 28–33.

5   *Times*, 26 and 27 Nov. 1920, and *Birmingham Daily Gazette*, 27 Nov. 1920.

6   Joanna Scutts, 'The True Story of Rupert Brooke', *New Yorker*, 23 April 2015.

7   Roy Foster, *Vivid Faces: The Revolutionary Generation in Ireland 1890–1923* (London, 2014), p. 331.

8   Hansard, House of Commons, vol. 883, Col. 564, 11 Dec. 1974.

9   Charles Townshend, *The British Campaign in Ireland, 1919–1921: the Development of Political and Military Policies* (Oxford, 1975), pp 16, 129–30.

10   These figures come from Eunan O'Halpin and Daithí Ó Corráin, *The Dead of the Irish Revolution 1916–1921* (New Haven, 2020).

Chapter One

1   Military Archives of Ireland (MAI), Bureau of Military History (BMH), WS 731 (Kathleen Barry Moloney), p. 10, cited hereafter as MAI, BMH, KBM WS.

2   O'Donovan, *Kevin Barry*, p. 60.

3   C.S. Andrews, *Dublin Made Me: An Autobiography* (Dublin, 1979), p. 135.

4   MAI, BMH, WS 1154 (Seán O'Neill), p. 7.

5   O'Donovan, *Kevin Barry*, passim.

6   Astri Erll, 'Families and Memories: Continuity and Social Change', *Journal of Comparative Family Studies* vol. 42, no. 3, (May–June 2011), p. 303.

7   MAI, MSPC, 1 DP 11069 Kevin Gerard Barry.pdf, Mary Barry to Frank Aiken, undated, Nov. 1937, and Dublin Corporation to Military Service Pensions Board, 8 Dec. 1939.

8   O'Donovan, *Kevin Barry*, p. 9.

9   See the family tree at https://digital.ucd.ie.

10   Donal O'Donovan, *Little Old Man Cut Short* (Bray, 1998), p. 94.

11   Patrick J. Carroll CSS, 'Kevin Barry's Secret', *America* (9 Dec. 1933), p. 225.

12   Kitby to Paddy, 10 Feb. 1963 (in my possession).

13   The cause of death is as recorded in the Register of Deaths.

14   O'Donovan, *Kevin Barry*, p. 25.

15   Ibid., p. 27.

16   Ibid., MAI, MSPC, 1 DP 11069 Kevin Gerard Barry.pdf, investigating officer's report, 20 Dec. 1939.

17   Information from Michael O'Rahilly, April 2020.

18   Shel, quoted in O'Donovan, *Kevin Barry*, p. 29.

19   O'Donovan, *Kevin Barry*, p. 32; Edward O'Toole, 'Bronze Age Burial, Ballyhacket Upper, Tullow, County Carlow', *Journal of the Royal Society of Antiquaries of Ireland*, vol. LXIV (1934), Part 1, pp. 141–2.

20 Gerry O'Donovan papers, Shel to Jim O'Donovan, undated (1960s?), second
    page (other pages missing). MAI, BMH, KBM WS, pp. 5–6; the 1901 census
    records Kate Kinsella, 39, unable to read, of 8 Fleet Street.
21 *Freeman's Journal*, 10 Apr. 1923.
22 Andrews, *Dublin Made Me*, p. 231.
23 *The Belvederian 1945*, pp. 13–14.
24 O'Donovan, *Kevin Barry*, pp. 33–4.
25 Extracts from a letter from Mary Barry to her California-based cousin Mary
    Dowling, quoted in *The Irish Independent*, 3 Mar. 1921.
26 MAI, BMH, KBM WS, p. 6.
27 He was a significant influence on me when preparing my MA thesis, ultimately
    published in revised form as *The Decline of the Union: British Government
    in Ireland, 1891–1920* (Dublin, 1987).
28 Andrews, *Dublin Made Me*, p. 118.
29 Duke to Lloyd George, 16 Apr. 1918, quoted in O'Halpin, *The Decline of the
    Union*, p. 155.
30 Trevor Wilson (ed.), *The Political Diaries of C.P. Scott 1911–1928* (London,
    1970), pp. 341–2, entries for 7 and 19–21 Apr. 1918.
31 Memorandum by French for cabinet, 8 Oct. 1918, quoted in O'Halpin,
    Decline of the Union, pp. 170.

Chapter Two

1 Quoted in Eunan O'Halpin, *Spying on Ireland: British Intelligence and Irish
   Neutrality During the Second World War* (Oxford, 2008), p. 175; information
   on O'Connell School from Colonel Terry O'Neill PhD, 23 Apr. 2020.
2 Charles Lysaght, *Brendan Bracken* (London, 1980), p. 29.
3 Charles Lysaght, email to author, 18 Apr. 2020.
4 UCDA, Kevin Barry Papers (KBP), 93/40 (1), *Our Boys* vol. 8, no. 2, Oct. 1921.
5 I donated this book to the Linen Hall Library, Belfast, in 1996, along with an
   autographed copy of Jawaharlal Nehru's *Autobiography*, which also carried
   Dan Breen's signature, following a Provisional IRA attempt to firebomb the
   building.
6 UCDA, KBP, P93/6, exercise copybook, undated (but Algebra homework is
   dated 'Jan' 1916).
7 UCDA, KBP, P93/6, exercise copybook, undated.
8 James Joyce, *A Portrait of the Artist as a Young Man* (1st ed., London, 1916;
   Viking ed., 1964), p. 71.

9   Andrews, *Dublin Made Me*, p. 148.

10 Carlow County Archives, Carlow Union Minute Book 127 (1918–19), undated, and 129 (1920–1), 6 Apr. 1921.

11 Bruce Bradley, 'Joyce, James (Augustine Aloysius)', *Dictionary of Irish Biography* (Cambridge, 2004), p. 1060.

12 Eunan O'Halpin, 'Personal Loss and the "Trauma of Internal War": The Cases of W.T. Cosgrave and Seán Lemass', in Melania Terrazas Gallego (ed.), *Trauma and Identity in Contemporary Irish Culture* (Berlin, 2020), pp. 159–81.

13 Jesuit Archives, Dublin, ADMN/20/192, Paidín O'Halpin to Fr Kiernan, 27 [Sept.] 1940. He entered in November 1941 and left the Society 'Parens indiget' on 29 March 1943 (his father Sergeant Hugh Halpenny was within weeks of death from kidney disease, and as the eldest of thirteen children he was probably needed at home).

14 *The Belvederian 1919*, pp. 7–8.

15 UCDA, KBP, P93/7, exercise copybook.

16 *Grammar and Composition on La Belle-Nivernaise* and *The Warwick Shakespeare: Henry V* (in possession of Ruth Sweetman).

17 O'Donovan, *Kevin Barry*, p. 41.

18 Cronin, *Kevin Barry*, pp. 10–11.

19 UCDA, KBP, P93/7.

20 TNA, HO 144/1457, P.J. Moloney journal, undated [June 1916].

21 O'Donovan, *Kevin Barry*, p. 41; Father Tom Counihan, 'Kevin Barry – Our Last Meeting', *The Belvederian* (1970), p. 103.

22 *The Belvederian 1970*, p. 43.

23 Tomás Ó Dochartaigh, *Cathal Brugha: A Shaol is a Thréithe* (Baile Átha Cliath, 1969), p. 17.

24 Kevin to Kitby, undated [but spring 1918], copy in my possession.

25 O'Donovan, *Kevin Barry*, p. 48.

26 *The Belvederian 1917*, p. 119.

27 *Times*, 23 Nov. 1996.

28 *The Belvederian 1919*, p. 45.

29 http://www.oldbelvedere.ie; *Freeman's Journal*, 30 Oct. 1920.

30 Jesuit Archives Dublin, J453/67, undated note by Father McGrath on the back of photographic print.

31 J.M. Winter, 'Britain's lost generation of the First World War', *Population Studies*, vol. 31, no. 3 (Nov. 1977), p. 449; British Library, MSS EUR F203/78 (Caroe papers), undated notes, 1970s.

32   Quoted in O'Donovan, *Kevin Barry*, pp. 51–4.

33   Kevin to Kathleen Carney, dated 'Sun 30 [should be 31] Oct 1920', photocopy provided by Michael O'Rahilly, Apr. 2020.

Chapter Three

1   Patrick McCarthy, *The Irish Revolution, 1912–23: Waterford* (Dublin, 2014), pp. 61–5.

2   Jim Moloney (1896–1981), speaking to me c. 1976. He returned to Tipperary in July 1920, becoming intelligence officer of the 4th Battalion, 3rd Tipperary Brigade. On 1 May 1921 he became adjutant when his brother Paddy was killed. From 1 July 1922 he was director of communications on Liam Lynch's staff. He and his brother Con (1898–1956), who was adjutant general and later deputy chief of staff, were captured in the Glen of Aherlow in March 1923. Con, badly wounded, was released in December 1923, and Jim in July 1924.

3   O'Donovan, *Kevin Barry*, pp. 43–4.

4   Ibid., pp. 45–6.

5   Charles Townshend, *The Republic; the Fight for Irish Independence* (London, 2005), pp. 73–8.

6   *An t-Óglách*, vol. 1, no. 8 (18 Dec. 1918).

7   Joost Augusteijn, *From Public Defiance to Guerrilla Warfare: The Experience of Ordinary Volunteers in the Irish War of Independence 1916–1921* (Dublin, 1996), pp. 116–17.

8   O'Halpin and Ó Corráin, *The Dead of the Irish Revolution*, pp. 11–12.

9   Ibid., p. 512.

10   Monaghan County Museum, Thomas Brennan papers, General Order No. 25, 16 June 1921.

11   Ibid., Training Order 1.7.21.

12   Andrews, *Man of No Property*, p. 95.

13   David R. Woodward (ed.), *The Military Correspondence of Field Marshal Sir William Robertson* (London, 1989), p. 1.

14   Commonwealth War Graves Commission, cwgc.org.

15   TNA, CO 904/144 Summary of police reports Feb. 1921; WO 35/160; WO 364/4251; MAI, BMH, WS 1296 (Thomas Costello), p. 17; WS 1308 (Henry O'Brien), pp. 14–15; WS 1337 (David Daly), pp. 20–22; WS 1504 (Séamus O'Meara), p. 44; MAI, A/0612 'IRA Casualties'.

16   https://jhse.org/centenary-execution-aby-bevistein.

17 Washington's birth certificate states he was born on 24 October 1904 in Salford.

18 Marnie Hay, *Na Fianna Éireann and the Irish Revolution, 1909–23: scouting for rebels* (Manchester, 2019), pp. 132–3.

19 MAI, BMH, WS 278 (Francis Daly), p. 16; WS 487 (Joseph O'Connor), p. 3; WS 813 (Pádraig Ó Conchubhair), pp. 6–7; WS 936 (Dulcibella Barton), p. 4; MSPC, WMSP34REF12204EdwardJMurray.pdf (Murray interview, 31 July 1940); *The Irish Independent*, 12 and 13 June 1917.

20 MAI, BMH, WS 1616 (John McGill), p. 2.

21 TNA, CO 904/142, Sept. 1920; HO 184/34; MAI, BMH, WS 1440 (Daniel Byrne), pp. 2–3; WS 1443 (Michael Fitzpatrick), p. 2; WS 1616 (John McGill), p. 4; *Nationalist and Leinster Times*, 18 Sept. 1920; *Wicklow People*, 18 and 19 Feb., 2 July 1921.

22 TNA, CO 904/142, Sept. 1920; MSP P, A/66 (1); MAI, BMH WS 1175 (Micheál Ó Ciardubháin), pp. 11–12; WS 1294 (Seán Whelan), pp. 20–2; MSP, WMSP34REF10356MichaelKirwan.pdf (Kirwan interview, 7 May 1936) and WMSP34REF24398JAMESWHELAN.pdf (Whelan interview, 15 Jan. 1937) *Nationalist and Leinster Times*, 25 Sept. 1920.

23 MAI, A/0649; MSPC, A/67; TNA, CO 905/15.

24 O'Halpin and Ó Corráin, *Dead of the Irish Revolution*, pp. 546–7.

25 TNA, WO 35/88B; WO 35/89; WO 35/150; WO 35/158; BHM WS 1298 (Patrick Doyle), p. 11; WS 1442 (Thomas Ryan), pp. 6–8; *Nationalist and Leinster Times*, 23 and 30 April 1921; *Leinster Express*, 23 and 30 April 1921.

26 TNA, CO 904/145 Summary of police reports May 1921; WO 35/154; WO 35/89; MAI, BMH, WS 410 (Thomas McNally), pp. 9–10; *Anglo-Celt*, 14 May 1921; UCDA, Mulcahy Papers, P7/A/18, OC ASU Cavan Brigade and OC Cootehill Battalion to GHQ, 11 and 10 May, and Mulcahy to GHQ Organiser, North Cavan, 24 May 1921.

27 TNA, WO35/70, raid report, 19 Sept. 1920; MAI, BMH, WS 628 (James Tully), p. 3; WS 650 (W. Kidd Davis), pp. 1–2; WS 865 (John Plunkett), pp. 31–4.

28 O'Donovan, *Kevin Barry*, pp. 81–2.

29 MAI, MSPC, W24SP1177AODHMACNEILL.pdf; O'Halpin, *Defending Ireland*, p. 136, 178.

30 Andrews, *Dublin Made Me*, p. 231.

31 Fearghal McGarry, *Eoin O'Duffy: a self-made hero* (Oxford, 2005), pp. 65–6.

32 MAI, BMH, WS 921 (Martin Finn), 24 February 1954.

33 Eunan O'Halpin (ed.), *MI5 and Ireland, 1939–1945: the Official History* (Dublin, 2003), p. 7.

34 TNA, CO 904/144 Summary of police reports March 1921; WO 35/148; MAI, BMH, WS 1361 (Gerald Davis), pp. 8–9; WS 1729 (Joseph Togher), p. 9; UCDA, Moss Twomey Papers P69/159 (73); Ormonde de l'Épée Winter, *Winter's Tale* (London, 1955), pp. 295–6.

35 O'Malley to Military Service Pensions Board, 15 Mar. 1938, in Jim Moloney's pension application file no. 4145 (extracts in my possession).

36 MAI, MSPC, MSP34REF57043 Brendan Muldoon.pdf.

37 MAI, MSPC, WMSP34REF59839CHARLESCULLINANE.pdf, Ó C_leánain to Military Service Pensions Board, 14 July and 5 Oct. 1942; *Cork Examiner*, 27 Oct. 1970.

38 Eunan O'Halpin, *Head of the Civil Service: A Study of Sir Warren Fisher* (London, 1989), pp. 82–4, 92–4.

39 Townshend, *The Republic*, p. 155.

40 Imperial War Museum (IWM), HW1/35, Wilson diary, 6 Feb. 1920.

41 IWM, HW1/35, Wilson diary, 2 Apr. 1920.

42 Ibid.

43 IWM, HW1/35, Wilson diary, 23 and 25 Sept. 1920.

44 IWM, HW1/35, Wilson diary, 28 Sept. 1920; Ross O'Mahony, 'The Sack of Balbriggan and Tit-For-Tat Terror' in David Fitzpatrick (ed.), *Terror in Ireland 1916–1923* (Dublin, 2013), pp. 58–74; Gerry White and Brendan O'Shea, *The Burning of Cork* (Cork, 2006).

45 MAI, BMH, WS 0663 (Joseph Dolan), p. 9.

46 Quoted in O'Donovan, *Kevin Barry*, p. 60; MAI, BMH, WS493 (Seamus Kavanagh), p. 8.

47 IWM, HW1/35, Wilson diary 31 Mar. 1920.

48 *The Irish Times*, 10 and 11 Nov., *Evening Herald*, 10 Nov., and *Irish Independent*, 11 Nov. 1920.

49 O'Donovan, *Kevin Barry*, pp. 64–5; MAI, MSPC, A/67/18.

50 MAI, MSPC, A/67/17.

51 McGarry, *Eoin O'Duffy*, pp. 51–5.

52 O'Donovan, *Kevin Barry*, pp. 68–9; *The Irish Times*, 4 Sept. 1920; MSPC A/67 (Carlow Brigade Activities). Kevin is listed as involved in the Aughavannagh raid, but not the Tullow affair, whereas Cullen is not listed

for Aughavannagh. These reports, compiled in the 1930s, were notoriously inaccurate.

53 O'Halpin and Ó Corráin, *The Dead of the Irish Revolution*, pp. 217–18, 255–6, 473–4.

54 *Irish Independent*, 4 Sept., and *Kilkenny People*, 4 Sept. 1920.

Chapter Four

1 O'Donovan, *Kevin Barry*, p. 79.

2 MAI, MSPC, W24SP2561 Seamus Kavanagh.pdf.

3 MAI, BMH, WS 493 (Seamus Kavanagh), p. 3.

4 Leitrim County Library, Charlie McGoohan memoir, p. 17.

5 MAI, BMH WS0493 (Seamus Kavanagh), p. 3; O'Donovan, *Kevin Barry*, p. 82.

6 *Irish Press*, 8 Dec. 1962. He died suddenly and was buried in Cork. As no press account of his funeral has been found, I cannot say whether any Barry family members attended.

7 MAI, MSPC, W24P2561 Seamus Kavanagh.pdf. For reports of the annual Mass, see, e.g., *Irish Press*, 17 Dec. 1934, 5 Nov. 1945, 15 Nov. 1947, 7 Nov. 1954; O'Donovan, *Little Old Man*, p. 56.

8 MAI, BMH WS 0493 (Seamus Kavanagh), p. 6; O'Donovan, *Kevin Barry*, p. 81.

9 Leitrim County Library, McGoohan memoir, p. 18; MAI, BMH, WS 1043 (J.V. Lawless), pp. 399–400 and WS 822 (William James Stapleton), p. 55.

10 MAI, BMH, WS 0865 (John Plunkett), p. 15, WS 1068 (Michael Brennan), p. 48, WS 1154 (Seán O'Neill), p. 10; William Kautt, *Ambushes and Armour: the Irish Rebellion 1919–1921* (Dublin, 2010), pp. 199–200.

11 TNA, WO71/360, court martial prosecutor's opening statement, 20 Oct. 1920, pp. 2–4.

12 Ibid.

13 MAI, BMH WS 0498 (Seamus Kavanagh), p. 12, and WS 1154 (Seán O'Neill), pp. 8–9.

14 TNA, CO 904/42, DMP report, 21 Sept. 1920.

15 TNA, CO 904/42, prosecutor's statement, p. 5, 20 Oct. 1920.

16 *Times*, 30 Oct. 1920.

17 *Hansard/commons/1920/nov/04/reprisals-police-and-military-1*.

18 Kieran Costello, 'Enniscorthy Courthouse Trials 1919', *The Past* no. 33 (2019), pp. 26–8.

19 Liz Curtis, *The Cause of Ireland: From the United Irishmen to Partition* (Belfast, 1994), p. 341; Frank Gallagher, *The Four Glorious Years 1918–1921* (1st ed., Dublin, 1953; 2nd ed., 2005), p. 105.

Chapter Five

1 King's College London, Liddell Hart Centre for Military Archives, Foulkes papers, 7/24, index of notes of 'Ernest O'Malley, Staff Captain', seized in June 1921.

2 MAI, BMH, WS340 (Oscar Traynor), p. 47.

3 TNA, CO904/42, DMP report, 23 Sept. 1920.

4 *Yorkshire Evening Post*, 25 Sept. and 1 Oct. 1920.

5 *Leeds Mercury*, 28 Sept. 1920.

6 TNA, WO141 46, minute by adjutant general, 18 Oct. 1920.

7 Information from Washington's gravestone as photographed at https://www.cairogang.com. A third son had died at the age of seven. The Weaste (Salford) register of graves also records Washington as fifteen years of age.

8 Parliamentary Archives, Lloyd George Papers (LGP), F/180/5/14, report by Macready for week ending 31 Oct. 1920.

9 MAI, BMH, KBM WS 731, p. 12.

10 *Evening Standard*, 1 Nov. 1920.

11 Bodleian Library, MS Eng c. 2803, undated memoir by A.P. Magill, p. 255; O'Halpin, *Decline of the Union*, pp. 198–9.

12 War Office, *Manual of Military Law 1914* (London, 1914), p. 6.

13 British Library, India Office Records, L/MIL/7/13314, Viceroy to Secretary of State for India, 28 Oct. 1920; Anthony Babbington, *The Devil to Pay: The Mutiny of the Connaught Rangers, India, July 1920* (London, 1991) and Michael Silvestri, *Ireland and India: Nationalism, Empire and Memory* (London, 2009), pp. 139–207, discuss the background to the mutiny and its suppression in detail.

14 A file on the preparation of the case, abstracted from Dublin Castle at some point after the Truce, is in the James O'Donovan papers in the NLI; O'Donovan, *Kevin Barry*, pp. 99–100.

15 TNA, WO35/62, circular to commanders, 11 June 1920.

16 David Foxton, *Revolutionary Lawyers: Sinn Fein and Crown Courts in Ireland and Britain, 1916–1923* (Dublin, 2008), p. 229.

17 Roger Sweetman, email to Eunan O'Halpin. 23 July 2020.

18 Captain A. Barrett to Kevin, 12 Oct. 1920 (original in possession of Ruth Sweetman).

19 MAI, BMH, KBM WS, p. 14.

20 O'Donovan, *Kevin Barry*, pp. 103–4.

21 MAI, KBM WS, p. 14. Andrew Bonar Law (1858–1923) was Lord Privy Seal and Conservative leader in the coalition.

22 O'Halpin, *Decline of the Union*, pp. 202–3.

23 *Irish Independent*, 14 May 1920.

24 William Murphy, 'Dying, Death and Hunger Strike: Cork and Brixton, 1920', in James Kelly & Mary Ann Lyons (eds), *Death and Dying in Ireland, Britain and Europe: Historical Perspectives* (Dublin, 2013), pp. 300–1.

25 Parliamentary Archives, LGP, F/31/1/43, Bonar Law to Lloyd George, 2 Sept. 1920.

26 Francis Costello, *Enduring the Most: The Life and Death of Terence MacSwiney* (Dingle, 1995), pp. 185–6; Parliamentary Archives, LGP, F/180/5/11, reports for 25 Sept. and 16 Sept. 1920; Anne Moore, 'Moore, Sir Norman, 1st baronet (1847–1922)', *Dictionary of National Biography* (Oxford, 2004, revd 2015, online).

27 TNA, CO 904/143 Daily summary of outrages Oct. 1920; MAI, BMH, WS 517 (Maurice Crowe), p. 8; WS 597 (Edmund O'Brien), p. 37; WS 1003 (Patrick Ahern), pp. 18–21; WS 1030 (John Joseph Hogan), pp. 9–11; WS 1065 (James Coss), p. 8; *Cork Examiner*, 18, 19 and 21 Oct. 1920; Peter Hart, *The IRA & its Enemies* (Oxford, 1998), pp. 248–9.

28 Michael Hopkinson (ed.), *The Last Days of Dublin Castle: The Mark Sturgis Diaries* (Dublin, 1999), p. 60 (26 Oct. 1920); MAI, BMH, WS 446 (Frank Hynes), p. 68; *Cork Examiner*, 26 Oct. 1920.

29 MAI, BMH, WS 446 (Frank Hynes), p. 68; *The Times*, 29 Aug. 1920; *Cork Examiner*, 26 Oct. 1920; *Clonmel Chronicle*, 27 Oct. 1920; Hart, *The IRA & its Enemies*, p. 85.

30 Westminster Diocesan Archives, Bourne papers, 5/36a, Cohalan to A.C. Dunlop, 19 Nov. 1920.

31 Costello, *Enduring the Most*, pp. 185–7.

32 Richard O'Rawe, *Blanketmen: An Untold Story of the H-Block Hunger Strike* (Dublin, 2005).

33 Winter, *Winter's Tale*, p. 292.

34 *Freeman's Journal*, 20 Oct. 1920.

35 MAI, KBM WS 208, p. 16.

36 Alan Clarke, *Diaries: In Power, 1983–1992* (London, 1993).
37 TNA, FCO87/204, C.W. Roberts (No. 10 Downing Street) to Ministry of Defence, 7 Aug. 1973.
38 IWM, Oral History Collection, #20097 (Michael Fitzroy Talbot Baines).
39 MAI, BMH, KBM WS, p. 16.
40 Robert Marshall, 'William Evelyn Wylie', *Dictionary of Irish Biography* (Cambridge, 2004).
41 Barry Bowman to Eunan O'Halpin, 28 Jan. 2020.
42 MAI, BMH, WS 731 (KBM), p. 18.
43 Dave Grossman, *On Killing: The Psychological Cost of Learning to Kill in War and Society* (New York, 1995), pp. 231–40.
44 Kevin to Kathleen Carney, 31 [misdated 'Sunday 30'] Oct. 1920, copy supplied by Michael O'Rahilly.
45 *Donegal News*, 4 Jan. and *FJ*, 22 July 1919. I am grateful to John McLoone for identifying this incident.
46 TNA, CO 904/111 Inspector-General's monthly report, Feb. 1920; MAI, BMH, WS 1041 (Thomas Doyle), p. 61; MAI, MSPC, W24SP1281PeterODwyer. pdf; MAI, MSPC, MSP34REF24701ThomasDSinnott.pdf (Sinnott interview, 1 May 1936); Wilson (ed.), *The Political Diaries of CP Scott*, p. 386, Scott's talk with Lloyd George, 4 June 1920.
47 https://jhse.org/centenary-execution-aby-bevistein, consulted 20 June 2020.

Chapter Six

1 TNA, CO904/42, P.J. Brady to Greenwood, 29 Oct. 1920.
2 Joseph J. Feeney, 'Hopkins and the MacCabe Family', *Studies* vol. 90, no. 359 (autumn 2001), pp. 300–5.
3 MAI, KBM WS, p. 31; A.C. Hepburn, *Catholic Belfast and Nationalist Ireland in the era of Joe Devlin 1874–1934* (Oxford, 2008), pp. 221–2.
4 Hopkinson (ed.), *The Last Days of Dublin Castle*, pp. 64–5 (31 Oct. 1920).
5 Parliamentary Archives, LGP, F/180/5/14, Macready's report for week ending 30 Oct. 1920; War Office, *Manual of Military Law*, pp. 315–16, carries the text of the declaration dated 29 July 1899.
6 Hopkinson (ed.), *The Last Days of Dublin Castle*, p. 48, 29 Sept. 1920.
7 TNA, CO904/42, memorandum by Campbell, 30 Oct. 1920; Hopkinson (ed.), *The Last Days of Dublin Castle*, 31 Oct. 1920, pp. 64–5.
8 IWM, French papers, 75/46/3, diary entry, 21 Oct. 1920.

9   IWM, French papers, 75/46/13, French to Greenwood, 1 Nov. 1920; O'Donovan, *Kevin Barry*, p. 136. Browne had been awarded an MC and Bar during his service in France.

10 Patrick Maume, 'James Henry Mussen Campbell', *Dictionary of Irish Biography*, pp. 290–1.

11 Parliamentary Archives. Campbell to Bonar Law, undated, BL 99/7/4.

12 Quoted in O'Donovan, *Kevin Barry*, p. 143.

13 MAI, BMH, WS 942 (Patrick Joseph Berry), p. 10.

14 MAI, MSPC, W24SP8076JamesLawless.pdf.

15 MAI, MSPC, WMSP34REF8865CharlesStewartBevan.pdf, interview 15 Jan. 1937; WMSP34REF8866AndrewJBermingham.pdf, interview 20 Dec. 1935.

16 MAI, BMH, WS 340 (Oscar Traynor), p. 49.

17 MAI, BMH, KBM WS, Appendix A, p. 14.

18 MAI, BMH, KBW WS, p. 39.

19 MAI, BMH, WS 631 (Bernard C. Byrne), p. 17.

20 MAI, BMH, WS 340 (Oscar Traynor), p. 48.

21 MAI, BMH, KBM WS, Appendix C. The pages are unnumbered after p. 1.

22 MAI, BMH, WS 340 (Oscar Traynor), p. 48.

23 MAI, BMH, WS 340 (Oscar Traynor), pp. 52–5; MSPC, WDP9287PeaderClancy.pdf and WMSP34REF63430RichardHayes.pdf; handwritten statement by John Fitzpatrick, 25 Jan. 1922 (in possession of Brian Fitzpatrick); Winter, *Winter's Tale*, pp. 322–3.

24 Andrews, *Dublin Made Me*, p. 140.

25 Babbington, *The Devil to Pay*, p. 50; India Office Records, L/MIL/7/13314, Viceroy to Montagu, 15 July 1920.

26 India Office Records, L/MIL/7/13314, Montagu to Viceroy, and reply, 28 and 31 Oct. 1920.

27 *Times of India*, 4 Nov. 1920.

28 *Donegal News*, 3 Dec. 1920.

29 MAI, MSPC, W1C514JamesDaly.pdf, Theresa Maher (niece) to Military Service Pensions Board, 11 June 1935.

30 MAI, MSPC, WDP23825WilliamComan.pdf.

31 MAI, MSPC, WCONRAN2JOHNFLANNERY.pdf.; Babbington, *The Devil to Pay*, p. 151; Silvestri, *Ireland and India*, pp. 139–209; Kate O'Malley, *Ireland, India and Empire: Indo-Irish radical connections 1919–64* (Manchester, 2008), p. 112.

Chapter Seven

1   MAI, BMH, WS 840 (Patrick J. Berry), p. 11.
2   MAI, BMH, WS 348 (Captain E. Gerrard, Royal Artillery), 3 Feb. 1950; Army Form W 3996 (in possession of Ruth Sweetman).
3   MAI, BMH, KBM WS, p. 21.
4   I am grateful to Ruth Sweetman for showing me the original.
5   1911 census, accessed via census.nationalarchives.ie; O'Donovan, *Kevin Barry*, p. 122.
6   *Evening Mail*, 30 Oct. 1920.
7   MAI, BMH, KBM WS, Appendix A, p. 17.
8   MAI, BMH, KBM WS, pp. 44–5.
9   Carroll, 'Kevin Barry's Secret', p. 225; Kitby to Paddy, 25 Nov. 1960.
10 MAI, BMH, WS 387 (Paddy Daly), p. 25–7.
11 MAI, BMH, WS 1226 (Michael Russell), pp. 2–9.
12 Reported in *Freeman's Journal*, 17 Oct. 1921.
13 MAI, JV Joyce diary, 26 Feb. and 5 Mar. 1942 (donated by Richard Barrett).
14 Joe Baker and Michael Liggett, *Belfast Executions* (Belfast, 2017), accessed at http://www.belfasthistoryproject.com, 3 Feb. 2020.
15 *Washington Post*, 12 Nov. 2018.
16 Hopkinson (ed.), *The Last Days of Dublin Castle*, p. 64, 31 Oct. 1920.
17 Winter, *Winter's Tale*, p. 292.
18 Royal Irish Academy, K.B. Nowlan papers, KBN 7/7/1/25, William Sweeney to the Director, Raidió Éireann, 21 Jan. 1966.
19 MAI, BMH, WS 0899 (Father Lawrence OSB), p. 2; *Irish Times*, 6 Nov. 1989.
20 Jesuit Archives, Dublin, Kevin to Gerry McAleer, 30 Oct. 1920, photocopy in possession of Damien Burke.
21 Eileen O'Neill, a friend of Kevin's, had attended his court martial. O'Donovan, *Kevin Barry*, p. 106.
22 Kevin to Kathleen Carney, 31 Oct. 1920 (copy provided by Michael O'Rahilly).
23 TNA, CO90/42, undated, Clarke to Street, 1 Nov. 1920.
24 Peter Hodgkinson, *British Battalion Commanders during the First World War* (Burlington, 2015), p. 48.
25 TNA, CO904/42, note by Governor Monro, 2 Nov. 1920.
26 MAI, BMH, WS 942 (Patrick J. Berry), p. 11.
27 MAI, KBM WS, pp. 47–8.

28 MAI, KBM WS, pp. 47–8.

29 *Cork Examiner*, 5 Sept. 1924.

30 IWM, French papers, 75/46/11, Macready to French, 17 Dec. 1921.

31 Churchill College Cambridge Archives, Amery papers, AMEL7/5, diary 20 Nov. 1942.

32 In 1989 I interviewed retired Lord Justice of Appeal Sir John Stephenson PC (1910–1998), who discussed his extensive dealings with Ireland from 1940 to 1942 while an officer in the security service MI5. He also described his activities in 1944–5 investigating British renegades in France and Germany. The only one whom he regarded as of any calibre and conviction was William Joyce. Stephenson's father Sir Guy Stephenson had been assistant director of public prosecutions when Roger Casement was tried in 1916, and his great uncle Lord Frederick Cavendish had been assassinated by the Invincibles in Phoenix Park in 1882.

33 Amery papers, AMEL7/8, diary 13 Dec. 1945; Patrick Maume, 'William Joyce', *Dictionary of Irish Biography*, pp. 1080–3, and Patrick Cosgrave, 'Amery, (Harold) Julian, Baron Amery of Lustleigh', *Dictionary of National Biography* (Oxford, 2004, online); author's interview with Karlo B. Paice (1906–2007), formerly of the Home Office, Brighton, 3 Apr. 1981.

34 Amery papers, AMEL7/8, diary 19 Dec. 1945.

35 Amery papers, AMEL7/8, diary 16–31 Dec. 1945.

36 Undated entry in Paddy's retirement autograph book, 1984, in my possession.

37 India Office records, L/F/7/2055, Monro to India Office, 10 May 1923, and India Office to Monro, 21 Apr. 1927.

Chapter Eight

1 Westminster Diocesan Archives, Bourne papers B5/36a, Francis Doheny to Bourne, 25 Nov. 1920.

2 Westminster Diocesan Archives, Bourne papers B5/36a, undated and unsigned t.s. letter from Denver, Colorado; Father B. Maguire PP (Inniskeen), to Bourne, 2 May 1921; *The Advocate* (Melbourne), 20 Nov. 1924.

3 Rory Sweetman, *Bishop in the Dock: The Sedition Trial of James Liston* (Auckland, 1997).

4 Westminster Diocesan Archives, Bourne papers B5/36a, Lloyd George to Bourne, 28 Nov. 1920.

5   Parliamentary debates, House of Commons, vol. 134, col. 683, 4 Nov. 1920.

6   Lambeth Palace Archives, Davidson papers, XIV, fols 75 and 82, 6 Feb. 1921.

7   Nicholas Mansergh, *The Unresolved Question: The Anglo-Irish Settlement and Its Undoing 1912–72* (London, 1991), pp. 282–9.

8   UCDA, P33/40 (1), quotations from *Our Boys* vol. 2, no. 2, Oct. 1920.

9   O'Donovan, *Kevin Barry*, pp. 167–8; Churchill College Cambridge Archives, Strang papers, 4/1, 'Tim' to William Strang, 13 Nov. 1920.

10   TNA, CO904/168, letter by Mrs J.A. Holloway, 2 Nov. 1920. I am grateful to Dr Eve Morrison for this document.

11   UCDA, P94/57, Jim to Kitby, 27 Jan. 1923.

12   Peter Hart, *The IRA at War 1916–1923* (Oxford, 2003), pp. 199–200.

13   Hopkinson (ed.), *The Last Days of Dublin Castle*, p. 142, 15 Mar. 1921.

14   Quoted in Anne Dolan and William Murphy, *Michael Collins: the Man and the Revolution* (Cork, 2018), p. 114.

15   Andrews, *Dublin Made Me*, pp. 149–50; *Report of the Labour Commission on Ireland* (1921), p. 8.

16   *Times*, 9 Feb. 1972.

17   *Evening Standard* and *Edinburgh Chronicle*, 1 Nov. 1920.

18   *Newcastle Chronicle*, 30 Oct.; *Daily Despatch*, 30 Oct.; *Le Nouvelliste de Lyon*, 1 Nov.; *Sheffield Independent*, 1 Nov.; *Hamburger Nachrichten*, 2 Nov.; *La Epoca*, 3 Nov.; *Casino and Kyogle Courier and North Coast Advertiser* [New South Wales], 3 Nov. 1920.

19   *Dillon Herald*, 2 Dec. 1920.

20   *The Cordovan Daily Times*, 29 Oct. 1920.

21   *Nottingham Evening Post*, 1 Nov.; *Idaho Republican*, 1 Dec. 1920; *Otago Witness* [New Zealand], 9 Nov. 1920; William Sheehan (ed.), *Fighting for Dublin* (Cork, 2007), p. 25; W.P. Crozier, *Ireland For Ever* (London, 1933), p. 202.

22   *Halifax Guardian*, 6 Nov. 1920.

23   *DZIENNIK CHICAGOSKI*, 1 Nov. 1920.

24   *San Luis Obispo Tribune*, 5 Nov. 1920.

25   *Mataura Ensign* and *Marlborough Express*, 2 Nov. 1920.

26   *Western Australian Record*, 18 Dec. 1920.

27   *Times of India*, 4 Nov. 1920; Conor Mac Neasa, *Our Martyr Boy, Kevin Barry, Victim of Britonism* (Buenos Aires, 1921), p. 3, copy in my possession courtesy of Michael O'Rahilly.

28   *Winnipeg Free Press*, 29 Oct. and *St John's Daily Star*, 2 Nov. and 29 Dec. 1920.

29 *Irish Times*, 17 Jan. 2009.

30 *Daily Sketch*, 1 Nov.; *Albuquerque Morning Journal*, 14 Dec. 1920.

31 Bibliothèque Nationale de France, https://gallica.bnf.fr.

32 UCDA, KBP, P93/44, Mervyn Wall to Kathy, 18 Jan. 1937.

33 M.A. Doherty, 'Kevin Barry and the Anglo-Irish propaganda war', *Irish Historical Studies*, vol. 32, no. 126 (Nov. 2000), pp. 221–2; Foster, *Vivid Faces* (London, 2013), passim.

34 Patrick J. Carroll CSS, 'Kevin Barry's Secret', *America* (9 Dec. 1933), p. 225.

35 Nehru Memorial Library, Delhi, Oral History Transcripts (Professor Abdul Majid Khan), Acc. 348, p. 36.

36 O'Malley, *Ireland, India and Empire*, pp. 1, 38, 96, 182; Dave Hannigan, *Terence MacSwiney: the Hunger Strike that Rocked an Empire* (Dublin, 2010), pp. 281–8.

37 http://sbsb.org.in.

38 https://www.sinnfeinbookshop.com.

39 *An Phoblacht*, 13 May 2010.

Chapter Nine

1 UCDA, Mulcahy Papers, P7/A/39, undated t.s. of report by William Gannon; MAI, BMH, WS 994 (George F. H. Berkeley), p. 85; WS 1280 (Éamon Broy), p. 116; *Freeman's Journal*, 11, 14, 15, 22 Feb. 1921; *Irish Independent*, 11 Feb. 1921.

2 TNA, WO 35/86B; WO 35/158; MAI, BMH, WS 547 (Joe Leonard), pp. 20–23; WS 628 (James Tully), p. 4; MAI, A/0612 'IRA Casualties'; UCDA, Republican Soldiers Casualty Committee, P156 (37); *Irish Independent*, 30 May 1921.

3 *Anglo-Celt*, 11 Dec. 1920; McGarry, *O'Duffy*, pp. 68–9.

4 TNA, CO 904/146 Summary of police reports June 1921; WO 35/159B; MAI, BMH, WS 574 (John McGonnell), p. 6; WS 575 (Joseph McKenna), p. 5; WS 1028 (James McKenna), p. 7; Monaghan County Museum, Marron Papers, Statement of Paddy Moran, Paddy McCluskey, Harry Lavery and Francie McKenna 3F; Statement of Patrick McGrory 2G1, Rev Joe Duffy Notebook 4 I; *Northern Standard*, 1 July 1921.

5 Daniel J. Murphy (ed.), *Lady Gregory's Journal Volume One* (Gerrard's Cross, 1978), pp. 302, 317, entries for 13 Oct. and 26 Dec. 1921.

6 *New Zealand Truth*, 8 Oct. 1921; *The Ashburton Guardian*, 13 Sept. 1921.

7 Defence Forces Ireland, *Army Equitation School: Promoting the Irish Horse* (Dublin, 2013), p. 33.

8 Kevin Barry (Las Vegas) email to Eunan O'Halpin, 24 Oct. 2018; *New York Times*, 5 Nov. 1997.

9 *Times*, 27 July 1966; *Evening Herald*, 24 Nov. 1977.

10 *Times*, 23 Feb. 1960.

11 *Times*, 27 July 1966; *Evening Herald*, 24 Nov. 1977; *Irish Times*, 4 Apr. 2003.

12 Kevin Barry Curran email to Eunan O'Halpin, 31 Oct. 2018.

13 *Nationalist and Leinster Times*, 25 Aug. 1989.

14 *Irish Times*, 28 Oct. 2018, https://www.irishtimes.com/sport.

15 *Hartford Daily Mail Courant*, 30 Mar. 1932.

16 'Richard O'Donovan', https://www.icu.ie.

17 *Nationalist and Leinster Times*, 31 Oct. 1986.

18 *Poughkeepsie Journal*, 17 Mar. 1977.

19 *Sunday Telegraph*, 28 Oct. 2001.

20 *Warwick Daily News*, 7 Oct. 1942; https://www.awm.gov.au.

21 23 Feb. 1960.

22 TNA, WO373/141/58.

23 http://www.bac-lac.gc.ca.

24 *Belfast Newsletter*, 7 Dec. 1938, 28 Oct. 1940, and 26 Mar. 1941.

25 *San Francisco Chronicle*, 17 Oct. 1998.

26 *The Times*, 31 Mar. 2003.

27 *Fall River Globe* [Massachusetts] 21 Jan. 1922.

28 *Belfast Newsletter*, 7 July 1926.

29 *Evening Post* [Wellington], 13 Feb. 1940.

30 *Limerick Leader*, 23 May 1970.

31 Hootenanny Singers, 'Have you heard of Kevin Barry', https://www.youtube.com/watch?v=fD44Y-TVWwc, accessed 3 Nov. 2018 .

32 Leonard Cohen, 'Kevin Barry', https://www.youtube.com/watch?v=dJ4INuSYr28, accessed 2 Mar. 2019.

33 Paul Robeson, 'Kevin Barry', https://www.youtube.com/watch?v=dJ4INuSYr28, accessed 2 Mar. 2019. The record was released by Topic Records in 1957.

34 Kevin Haddick Flynn, 'Seán South of Garryowen', *History Ireland*, Vol. 15, No. 1 (Jan. – Feb. 2007), pp. 36–41; South's letter in *Limerick Leader*, 26 Jan. 1949; extract from the BBC's *Who Do You Think You Are?*, 25 July 2018, http://youtube.com/watch?v=vSSSQjBm964, accessed 2 Mar. 2019.

35 https://www.rte.ie/entertainment; Kautt, *Ambushes and Armour*, pp. 194–7.
36 O'Donovan, *Kevin Barry*, pp. 212–32. Kevin Galligan, *Peter Paul Galligan* (Dublin, 2012), pp. 99–100, carries another poem on Kevin written days before his death. I am grateful to Síofra O'Donovan for permission to quote from her father's poem.

Chapter Ten

1 MAI, BMH WS 731, Appendix A (Kitby to Jim O'Donovan, 10 Dec. 1948) and Kitby's notes of 22 Jan. 1952 explaining what transpired from her exchanges with Mulcahy and MacNeill.
2 Gerry O'Donovan papers, Kitby to Jim O'Donovan, 25 Aug. 1964. O'Donovan's *Irish Press* articles had appeared on 1 and 2 Nov. 1963.
3 UCDA, P93/44 (1–5), Kitby to 'John' (Cronin), 13 Dec. 1933, Cronin to Department of Justice, 29 Oct. 1936, and Mervyn Wall to Kitby, 18 Jan. 1937.
4 New York University, Tamiment Library, Seán Cronin papers, TAM460.
5 https://www.ebay.ie/itm.
6 *Irish Press*, 6 Oct. 1989.
7 *Irish Times*, 17 Jan. 2009; O'Donoghue, *The Devil's Deal*.
8 Orange Stationery Office Book marked 'Book No 1', Dan Breen diary, 5 May 1945 (private collection); Michael Gorman, *Were Those the Days?* (privately printed, 2017), p. 63.
9 Gorman, *Were Those the Days?*, pp. 45–6.
10 *Irish Examiner*, 27 Sept. 2016.
11 UCDA, Kathleen Barry Moloney Papers (KBMP), P94/105, Kitby to Confederate Films, Liverpool, 21 June 1962.
12 *Mein Leben Für Irland*, https://www.youtube.com/watch?v=opxEmGZEtxU.
13 *Irish Times*, 27 May, 23 June, 14 Aug. 1959; *Cork Examiner*, 24 June 1959.
14 https://www.savannahnow.com/news; https://www.fft.ie.
15 *Irish Press*, 3 Nov. 1958.
16 *Irish Press*, 6 Jan. 1932 and 2 Nov. 1933.
17 UCDA, P278/56, Cumann Chaomhghín to John V. Burke, 26 Feb. 1934.
18 Jay Winter, 'Beyond Glory? Cultural Divergences in Remembering the Great War in Ireland, Britain and France', in John Horne and Edward Madigan (eds), *Towards Commemoration: Ireland in War and Revolution, 1912–1923* (Dublin, 2013), pp. 140–1.
19 George L. Mosse, *Fallen Soldiers: Reshaping the Memory of the World Wars* (Oxford, 1990; pbk, 1991), p. 84.

20 O'Donovan, *Little Old Man*, pp, 48–52.

21 https://www.ucd.ie/news.

22 *The Irish Times*, 23 May 1953; https://societies.ucd.ie.

23 http://www.ucd.ie.

24 Hansard, House of Lords, vol. 198, 10 July 1956, col. 759.

25 Hansard, House of Commons, vol. 883, col. 564, 11 Dec. 1974. The left wing 'Angry Brigade' bombed his house, without inflicting any injuries on its occupants.

26 Hansard, House of Commons, vol. 23, col. 683, 11 May 1982.

27 Hansard, House of Commons, vol. 498, col. 123, 28 Oct. 2009.

28 *Dáil Debates*, 5 Feb. 1936.

29 *Dáil Debates*, 20 Apr. 1967.

30 *Dáil Debates*, 14 Oct. 1992.

31 *Dáil Debates*, 21 Feb. 2006.

32 Brian Heffernan, 'Discerning the Spirits: the Irish Jesuits and Political Violence, 1919–1921', *Studies* vol. 103, no. 412 (Winter 2014/15), pp. 552–61.

33 *The Mungret Annual 1921*, p. vi.

34 Denis G. Marnane, *The 3rd Brigade: A History of the Volunteers/IRA in South Tipperary, 1913–21* (Nenagh, 2018), pp. 425–7; *The Mungret Annual 1920*, p. 236, and *The Mungret Annual 1921*, p. 223.

35 Heffernan, 'Discerning the Spirits', pp. 552–61.

36 Olivia Frehill, 'Republican Dissent Among Irish Jesuits during the Civil War, 1922–23', *Studies* vol. 107. no. 425 (Spring 2018), pp. 57–75.

37 Foster, *Vivid Faces*, p. 227; Charles Townshend, *Easter 1916: the Irish Rebellion* (London, 2005), pp. 96–102. I am grateful to Dr Jan Graffius, archivist of Stonyhurst College, for last-minute information on the Stonyhurst Officers' Training Corps records; Noonan, *The IRA in Britain*, pp. 204–7.

38 Louis McRedmond, 'Clongownians in Politics', in William Menton (ed.), *The Clongowes Union Centenary Chronicle* (Dublin, 1997), p. 232. Reginald Dunne (1892–1922), OC of the IRA in London, was an alumnus of St Ignatius College SJ, Enfield, London.

39 MAI, MSP34REF4143 Cornelius Moloney.pdf.

40 https://www.staloysius.org/; variants of this maxim are sometimes attributed to Saint Ignatius Loyola, founder of the Jesuit Order.

41 For a sympathetic study, see Mary Kenny, *Germany Calling: A personal biography of Lord Haw-Haw, William Joyce* (London, 2004).

42 Quoted in O'Donovan, *Kevin Barry*, p. 196.

43 Statute of the Council of Europe (London, 1949), https://rm.coe.int, accessed 30 Apr. 2020.

44 Kerry County Archives, Con Casey papers, P36A/9/50, Tess Carney to Casey, 21 Jan. 1996; *An Phoblacht*, 17 Feb. 2000.

45 *Irish Times*, 10 Oct. 2001.

46 *Examiner*, 13 Oct. 2001.

47 *Irish Times*, 2 and 3 Oct. 2001.

48 *Irish Times*, 6 and 13 Oct. 2001.

49 *Irish Times*, 13 and 31 Oct. 2001.

50 MAI, 1D343 Patrick Maher.pdf. Despite uncertainty surrounding his Volunteer status, his mother secured a £75 dependant's gratuity. His stepbrother failed in a further claim in the 1960s.

51 MAI, W134ThomasTraynor.pdf.

52 MAI, 1D26PatrickDoyle.pdf

53 *Irish Times*, 15 Oct. 2001.

54 *An Phoblacht*, 20 Jan. 2000; *Belfast News Letter*, 8 Apr. and 24 June 1942; *The Irish Press*, 28 April and 30 May 1942; *Irish Independent*, 3 Sept. 1942. Murphy's widow Brigid and four youngest children were awarded £2,000 in criminal injuries compensation in June 1942.

55 *An Phoblacht*, 18 Oct. 2001.

56 *Sunday Independent*, 20 Oct. 2001.

57 https://republicansinnfein.org/hunger-strike-roll-of-honour.

58 Photographs of the event, together with an error-strewn account of Kevin's circumstances, can be seen at www.glasnevintrust.ie.

Chapter Eleven

1 *Irish Independent*, 3 Mar. 1921, quoting an undated letter from Mary Barry to Mary Dowling as published in the 'San Francisco Leader' (probably *The Leader*, a weekly of the time). Due to Covid-19 restrictions between March and June 2020 I was unable to travel to Tombeagh to review the originals of the family's letters to and from Mick.

2 O'Donovan, *Kevin Barry*, pp. 184–5.

3 NAI, CS/HC/PO/4/95, 1942 Calendar of grants of probate of wills and letters of administration.

4 MAI, 1DP 11069 Kevin Gerard Barry.pdf.

5 UCDA, KBMP, P94/111, draft note to de Valera, undated; *Irish Times*, 21 Aug. 1953.

6   Interview with Michael O'Rahilly, April 2020.
7   O'Donovan, *Kevin Barry*, p. 182; MAI, MSPC, RO577.pdf, Carlow Brigade committee to Department of Defence, 2 Apr. 1937 and attached list.
8   https://api.parliament.uk, cols. 2021W–2022W.
9   *Irish Times*, 21 Jan. 2020.
10 MAI, BMH, WS 1682 (Peg Broderick), p. 5.
11 MAI, MSPC, A67 Carlow Brigade.pdf.
12 Data from https://electionsireland.org.
13 Kevin Barry to Paddy Moloney, undated [*c*.19 Jan. 1974] (in my possession).
14 O'Donovan, *Kevin Barry*, p. 189.
15 Andrews, *Dublin Made Me*, p. 94.
16 MAI, J.V. Joyce diary, 26 Feb. 1942.
17 *Irish Times*, 29 Sept. 1962.
18 'Obituary', *Irish Press*, 13 Jan. 1969.
19 *San Francisco Chronicle*, 2 May 1922.
20 *New York Herald*, 30 May 1922.
21 Eve Morrison, 'One woman's Civil War in Ireland', *Irish Times*, 23 May 2013; MAI, BMH, KBM WS, p. 6.
22 Quoted in Tomás Ó Dochartaigh, *Cathal Brugha: a shaol is a thréithe* (Dublin, 1969), pp. 250–1.
23 Kitby to Monty, 27 Feb. 1923 (in the author's possession).
24 Villanova University Falvey Library, Villanova Digital Collection, Joseph McGarrity papers, undated handbill, accessed 23 Apr. 2020; MAI, MSPC, WMSP34REF1359CORNELIUSMOLONEY.pdf, Kathleen Barry Moloney to Military Service Pensions Board, 12 Dec. 1936, writing in support of Con Moloney's claim to have served as adjutant general from July 1922.
25 MAI, MSPC, WMSP34REF1359CORNELIUSMOLONEY.pdf, Tadgh Qullinan to Military Service Pensions Board, 10 Dec. 1936.
26 Andrews, *Dublin Made Me*, p. 281.
27 Florence O'Donoghue, *No Other Law: the Story of Liam Lynch and the Irish Republican Army, 1916–1923* (Dublin, 1954), p. 301; *San Francisco Chronicle*, 11 Apr. 1923.
28 National Library of Ireland, Florence O'Donoghue papers, MS31428, Moss Twomey to O'Donoghue, 31 May 1954.
29 Father C.J. Carroll to Elgin Barry, 12 Dec. 1933 (original in my possession).
30 UCDA, KBMP, P94/121, Kathy Barry to Jim Moloney, 8 July 1924.

31 Dianne Hall, 'Irish Republican Women in Australia: Kathleen Barry and Linda Kearns' tour in 1924–5', *Irish Historical Studies* (2019), 43 (163), pp. 73–4.

32 *Bundaberg Mail* [Queensland], 23 Jan., and *The Catholic Press*, 12 Feb. 1925.

33 Hall, 'Irish Republican Women', p. 84.

34 *The Advocate* [Melbourne], 20 Nov. 1924; *Freeman's Journal* [Sydney], 5 Mar. 1925.

35 Hall, 'Irish Republican Women', pp. 89–90.

36 *The Worker* [Brisbane], 22 Jan. 1925.

37 Kitby to Jim, 1 Jan. 1968 (copy in my possession).

38 C.S. Andrews, *Man of No Property* (Dublin, 1982), p. 94.

39 Gorman, *Were Those the Days?*, p. 46; Kitby to Paddy, 25 Nov. 1960.

40 Information from Jeanne Winder, 1 July 2020.

41 Michael O'Rahilly interview, April 2020; Gorman, *Were Those the Days?*, pp. 45–6.

42 MAI, Halpenny Hugh 24DSP7076, Woods to Military Service Pensions Board, 31 July 1925.

43 MAI, MSPC, 34D2305 Hugh Edward Halpenny 2.pdf, Annie Halpenny to the Military Service Pensions Board, 6 May 1943.

44 Minister's private secretary to referee, Military Service Pensions Board, 11 Dec. 1935, Jim Moloney's pension application file no. 4145 (extracts in my possession).

45 Kitby to Paddy Moloney, undated [page 1 missing], Apr. 1964; Raymond Molony, 'Flying in the Free State', *An Cosantóir*, Dec. 2019–Jan. 2020, pp. 36–7. Billy Hannon's anti-Treaty half-siblings attended his funeral in 1943.

46 Kitby to Paddy Moloney, 18 July 1963 (in my possession); TNA, WO372/9/2736.

47 MAI, WS 731 (Kathleen Barry Moloney), p. 13; *Irish Times*, 3 Apr. 1957.

48 Kitby to Paddy Moloney, 2 Feb. 1966 (in my possession).

49 Ibid.

50 Kitby to Paddy Moloney, 11 Oct. 1962.

51 Kitby to Paddy Moloney, 11 Oct. 1962, and 24 and 30 Mar. 1966 (in my possession).

52 *Irish Independent*, 10 Jan., *Irish Press*, 13 Jan., *Irish Times*, 11 and 13 Jan. 1969; O'Donovan, *Kevin Barry*, p. 51. Although reported present by *The Irish Press*, I was on a school trip to Austria.

53 Andrews, *Dublin Made Me*, p. 297.

54 MAI, MSPC, 34D1673 James Keenan.pdf gives details of War of Independence veteran James's sons Seán, David and James, who were interned at the time of his death in October 1943.

55 Kitby to Paddy Moloney, 3 Mar. 1966 (in my possession).

56 *Irish Independent*, 9 Mar. 1923.

57 Arthur Conan Doyle, *Our American Adventure* (London, 1923), p. 123; *Times*, 29 July 1920.

58 Mary O'Halpin to Paddy Moloney, 1 Sept. 1954 (in my possession).

59 Laurence White, 'Helen Moloney', *Dictionary of Irish Biography* online, 2017; Bart Felle, 'Radiant Legacy: Helen Moloney', *Irish Arts Review* (Spring 2020), pp. 120–5.

60 *Irish Press*, 20 Feb. 1978.

61 Gorman, *Were Those the Days?*, p. 45; my conversations with Paddy Moloney, 1970s.

62 *Irish Times*, 8 Nov. 1952. His MA thesis and some significant *Irish Times* records, can be found in UCDA, P95 (Patrick Barry Moloney papers).

63 Katherine to Paddy, undated but between 15 and 22 Aug. 1960 (in my possession).

64 *Irish Times*, 16 Oct. 2004; James Liddy, 'A Memoir of Katherine Barry Moloney Kavanagh', *The London Magazine* (Oct.–Nov. 2003), pp. 24–31.

65 Judy to Helen, 21 Oct. 1970, copy in my possession.

66 Judy to Helen, 28 Dec. 1970, copy in my possession. In 1970 Seán Garland (1934–2018) was then adjutant general of the Official IRA, and Tomás Mac Giolla (1924–2010) the President of Official Sinn Féin.

67 Helen Moloney to 'Mike' [unidentified], 19 Mar. 1971 (copy in my possession).

68 *Irish Times*, 10 Mar. 1971.

69 Elgin to Kitby, 13 Nov. 1924, quoted in Paul M. Taylor, *Heroes or Traitors? Experiences of Southern Irish Soldiers Returning from the Great War 1919– 1939* (Liverpool, 2015), p. 213.

70 Information from Ruth Sweetman, 24 Apr. 2020.

71 I saw correspondence relating to this transaction in Elgin's papers when they were still in family hands.

72 Eithne MacDermott, *Clann na Poblachta* (Dublin, 1998), p. 10.

73 I have been unable to find his War of Independence medal file in the MAI database.

74 O'Donovan, *Little Old Man*, p. 47.

75 O'Donoghue, *The Devil's Deal*, pp. 171–2; O'Donovan, *Little Old Man*, pp. 83–5.
76 MAI, MSPC, W1AB944JamesLaurenceODonovan.pdf and WMSP34REF1590 JamesLaurenceODonovan.pdf.
77 O'Donovan, *Little Old Man*, pp. 40–5; *The Irish Press*, 5 June 1979; my conversations with Bob Bradshaw, 1976 and Todd Andrews, 1983.
78 Information from Professor Iseult Honohan, 28 Apr. 2020.
79 O'Donovan, *Little Old Man*, pp. 176–7.
80 Ibid., p. 106
81 *Irish Times*, 17 Jan. 2009; O'Donovan, *Little Old Man*, p. 175.
82 O'Donovan, *Little Old Man*, pp. 5, 133–5.
83 MAI, KBM WS, enclosure at p. 13 of copy of her memorandum [for Jim O'Donovan] dated 10 Dec. 1948; O'Donovan, *Kevin Barry*, p. 58, quoting Peggy to Jim O'Donovan, undated [1965].
84 Manmohini Zutshi Saghal, *An Indian Freedom Fighter Recalls Her Life* (New York, 1996), pp. 86–97.
85 India Office Records, L/P.J. /7/332 has papers on Bina Das; Nehru Memorial Library, Oral History Transcript Acc No 271 (Mrs GMS Captain), p. 12.
86 MAI, MSPC, WMSP34REF1991MARGARETSKINNIDER.pdf.
87 MAI, MSPC, WMSPREF342736 HannahHanley.pdf, interview with advisory board, 30 July 1937; MAI, BMH, WS 1527 (Liam O'Dwyer).
88 MAI, MSPC, MSP34REF21421 THOMASINALYNDERS.pdf.
89 MAI, MSPC, MSP34REF20579 Margaret Cromien.pdf, interview with Pensions Board, 8 July 1932; Seán Cromien (son) to Eunan O'Halpin, 28 July 2009. Margaret eventually married her 1916 sweetheart's brother.
90 MAI, BMH WS755 (Seán Prendergast), p. 468.
91 Quoted in Morrison, 'One woman's Civil War'.
92 The People's History Museum, Manchester, Palme Dutt papers, CD/IND/06/05, Muriel MacSwiney to Palme Dutt, 12 Mar. 1966.
93 I am grateful to Manus O'Riordan for this information on Muriel, whom he met as a teenager and corresponded with intermittently in the 1960s.
94 Costello, *Enduring the Most*, p. 240.
95 Máire Brugha, *History's Child: A Memoir from the Only Child of Terence MacSwiney* (Dublin, 2005).
96 MAI, MSPC, DP19903 TerenceMacSwiney.pdf, Muriel to Department of Defence, 15 Apr. 1953.
97 Stephen Murphy (a first cousin of Máire's) to solicitors W.H. Thompson and Co., London, 6 Mar. 1975 (copy in my possession); Palme Dutt papers,

CD/IND/DUTT/06/05, Muriel MacSwiney to R. Palme Dutt, 1 and 12 Mar. 1966, 16 Nov. 1967, 30 Aug. and 13 Dec. 1968.

98   UCDA, KBMP, P94/33, undated draft letter to Oscar Traynor.

99   *Dáil Debates, Treaty,* no. 8, col. 122 (21 Dec. 1921).

100   *Nenagh Guardian*, 19 Oct. 1940, 18 Oct. 1941, 20 Oct. 1945; Eunan O'Halpin and Mary Staines, '"Between Two Hells": The Social, Political and Military Backgrounds and Motivations of the 121 TDs Who Voted For or Against the Anglo-Irish Treaty in January 1922', in Liam Weeks and Mícheál Ó Fathartaigh (eds), *The Treaty* (Dublin, 2018), pp. 113–35; transcript of military service pension board interview with James Moloney, 3 Mar. 1936 (copy in my possession).

101   Parliamentary Archives, LGP, F/180/5/11, report by Dr Griffith of views of Sir Norman Moore (1847–1922) and another specialist, 25 Sept. 1920; IWM, Wilson papers, HW1/34, diary, 31 Oct. 1920.

Conclusion

1   Eunan O'Halpin, 'Seán Lemass's silent anguish', *Irish Times*, 20 Jul. 2013.

Bibliography

Archives, Repositories and Papers in Private Hands

India
Jawaharlal Nehru Memorial Library and Archives
Oral History transcripts

Ireland
Carlow County Library and Archives
Carlow Union Minute Books 127 and 129

Kerry County Archives
Con Casey papers

Leitrim County Library
Charlie McGoohan memoir
Oral History Collection

Material in Private Hands
Dan Breen journal
Kevin Barry letter to Kathleen Carney
Kevin Barry notice of court martial and confirmation of sentence
Kevin Barry St Mary's and Belvedere school books
Michael Barry correspondence and ephemera (Barry family, Tombeagh)
Patrick B. Moloney additional correspondence (deposited in UCD Archives, Aug. 2020)
Gerry O'Donovan papers

Military Archives of Ireland
Bureau of Military History records
J.V. Joyce Diaries
Military Service Pensions Project

Monaghan County Museum
Thomas Brennan papers
Father Marron papers

National Library of Ireland
Liam Deasy papers
Florence O'Donoghue papers
James O'Donovan papers
Sean O'Mahony papers

Royal Irish Academy
Kevin B. Nowlan papers

University College Dublin Archives
Kevin Barry papers
Katherine Barry Moloney papers
Richard Mulcahy papers
Republican Soldiers Casualty Committee papers

United Kingdom
Bodleian Library, Oxford
A.P. Magill papers

British Library
India Office records
Sir Olaf Caroe papers

Churchill College Cambridge Archives Centre
Leopold Amery papers
William Strang papers

Imperial War Museum, London
Field Marshal Lord French papers
Sir Henry Wilson papers

Kings College London Liddell Hart Centre for Military Archives
Foulkes papers

Lambeth Palace Library and Archive
Archbishop Davidson papers

People's History Museum, Manchester
Palme Dutt papers

Public Record Office of Northern Ireland
Ministry of Home Affairs HA5

Stonyhurst College Archives
Information from Archivist on Officers Training Corps records

The National Archives, London
CO904
CO905
HO144
WO 35
WO71

Parliamentary Archives
Bonar Law papers
Lloyd George papers

Westminster Diocesan Archives
Cardinal Bourne papers

United States
New York University Tamiment Library
Seán Cronin papers

Villanova University Library
Joseph McGarrity papers

Newspapers

Albuquerque Morning Journal (New Mexico)
Anglo-Celt
Belfast Newsletter
Bundaberg Mail (Queensland, Australia)
Casino and Kyogle Courier and North Coast Advertiser (New South Wales, Australia)
Daily Sketch (London)
Dillon Herald (Dillon, South Carolina)

Donegal News
Dublin Evening Mail
Dziennik Chicagoski (Chicago)
Edinburgh Chronicle
Evening Herald
Evening Standard (London)
Fall River Globe (Massachusetts)
Freeman's Journal
Freeman's Journal (Sydney, Australia)
Halifax Evening Courier
Halifax Guardian (Nova Scotia)
Hamburger Nachrichten (Hamburg)
Hartford Daily Mail Courant (Connecticut)
Idaho Republican (Blackfoot, Idaho)
Irish Examiner
Irish Independent
Kilkenny People
La Epoca (Madrid)
Le Nouvelliste Lyon (Lyon)
Leeds Mercury
Leinster Express
Marlborough Express (Blenheim, New Zealand)
Matuaru Ensign (Gore, New Zealand)
Nationalist and Leinster Times
Nenagh Guardian
New Zealand Truth (Auckland, New Zealand)
Northern Standard
Nottingham Evening Post
Otago Witness (New Zealand)
Poughkeepsie Journal (New York)
San Francisco Chronicle
San Luis Obispo Tribune (California)
Sunday Telegraph (London)
The Advocate (Melbourne, Australia)
The Ashburton Guardian (Ashburton, New Zealand)
The Catholic Press (Melbourne, Australia)
The Cordovan Daily Times (Alaska)

The Irish Press
The Irish Times
The Leader (San Francisco)
The New York Times
The Sheffield Independent
The Times (London)
The Western Australian Record (Perth, Australia)
The Worker (Brisbane, Australia)
Times of India
Warwick Daily News (Queensland, Australia)
Washington Post (Washington DC)
Western Australian Record (Perth)
Wicklow People
Winnipeg Free Press (Manitoba, Canada)
Yorkshire Evening Post

Journals and Magazines

America
An Cosantóir
An Phoblacht
An t-Óglách
History
History Ireland
Irish Arts Review
Irish Historical Studies
Journal of Comparative Family Studies
Journal of the Royal Society of Antiquaries of Ireland
Our Boys
The Past
Studies
The Belvederian
The Harrovian
The London Magazine
The Mungret Annual
The New Yorker

Books and Chapters

Ainsworth, John	'Kevin Barry, the Incident at Monk's Bakery and the Making of an Irish Republican Legend', *History*, July 2002, vol. 87, no. 287 (July 2002), pp. 372–87
Andrews, C.S.	*Dublin Made Me: An Autobiography* (Dublin, 1979)
Augusteijn, Joost	*From Public Defiance to Guerrilla Warfare: The Experience of Ordinary Volunteers in the Irish War of Independence* (Dublin, 1996)
Babbington, Anthony	*The Devil to Pay: The Mutiny of the Connaught Rangers, India, July 1920* (London, 1991)
Baker, Joe and Michael Liggett	*Belfast Executions* (Belfast, 2017), accessed via http://www.belfasthistoryproject.com/belfastexecutions/, 1 Feb. 2020
Beatty, Aidan	*Masculinity and Power in Irish Nationalism, 1848–1938* (London, 2015)
Bradley, Bruce	'Joyce, James Augustine Aloysius', *Dictionary of Irish Biography* (Cambridge, 2009)
Brugha, Maire	*History's Child: A Memoir from the Only Child of Terence MacSwiney* (Dublin, 2005)
Carroll, Patrick J.	'Kevin Barry's Secret', *America* (9 Dec. 1933), pp. 224–6
Clarke, Alan	*Diaries: In Power, 1983–1992* (London, 1993)
Cosgrave, Patrick	'Amery, (Harold) Julian, Baron Amery of Lustleigh', *Dictionary of National Biography* (Oxford, 2004)
Costello, Francis	*Enduring the Most: The Life and Death of Terence MacSwiney* (Dingle, 2005)
Costello, Kieran	Enniscorthy Courthouse Trials 1919', *The Past*, no. 33 (2019), pp. 25–34
Cronin, Sean	*Kevin Barry* (Tralee, 1965)
Crozier, W.P.	*Ireland for Ever* (London, 1933)
Curtis, Liz	*The Cause of Ireland: From the United Irishmen to Partition* (London, 1994)
Davidson, F.J.A.	*Grammar and Composition on La Belle-Nivernaise* (Toronto, 1903)
Defence Forces Ireland	*Army Equitation School: Promoting the Irish Horse* (Dublin, 2013)

Doherty, M.A. — 'Kevin Barry and the Anglo-Irish propaganda war', *Irish Historical Studies*, vol. 32, no. 126 (Nov. 2000), pp. 217–31

Dolan, Anne and William Murphy — *Michael Collins: The Man and the Revolution* (Cork, 2018)

Doyle, Arthur Conan — *Our American Adventure* (London, 1923)

English, Richard — *Armed Struggle: the History of the IRA* (London, 2004)

English, Richard — *Irish Freedom: The History of Nationalism in Ireland* (London, 2003)

Erll, Astri — 'Families and Memories: Continuity and Social Change', *Journal of Comparative Family Studies*, vol. 42, no. 3 (May–June 2011), pp. 300–13

Feeney, Joseph J. — 'Hopkins and the McCabe Family', *Studies*, vol. 90, no. 395 (autumn 2001)

Felle, Bart — 'Radiant Legacy: Helen Moloney', *Irish Arts Review* (Spring 2020), pp. 120–5

Fitzpatrick David (ed.) — *Terror in Ireland, 1916–1923* (Dublin, 2012)

Fogerty, Des — *Sean South of Garryowen* (Ennis, 2006)

Foster, Roy — *Vivid Faces: The Revolutionary Generation in Ireland 1890–1923* (London, 2014)

Foxton, David — *Revolutionary Lawyers: Sinn Fein and Crown Courts in Ireland and Britain, 1916–1923* (Dublin, 2008)

Frehill, Olivia — 'Republican Dissent Among Irish Jesuits during the Civil War, 1922-23', *Studies*, vol. 107, no. 412 (Spring 2018), pp. 57–75

Gallagher, Frank — *The Four Glorious Years 1918-1921* (Dublin, 1953; 2nd ed., 2005)

Gallego, Melania Terrazas (ed.) — *Trauma and Identity in Contemporary Irish Culture* (Berlin, 2020)

Galligan, Kevin — *Peter Paul Galligan* (Dublin, 2012)

Gorman, Michael — *Were Those the Days?* (Dublin, 2017)

Grossman, Dave — *On Killing: The Psychological Cost of Learning to Kill in War and Society* (New York, 1995)

Hall, Dianne — 'Irish Republican Women in Australia: Kathleen Barry and Linda Kearns' tour in 1924–5', *Irish Historical Studies* (2019), 43 (163), pp. 73–4

Hannigan, Dave — *Terence MacSwiney: The Hunger Strike that Rocked an Empire* (Dublin, 2010)

Hart, Peter — *The IRA at War, 1916–1923* (Oxford, 2003)

Hart, Peter — *The IRA & Its Enemies: Violence and Community in Cork, 1916–1923* (Oxford, 1998)

Hay, Marnie — *Na Fianna Eireann and the Irish Revolution, 1909–23: Scouting for Rebels* (Manchester, 2019)

Heffernan, Brian — 'Discerning the Spirits: the Irish Jesuits and Political Violence, 1916-1921', *Studies*, vol. 103, no. 412 (Winter 2014/15), pp. 552–61

Hepburn, Anthony — *Catholic Belfast and Nationalist Ireland in the era of Joe Devlin 1874–1934* (Oxford, 2008)

Hodgkinson, Peter — *British Battalion Commanders during the First World War* (Burlington, 2015)

Hopkinson, Michael (ed.) — *The Last Days of Dublin Castle: The Diaries of Mark Sturgis* (Dublin, 1999)

Horne, John and Edward Madigan (eds.) — *Towards Commemoration: Ireland in War and Revolution, 1912–1923* (Dublin, 2013)

Joyce, James — *A Portrait of the Artist as a Young Man* (1st ed., London, 1916; Viking ed., 1964)

Kautt, William — *Ambushes and Armour: the Irish Rebellion 1919–1921* (Dublin, 2010)

Kelly, James and Mary Ann Lyons (eds), — *Death and Dying in Ireland, Britain and Europe: Historical Perspectives* (Dublin, 2013)

Kenny, Mary — *Germany Calling: A personal biography of Lord Haw-Haw, William Joyce* (London, 2004)

Levett, Richard Byrd — *Letters of an English Boy: Being the Letters of Richard Byrd Levett, Kings Royal Rifle Corps* (London, 1918)

Lysaght, Charles — *Brendan Bracken* (London, 1980)

Mac Ruairi, Marcus — *In the Heat of the Hurry: Republicanism in County Down* (Castlewellan, 1997)

MacDermot, Eithne — *Clann na Poblachta* (Dublin, 1998)

Mansergh, Nicholas — *The Unresolved Question: The Anglo-Irish Settlement and Its Undoing 1912–72* (London, 1972)

Marnane, Denis G.	*The Third Brigade: A History of the Volunteers/IRA in South Tipperary, 1913–21* (Thurles, 2018)
Marshall, Robert	'William Evelyn Wylie', *Dictionary of Irish Biography* (Cambridge, 2009)
Maume, Patrick	'William Joyce', *Dictionary of Irish Biography* (Cambridge, 2009)
McCarthy, Patrick	*The Irish Revolution 1912–23: Waterford* (Dublin, 2015)
McDermott, Eithne	*Clann na Poblachta* (Dublin, 1998)
McGarry, Fearghal	*Eoin O'Duffy: A Self-Made Hero* (Oxford, 2005)
McNessa, Conor	*Our Martyr Boy: Kevin Barry, Victim of Britonism* (Buenos Aires, 1921)
McRedmond, Louis	'Clongownians in Politics', in Menton (ed.), *Clongownian Union Centenary Chronicle*, pp. 231–47
Menton, William (ed.)	*The Clongowes Union Centenary Chronicle* (Dublin, 1997)
Meyer, Jessica	*Men of War: Masculinity and the First World War in Britain* (London, 2009; pbk., 2011)
Moore, Anne	Moore, Sir Norman, 1st baronet (1847–1922), *Dictionary of National Biography* (Oxford, 2004)
Moore Smith, G.C. (ed.)	*The Warwick Shakespeare: The Life of Henry V* (London, undated)
Morrison, Eve	'Tea, Sandbags and Cathal Brugha: Kathy Barry's Civil War', in Una Frawley (ed.), *Women and the Decade of Commemorations* (Bloomington, forthcoming 2021)
Mosse, George	*Fallen Soldiers: Reshaping the Memory of the World Wars* (Oxford, 1990; pbk, 1991)
Murphy, Daniel J. (ed.)	*Lady Gregory's Journal Volume 1* (Gerrard's Cross, 1978)
Murphy, William	'Dying, Death and Hunger-Strike: Cork and Brixton, 1920', in Kelly and Lyons (eds), *Death and Dying in Ireland, Britain and Europe: Historical Perspectives*, pp. 297–316
Nehru, Jawaharlal	*An Autobiography* (London, 1936)

Noonan, Gerard   *The IRA in Britain, 1919–1923: "In the Heart of*
                         Enemy Lines" (Liverpool, 2014)

Ó Dochartaigh, Tomás   *Cathal Brugha: A Shaol is a Thréithe* (Dublin, 1970)

O'Donoghue, David   *The Devil's Deal: The IRA, Nazi Germany and the*
                         Double Life of Jim O'Donovan (Dublin, 2010)

O'Donovan, Donal   *Kevin Barry and His Time* (Dublin, 1989)

O'Donovan, Donal   *Little Old Man Cut Short* (Bray, 1998)

O'Halpin, Eunan   *The Decline of the Union: British Government in*
                         Ireland, 1892–1920 (Dublin, 1987)

O'Halpin, Eunan   *Head of the Civil Service: A Study of Sir Warren*
                         Fisher (London, 1989)

O'Halpin, Eunan (ed.)   *MI5 and Ireland, 1939–1945: The Official History*
                         (Dublin, 2003)

O'Halpin, Eunan   *Spying on Ireland: British Intelligence and Irish*
                         Neutrality During the Second World War (Oxford,
                         2008)

O'Halpin, Eunan   'Personal Loss and the "Trauma of Internal War":
                         the cases of W.T. Cosgrave and Seán Lemass', in
                         Gallego (ed.), *Trauma and Identity in Irish Culture*,
                         pp. 159–81

O'Halpin, Eunan & Ó   *The Dead of the Irish Revolution* (London, 2020)
Corráin, Daithí

O'Halpin, Eunan &   'Between Two Hells: The Social, Political and
Staines, Mary   Military Backgrounds of the 121 TDs who voted for
                         or against the Anglo-Irish Treaty in January 1922',
                         in Weeks and Ó Fathartaigh (eds), *The Treaty*, pp.
                         113–35

O'Mahony, Ross,   'The Sack of Balbriggan and Tit-For-Tat Terror', in
                         Fitzpatrick (ed.), *Terror in Ireland*, pp. 58–74

O'Malley, Kate   *Ireland, India and Empire: Indo-Irish Radical*
                         Connections, 1919–64 (Manchester, 2008)

O'Neill, Ciaran   *Catholics of Consequence: Transnational Education,*
                         Social Mobility, and the Irish Catholic Elite, 1850–
                         1990 (Oxford, 2014)

O'Rawe, Richard   *Blanketmen: An Untold Story of the H-Block*
                         Hunger Strike (Dublin, 2005)

O'Toole, Edward J.   'Bronze Age Burial, Ballyhacket Upper, Tullow, County Carlow', *Journal of the Royal Society of Antiquaries of Ireland*, vol. LXIV (1934), part 1, pp. 141–2

Saghal, Manmohini Zutshi   *An Indian Freedom Fighter Recalls Her Life* (New York, 1996)

Scutts, Joanna   'The True Story of Rupert Brooke', *The New Yorker*, 23 April 2015

Sheehan, William   *Fighting for Dublin* (Cork, 2007)

Silvestri, Michael   *Ireland and India: Nationalism, Empire and Memory* (London, 2009)

Sweetman, Rory   *Bishop in the Dock: the Sedition Trial of James Liston* (Auckland, 1997)

Taylor, Paul   *Heroes or Traitors? Experiences of Southern Irish Soldiers Returning from the Great War 1919–1939* (Liverpool, 2015)

Townshend, Charles   *The British Campaign in Ireland 1919–1921: The Development of Political and Military Policies* (Oxford, 1975)

Townshend, Charles   *Easter 1916: The Irish Rebellion* (London, 2005)

Townshend, Charles   *The Republic: The Fight for Irish Independence* (London, 2013)

Weeks, Liam & Ó Fathartaigh, Mícheál (eds)   *The Treaty* (Dublin, 2018)

White, Gerald, and Brendan O'Shea   *The Burning of Cork* (Dublin, 2006)

White, Laurence   'Helen Moloney', *Dictionary of Irish Biography* online (Dublin, 2017)

Wilson, Trevor (ed.)   *The Political Diaries of C.P. Scott 1911-1928* (London, 1970)

Winter, Jay   'Beyond Glory? Cultural Divergences in Remembering the Great War in Ireland, Britain and France', in Horne and Madigan (eds), *Towards Commemoration*, pp. 134–45

Winter, Jay	'Britain's Lost Generation of the First World War', *Population Studies*, vol. 31, no. 3 (Nov. 1977), pp. 449–66
Winter, Ormonde de l'Épée	*Winter's Tale: An Autobiography* (London, 1955)
Woodward, David R. (ed.)	*The Military Correspondence of Field Marshal Sir William Robertson* (London, 1989)

Online Sources

Note that the URLs below may no longer serve to locate the item cited

BBC Television	'Who Do You Think You Are?', 25 July 2018 https://www.youtube.com/watch?v=vSS5QjBm964, accessed 2 Mar. 2019
Charlie & the Bhoys	'Sean South of Garryowen', https://www.youtube.com/watch?v=VdGMkYFTTrg, accessed 2 Mar. 2019
Hootenanny Singers	'Have you heard of Kevin Barry?' https://www.youtube.com/watch?v=fD44Y-TVWwc, accessed 3 Nov. 2018
Leonard Cohen	'Kevin Barry' https://www.youtube.com/watch?v=dJ4INuSYr28, accessed 2 Mar. 2019
Lonnie Donegan	'Kevin Barry' https://www.youtube.com/watch?v=5LY3EVG05Vw, accessed 2 Mar. 2019
Max W. Kimmich (director)	'Mein Leben für Irland' (My Life for Ireland) https://www.imdb.com/title/tt0033895/
McGonigle, Michael	'Kevin Barry Song', https://www.itma.ie/digital-library, accessed 2 Mar. 2019
Paul Robeson	'Kevin Barry' https://www.youtube.com/watch?v=BSjO9rIwn5M, accessed 4 June 2020
Pete Seeger	'Kevin Barry' https://www.youtube.com/watch?v=8SR3B7Xq_S0, accessed 2 Mar. 2019
Rod Stewart	'Grace' https://www.youtube.com/watch?v=ZdnR4Q4zvMY, accessed 5 Nov. 2019

Index

accidental shootings 8, 42, 208
Abba (pop group) 137
Adams, Gerry 161, 162
Ahern, Bertie 157, 162
Aiken, Frank 165, 169, 181, 185
Albert, Father B. 106, 111
Allen, Seán 78
Amery, Jack 113–115
Amery, Leo 113–115, 209
Ancient Order of Hibernians (AOH) 37,
   129
Anderson, John 53, 94, 149
Anderson, Michael 144
Andrews, David 159, 186
Andrews, Todd 26, 43, 102, 123, 169,
   172, 177; about Jim Moloney
   185–186, 196
Anglo-Irish poets 24
Anglo-Irish tensions: during Economic
   War 120
Anglo-Irish War 4
Angry Brigade bombers 5
anti-British emotions 123
An t-Óglach (monthly journal): 'Training
   Notes' 39
AOH. See Ancient Order of Hibernians
Aontacht Éireann 158
Armagh prison, republic women struggle
   in 82
armed services, British 134; minimum
   age for conscription 43
Armistice Day 194
Artt, Kevin Barry 135
Ashe, Thomas 19, 79, 96
assassinations: Easter Monday 1916 5,
   17–18

Aston, Ernest 73, 93, 198
Aughney, Honora 185
Augusteijn, Joost 40, 45
Australia: fund raising by Kitby Barry
   in 174–177; soldiers named Kevin
   Barry 134–135

Balfe, Edward 68
Banks (Lance Sergeant) 65, 86
Barnes, Peter 149
Barrett, A. 77, 105
Barrett, Dick 48
Barrett, Joan 178
Barry, Elgin (Kevin's sister) 14, 18, 19,
   193–199; failed rescue plan with
   Kitby and 98–99; and Kitby Barry
   171–172; women's hunger strike
   193–194
Barry, Jimmy 16
Barry, Judith (Kevin's aunt) 11, 15
Barry, Julia Mary Josephine 'Shel' 14
Barry, Kathleen 'Kitby' (Kevin's sister)
   14, 16, 50, 75, 166–167; in Australia
   174–177; about Cathal Brugha
   183–184; children 177, 180,
   188–193; with Constance Markievicz
   170; death of 185; failed rescue plan
   along with Elgin 98–99; as general
   secretary of IRPDF 171–172, 174;
   into independence struggle 170;
   invitation to High Mass in Pro-
   Cathedral 184; joined Cumann na
   mBan 170; last words with Kevin
   107; link between de Valera and
   Lynch 172; married Jim Moloney
   174; Mulcahy and 141; Publicity

Sales Advisor in ESB 177; reproving factual errors of O'Donovan 141; witness statement to BMH 7, 10, 142; worked for Austin Stack 170

Barry, Kevin 207–211; absence of contact with family 75; as active Volunteer 9; affidavit 89, 119–120; avenging 122–127; at Belvedere College SJ 26; bold statements and platitudes as doodles 29–31; in British political discourse 149–150; British propaganda response 94; capture of 63; in C Company, 1st Battalion, Dublin Brigade 38; in C Company, 3rd Battalion, Carlow Brigade 55; childhood of 10–11; commemoration/invocation after trial/death of 123–126; commiseration for 121; defending 70–91; education 16–17; execution of 9; final hours of 112; final meeting with family members 106–107; friend's execution 22; friendships and fitting in 32; in H Company, 1st Battalion, Dublin Brigade 55; ill-treatment in prison 85; impact following execution of 117–122; inadequate defence for 78, 82; interest in sports 33–34; Jesuits and 26–32, 152–155; joined as Volunteer in Dublin 19; King's Inn operation 8–9, 55; letter to Gerry McAleer 110; letter to Kathleen Carney 110; memorials for 145–149; namesakes 131–133; at O'Connell School 22–24; about prejudice 25; reinterment of 156; as republican martyr 1; rescue plans 96–102; as Section Commander 39; seeking reprieval for 93–96; in songs and stories 136–139; at St Mary's College 24; in the Oireachtas 150–152; torture during interrogation 66–68; training and military service 37–59;

trial proceedings 84–87; as university student 35–36; valedictions of 105; as Volunteer at earlier age 43–44; weapon raids under Matt Cullen 56–58

Barry, Kevin (rugby player) 132

Barry, Kevin (boxer) 132

Barry, Kevin (American playwright) 133

Barry, Kevin (Limerick author) 133

Barry, Kevin James 134–135

Barry, Margaret Dolores 'Peggy' (Kevin's sister) 14, 198

Barry, Mary (Kevin's mother) 10, 12–14, 62, 100, 120, 147, 164; after Kevin's death 164–167; pension for 165–166; visiting Kevin's grave 112–113

Barry, Mary Christina 'Monty' (Kevin's sister) 14, 137, 165, 195–196

Barry, Michael (Kevin's grandfather) 12

Barry, Michael 'Mick' (Kevin's brother) 14, 209–210; arrested in Tombeagh 164, 167; convicted by court martial 167; and de Valera 169; joined as Volunteer in Carlow 19; Rathvilly company of the Volunteers 17; as republican candidate in Carlow/ Kilkenny constituency 168; Vice OC listing, 3rd Battalion, Carlow Brigade 168

Barry, Sheila 'Shel' (Kevin's sister) 14, 16–19, 31–2, 165, 167, 195, 205, 210; active in Cumann na mBan 195

Barry, Thomas (Kevin's father) 10–11, 15, 117

Bartsch, Barry Kevin 135

Battle of Hacketstown 13

Beatty, Adrian 2

Bell, Alan 73

Belvedere College SJ, Jesuit community in 26–27

The Belvederian: captioned 'Pillars of the House' 34

Bermingham, Andrew 98

Berry, J. 71

Berry, Patrick 97
Bevan, Charlie 98
Bevistein, Aby 91
Bhagat Singh 127
Birmingham pub bombings 5, 149
Black and Tans 52, 54; execution during
    War of Independence 159
Blake, Eliza 130
Blood Red Roses (album) 138
Bloody Sunday (Derry) 123
Bloody Sunday (Dublin) 3, 48–49, 70,
    100, 117, 122, 208
Blueshirt movement 130, 147
BMH. *See* Bureau of Military History
Boland, Kevin 158
Bonaparte, Napoleon 137
Bonfield, Bobby 18, 48
Bourne, Cardinal Francis 117–118
Bowman, Barry 87–88
Boy George (George O'Dowd) 138
boy soldiers 44
Bracken, Brendan 23, 114
Breen, Dan 143
Brennan, Joe 183–184
Britain: Germany war against 143;
    Littlejohn affair 84; naming
    Kevin Barry during 1920s and
    1930s 131
British: commemorative culture 2; killing
    of intelligence agents in Dublin
    83; killings of unarmed officers 5;
    at King's Inn 8–9, 64; Ludendorff
    offensive 20; misdeeds in Ireland
    118–119; Moplah revolt in India
    102; propaganda response to Kevin's
    case 94; response to increasing IRA
    activity 51–54; violent deaths of
    soldiers 8
Broderick, Peg 168
Brooke, Rupert 3–4
Browne SJ, Father Francis 95
Brugha, Cathal 175; arranging bombing
    offensive in Britain 155; as chairman
    of Dáil Eireann 28; gendered attitude

of 171; recollections of 183–184;
    sports activity 33; wounded in South
    Dublin Union fighting 27
Brugha, Máire MacSwiney 183, 203
Brugha, Rory 184, 186
Brunswick Street ambush 156
Bryan, Colonel Dan 49
Bryan, Thomas 138, 156
Bulfin, Nora 179
Bureau of Military History (BMH);
    witness statements for Kevin's case 7,
    10, 88, 108, 142; other statements of
    King's Inn events 61, 99
Burke, Jock 28
Burke, Seamus 154
Byrne, Bernard C. 99
Byrne, J.C. 107
Byrne, John 'Hoppy' 201
Byrne, Sir Joseph 51–52

Cagney, James 144
Cahill, Joe 161–162
Callanan SC, Frank 88
Campbell, James 79, 94
Caomhín de Barra 31
capital punishments 149, 150
Carlow: Barry family in 29; deaths
    from political conflict 46; Kevin
    Barry during childhood 11; Kevin's
    minor operations in 37–38, 55;
    Michael Barry in 207, 209; War of
    Independence in 45–47
Carney, Kathleen 36, 89; Kevin's letter
    to 110
Carney, Tess 157
Carroll, John Joe 9, 60, 97
Carson, Edward 20
Catholics, shootings 58
Chetwynd-Stapylton, B.H. 84
Christian Brothers 23
Christian 'Cross of Sacrifice' 147
Christina, Mary 14
Churchill, Winston 6; general election
    defeat of 114; Tudor and 54;

violence to crush Irish separatist disorder 52

Church Street affray 41, 47; capture and interrogation 65–69; operation 62–65; planning 60–62

civil war 4, 48; anti-Treaty side in 49, 126, 174, 195; Free State abuses during 154; UCD students killed during 146

Clancy, Peadar 96, 99–101

Clann na Poblachta 113

Clare, Dr Anthony 148

Clarke, Alan 84

Clarke, Joe 185

Clarke, Kathleen 146

Clery, Reggie 27

Clongowes Wood College SJ 27, 153–5

close-up killings 48

Clune, Conor 101

Cohen, Leonard 138

Colley, George 189

Collins, Michael 39, 175

Coman, William 104

Comerford, Máire 178, 185

Commonwealth War Graves Commission 44

Condon, John 43

Connaught Rangers: deaths 70, 74, 88, 102; Irish pension for 104

Connaught Rangers Mutineers Association 104

Conner, Rearden 145

conscription crisis/threat 19–21

Constance Markievicz 139, 170, 200

Conway, Tom 187

Cooney, Andy 49

Cork jail, hunger strike deaths in 80

Cosgrave, W.T. 27, 154, 168; death sentence to life imprisonment 86

Costello, M.J. 185

Counihan SJ, Tom 28, 32, 152, 185

Craig, James 80

Cromien, Jack 201

Cromien, Margaret 201

Cronin, Peggy. *See* Barry, Margaret Dolores

Cronin, Seán 10; *Kevin Barry* (booklet) 141–142

Cronin, Anthony (Tony) 190

A Crowded Year (O'Donovan) 139, 156, 164, 210

Crown forces: deaths 122; defending 113; IRA activity against 47; unofficial reprisals and dubious killings of 117

Crozier, F. 124

Cuilleánain, Cormac Ó 50

Cullen, Matt 56–57, 58

Cullens, Eddie 108

Cullen, Tom 62

Cumann na gCáilíni 188

Cumann na mBan 168, 200

Curran, Kevin Barry 133

Curtis, Liz 68

Cushnan, Samuel 108

Daiken, Leslie 139

Dáil Éireann (Irish assembly) 28, 38, 156; establishment of 21, 51; removal of six university seats 150

Dalton, Charlie 208

Daly, C. 162

Daly, James 88, 102–104, 209

Daly, Paddy 107

Darcy, Galwayman Louis 49

Darcy, Patrick 108

Das Bina 200

Dasgupta, Kamala 199–200

Davidson, Archbishop Randall 119

Davy, Eugene 34

Deasy, Pat 45

death penalty 150, 162, 164

Delaney, Timothy 46

De mortuis nil nisi bonum ('Of the dead, say nothing but good') 1

Dempsey, George 29

de Valera, Éamon 166, 183, 210;
in Kitby's funeral 185; Michael
Barry antagonism towards 169; in
Tombeagh during civil war 169
de Valera, Sineád 172
Devlin, Joe 93
Devonshire Regiment, handling of
prisoners 68
Devoy, John 113
Distinguished Service Order (DSO) 83
Doherty, M.A. 126
Dolan, Joe 55
Dominic, Fr 125
Donegan, Lonnie 137
Douglas, James 9
Dowling, James 13
Dowling, Laurence 13
Dowling, Mary. *See* Barry, Mary
Dowling, Patrick 11, 166
Dowling, Seán 48, 185
Doyle, Arthur Conan 187
Doyle SJ, Father Charlie 27
Doyle, John 46
Doyle, Louisa 161
Doyle, Patrick 156, 161
Doyle SJ, Father Willie 27
Drumcondra ambush 156
DSO. *See* Distinguished Service Order
Dublin: Dáil Éireann inauguration 21;
dairy business of Barry's in 15;
English Catholic officers killed on
Bloody Sunday 118; IRA's shooting
in 3, 8; killing of British intelligence
agents/soldiers in 83, 92; King's Inn
operation 8–9
Dublin Made Me memoir (Andrews)
185–186
Duffy, Gavan 188
Duffy, George Gavan 154
Duffy, Owen 130
Duggan, Eamon 76–77
Duke, H.E. 20
Dunne, Reginald 155
Dutt, Rajani Palme 204

Dwyer, James 18
Dwyer, Michael 13

Easter Rising 5, 98, 154
Economic War 120
Ede, Chuter 114
Egan, John 169
Electricity Supply Board (ESB) 177
Ellis (Kevin's hangman) 109
Ellison, Rev Charles S.S. 58
Emmet, Robert 147, 156
English, Richard 1, 6
Ennis, Tom 96
ESB. *See* Electricity Supply Board
exhumations, in Mountjoy prison
156–163

Fanning, Ronan 158
Ferdinand, Archduke Franz 90
Fianna Éireann 18; separatist movement
from young age 44
Fianna Fáil 150–151, 185; Ard Fheis
of 158; Kevin Barry student
cumann 148
The Fields of Athenry (song) 138
Fine Gael party 130
Finlay, Canon John 58–59
Finlay, Fergus 158
Finn, Martin 49
Finucane, Brendan 'Paddy' 22
Fisher, Sir Warren 52
Fitzgerald, Michael 70, 206; dead in
Cork jail 80
Fitzpatrick, John 100–101
Fitzpatrick, May 56
Flood, Frank 146; execution of Kevin's
friend 22, 138, 146; unfairly
forgotten 161
Foley, Edmund 156
Foley, Frank 156
'The Forgotten Ten' 156–163
Foster, Roy 4
Foxton, David 76
Frawley, John 137

Freeman's Journal: captioned 'Master Kevin Barry' 34
'Free State' Forces 172
Frehill, Olivia 153
fundraising: to support anti-Treaty in civil war 174; for 'war-stricken Volunteers' 130
Furlong, Thomas 139

Gaelic script 32
Gageby, Douglas 49
Gallagher, Frank 68
Galway IRA 130
Gandhi, M. 127
Gardai and Defence Forces 161
Garland, Seán 192
Gaughan, John 46
gender violence 168
general massacre, fear of 79–80
General Officer Commanding (GOC) 74
Gerard, Kevin 168
Germany, war against Britain 143
GHQ 39, 57, 70, 82; General Order no. 25 43
Gibney, Jim 162
Glasnevin cemetery 157–158, 160; funeral mass at 161
Glenalmond College 2
GOC. *See* General Officer Commanding
Goertz, Hermann 196
Gollancz, Victor 143
Goodbye, Twilight: Songs of the Struggle in Ireland (anthology) 139
good death, dying 107–109
Good Friday Agreement of 1998 157
Gorman, Michael 143, 178, 179, 189
Goulding, Cathal 185, 193
Grace (melodic dirge) 138
The Grave of a Rebel 139
Graves, Robert 4
Great War 2; volunteers at earlier age 43–44
Green, Johanna 56, 57

Greenwood, Hamar 53, 54, 66, 73, 95, 113, 120
Gregory, Augusta 130
Grimley, Liam 47

Hackett, Michael 46
Hall, Dianne 173
Halliday, Professor Fred 152
Halpenny, Annie: pension for 180–181
Halpenny, Hugh 180
Hanley, Hannah 201
Hannon, William 182
Hapsburg law 91
Hardy, J. 101
Harnett SC, Hugh 88
Harrison BL, Alice 88
Hattersley, Roy 150
Haughey, Charles 142, 189, 198
H-Block hunger strikers 163
Healy, Tim 75, 77–78
Heath, Edward 84, 150
Herron, Anthony 89–90
Higgins, Eva 137
Hinchcliffe, H. 128
Hitler, Adolf 143
Hobson, Bulmer 18
Hogan, Sarsfield 126
Holloway, J.A. 121
Holyfield, Evander 132
Hootenanny Singers 137
Hopkins, Gerard Manley 93
Horan, Timothy 78
horse, named after Kevin 131
Houston Riot 108
Hughes, Kevin Barry 135
Humphries, Thomas 64, 71, 87
hunger strikes 82, 127; force-feeding during 79; Volunteers 70, 79
Hutchinson, John 13
Hutchinson, Margaret 13
Hyde, Seán 49

India: Connaught Rangers deaths 70, 74, 88, 102; MacSwiney death impact in 126–127

intercommunal violence 92
IRA. *See* Irish Republican Army
IRB. *See* Irish Republican Brotherhood
Ireland: compulsory military service in
20; producing revolutionary leaders
152; punishment for political crimes
during 1916–21 89–91; recognition
of Kitby Barry 175
Ireland Today 140; strategic planner of
'S-Plan' 140
Irish Catholics 118
Irish Club in Wellington, New Zealand
137
Irish Jesuit 152–155
An Irishman's Diary (essay) 159
Irish nationalism 19
Irish pension 104
The Irish Press 100
Irish rebellions 102–104
Irish Republic 156–157
Irish Republican Army (IRA):
Birmingham pub bombings 149;
Bloody Sunday killings 3, 48–49, 70,
100, 117, 122; British response to
increasing activity of 51–54; King's
Inn operation 8–9, 55, 60–69; and
Protestant 58–59; shooting in Dublin
3; 'S-Plan' British bombing campaign
140, 149; 'The Forgotten Ten' in
Mountjoy prison 156–163; weapon
raiding 57–58
Irish Republican Brotherhood (IRB) 18,
39, 156
Irish Republican Prisoners Dependents
Fund (IRPDF) 172, 174
The Irish Times 169
Irish Volunteers 21; battalions 7–9;
Carlow 38; conscription crisis 21;
constrained firearms training 41;
pre-Rising 39; public defiance
towards guerrilla warfare 45; and
Sinn Féin 20; tactical training and
drilling for 39–40
Irish women, military role of 199–204

Irish Women's Franchise League 92
IRPDF. *See* Irish Republican Prisoners
Dependents Fund

Jesuit education 26–32
Jesuit, in memory of Kevin 152
Jones, Alfred 176
Jones, John 120
Josipovic, Anton 132
Joyce, James 26
Joyce, Colonel J.V. 108
Joyce, William 114, 155, 209
judicial leniency 89–90

Kaan, Pierre 202
Kavanagh, Patrick 179, 190–191, 209
Kavanagh, Seamus 60–62, 64
Kearns, Linda 171, 173, 175
Keenan, Seán 186
Kells, Henry 48
Kelly, J.J. 170
Kelly, Luke 185
Kelly, Patrick 200
Kennedy, Patrick 128
Kevin Barry. *See* Barry, Kevin
Kevin Barry (booklet) 141–142
Kevin Barry (song) 4, 136–137,
151–152, 162; in every pub in
Ireland 149
Kevin Barry and His Time (O'Donovan) 1
Kevin Barry Bar, Savannah 145
Kevin Barry basketball club (Hartford,
Connecticut) 134
Kevin Barry Chess Club 134
Kevin Barry club, Carlow 133–134
Kevin Barry Memorial Hall 104
Kevin Barry Memorial Medal 148
Kevin Barry Trophy 134
killing, of unarmed British officers 5
King, H.L. 128
King's Inn operation 8–9, 55; Kavanagh's
account of events 61; Kitby's account
as told by Kevin Barry 65; weapons
used in 87; witnesses in 65, 86–87

Kingston, J.A. 24
Kinsella, Kate 17, 32, 171
Kissane, Tom 47
Kitby, Barry. *See* Barry, Kathleen
Knocklong railway station incident 156

Lacey, John 90
Lancashire Fusiliers 66
Law, Bonar 95–96
Lawless, J.J. 63, 98
Lawrence and Wishart publishers 139
Left Book Club 143
Leinster Regiment 102
Leitrim Volunteers 61
Lemass, Seán 22, 208
Liddy, James 191
Liston, Joseph (Bishop) 118
'Littlejohn affair' 84
Lloyd George, David 6, 90, 118; assuring
    Kitby about Kevin's case 93–94;
    compulsory military service in
    Ireland 20–21; determined to crush
    Irish disorder 52
Logan, Katherine 195
Lord French (viceroy) 51, 53, 74, 94–95
Lucey, Christy 153
'Ludendorff offensive' 20
Luka Bloom. *See* Moore, Kevin Barry
Lynch, Declan 158
Lynch, Liam 91, 155, 171–172, 204;
    killed 173
Lynders, Thomasina 201

MacBride, Seán 113, 141, 156, 181, 185,
    194
MacCabe, John Francis 93
MacCurtain, Tomás 51, 79, 81
MacDonagh, Thomas 148
MacDonnell, Mike 58
MacEoin, Seán 112–113, 205
MacGiolla, Tómas 185, 192
MacMahon, Fr 109
MacNeill, Eoin 18
MacNeill, Hugo 48, 141

MacNeill, James 181
MacNeill, Josephine 181
Macpherson, Ian 53
Macready, General Sir Nevil (1st Bart)
    53–54, 72, 74, 94, 95, 115, 209
Macready, Sir Nevil (3rd Bart) 115
MacSwiney, Annie 80, 194, 202
MacSwiney, Mary 80, 81, 178, 194, 202,
    205, 210
MacSwiney, Muriel 80, 171, 172,
    201–203
MacSwiney, Terence 122, 123, 153, 203,
    206, 207, 209, 210; death impact
    in India 126–127; hunger strike 70,
    79–80, 83, 205–206
Magner, Canon 58–59
Maher, Bapty 36, 195
Maher, Patrick 156, 160
Maher, Triona 14, 16
Main, Kevin Barry 136
Malabar Rebellion 102
Mandela, Nelson 127
Mannix, D. (archbishop of Melbourne)
    118, 137, 176
Manual of Military Law of 1914 73
Marecco, Anne 170
'Maynooth Rule' 184
McAleer, Gerry 33–34, 36, 165, 182;
    Kevin's letter to 110
McCardle, Ellen 13
McCarville, Eileen 185
McCullough, Joe 185
McDonnell, Joseph 26
McDonnell, Mick 56, 208
McDonough, George 72
McGahon, Brendan 151
McGilligan, Anna 181
McGilligan, Patrick 154, 181
McGill, John 45
McGoohan, Charlie 61, 63
McGrath, Fearghal 35
McGrory, Patrick 129
McGuinness, Martin 161
McKay, W.G. 105

McKee, Dick 62, 66, 99–101
McKelvey, Joe 48
McKenna, Kevin Barry 133
McLoughlin, T.A. 177
McNeill boys 18
McNulty, Kevin Barry 135
McQuillan, Kevin Barry 135
Meath Chronicle 129
Mein Leben für Irland (My Life for
    Ireland, film) 144
Mellowes, Liam 48
Meyer, Jessica 2
military law 73
Military Service Pensions Act (1934) 56
Miller, Melville 'Sandy' 185
Mitchell, William 159
Mobil Oil 115
Moloney, Con 155, 187
Moloney, Helen 188, 192
Moloney, Jim 16, 155, 178–179, 185–187;
    hunger strike in Newbridge 194; in
    IRB 39; letter to Kitby 122
Moloney, Judy 188, 191–193
Moloney, Katherine 188, 190–191
Moloney, Mary 189, 192; secretarial job
    in OEEC 188
Moloney, Dr Michael 148
Moloney, Paddy 114, 180, 208; killed
    23, 115, 153
Moloney, Patrick (Paddy) Barry 18, 115
Moloney, P.J. 21, 32, 189, 205; released
    from hunger strike 79
Monaghan IRA 129–130
Monk's Bakery clash 60, 72
Monro (Governor) 112, 115–116
Montagu, E.S. 102
Monty. *See* Barry, Mary Christina
Moore, Kevin Barry 133
Moore, Norman 80
Moplah revolt 102
Moran, Patrick 156
Morris, Ellen 90
Morton, E. 84
Mountjoy prison 97; 'hang house' 150;

reinterment of 'The Forgotten Ten'
    156–163
Moyna, Kevin Barry 133
Mulcahy, Dick 47
Mulcahy, Richard 141
Muldoon, Brendan 50
The Mungret Annual 1921 153
Mungret College SJ 23, 114, 153
Murphy, James 128
Murphy, John A. 162
Murphy, Joseph 70, 206, 209; dead in
    Cork jail 80–81
Murphy, Patrick 162
Murphy, Seán 188
Murray, Don 144
Murray, Eamon 44
Myers, Kevin 162

Nathan, Seán 201
National Graves Association 157–158
National University of Ireland 151
National Volunteers 57
Nazi Germany 143
Nehru, Jawaharlal 127
Nixon, Christopher 15
Noble, Bridget 201
North Dublin Union 60, 65
Northern Ireland, peace process 157
North Wexford Brigade 90
Nowlan, Kevin B. 131

O'Brien, Patrick 144
O'Broin, Leon 193
O'Connell, 'Ginger': kidnapping of 155
O'Connell School 22–24
O'Connor, Kevin Barry 132–133
O'Connor, Rory 48, 155
O'Connor, T.P. 119
Ó Dochartaigh, Tomás 184
O'Donnell, Kevin Barry 135
O'Donoghue, David 142–143
O'Donoghue, Florence 173
O'Donovan, Donal (Kevin's nephew) 10,
    15, 47, 60, 105, 207; *A Crowded*

Year essay 139, 156, 164, 210;
Kevin Barry and His Time book 1,
    88–89, 142; relationship with Jim
    O'Donovan 197–198; about Royal
    Irish Fusiliers in West Germany 182
O'Donovan, Gerry 198
O'Donovan, Jim 10, 155, 184, 186,
    196–197; architect for S-Plan 195;
    and de Valera 197; links with Nazi
    Germany 143; *War of Independence*
    film, character resembling 145;
    writing about Kevin 140–144
O'Donovan, Síofra 139
O'Dowd, George (Boy George) 138
O'Duffy, Eoin 49
O'Dwyer, Dermot 50
official reprisals 54
O'Flanagan, Michael 173, 176
O'Halpin, Paidín 139, 177, 179, 180, 189
O'Hanlon, Michael 49
O'Higgins, Kevin 146, 188
Ó hUadhaigh, Seán 66, 75, 77, 83, 85,
    100
Oireachtas (Irish legislature), Kevin's
    memory in 150–152
O'Kelly, J.J. 173, 176
Old Belvedere clubhouse, Dublin 134
O'Malley, Donogh 151
O'Malley, Ernie 22–23, 49, 70, 108, 178,
    208
O'Neill, Charlie 165
O'Neill, Eily 111
O'Neill, Seán 62, 63–64
O'Neill, Terry 22
Onslow, Cranley 83–84, 105
Onslow, Lady Pamela 84
Opus Dei movement 152
O'Rahilly, Michael 13, 179
O'Rahilly, Michael Joseph: died in Easter
    Rising 19, 191, 209
O'Rahilly, Richard 'Mac' (Kevin's
    nephew) 21, 146, 191, 194, 197, 209
O'Rahilly, Ruth (Kevin's niece) 13, 76,
    163, 179

Orange songs 162
O'Reilly, Stephen 128
O'Riordan, Aodhán 163
O'Shea, Kerry 144
O'Sullivan, John Marcus 154
O'Sullivan, John 'Slag' 91
O'Sullivan, Michael 209
Otago Trotting Association 131
O'Toole, Fintan 158, 162
O'Toole, Ned 16
Our American Adventure (book) 187
Owen, Wilfred 4

Palmer, Colonel 87
Parnell, Charles Stewart 12, 17
Parnell, John Henry 12
Pearse, Margaret 172
Pearse, Patrick 207
Pearson, Alfred 45
Penrose, Willie 151
Phipps, C.F. 84
Pilkington, F.C. 84
'Pillars of the House' photograph 34,
    125, 146
Plant, George 108, 169
Plunkett, Horace 19
Plunkett, Jack 100
Plunkett, Joseph 27, 138, 154, 206
political killings 89
Pollington, George 55–56
Pound, Stephen 150
prejudice, Kevin Barry about 25
press denunciations, about funeral mass
    at Glasnevin cemetery 162–163
Princip, Gavrilo 90
Proctor, Edward 105
Protestants, arms raids on 58
punishments, for political crimes in
    Ireland (1916–21) 89–91

Quinlan, Geraldine 160

racism, awareness of 25
Radley College 2

Rawlinson, Peter 4–5, 150
Redmond, John 19–20, 56, 174
Redmond, William 56–57, 174
Reid, John 134
reprisal killings 79
Restoration of Order in Ireland Act
    (ROIA) 74, 82
RIC. *See* Royal Irish Constabulary
Rice family (Co. Down) 205
Richards, James 'McCormack' 149
The Rising of the Moon (play) 130
Robertson, William Sir 43
Robeson, Paul 138
Robinson, Mick 47
Robinson, Seamus 178
Rogers, Alf 153
ROIA. *See* Restoration of Order in
    Ireland Act
Rossa, O'Donovan 158
Rossiter, John 42
Royal Irish Constabulary (RIC) 20, 51
Ruddock, Alan 158
Rush, Kevin 178
Ryan, Bernard 156
Ryan, Frank 144
Ryan, Tom 32

Sassoon, Siegfried 4
Savannah pub 145
'Scariff martyrs' 153
Scoil Bhríde school 154, 188
Scott, C.P. 20
Seán South of Garryowen 138
Seeger, Pete 138
Seltzer, Walter 144
Sen, Ajuna 200
Shaheed Bhagat Singh Brigade 127
Shake Hands with the Devil
    (film) 144
Shaw, Celia 122
Sheehan, Michael Joseph 44
Sherlock, Lorcan 94
Sherwin, Seán 158
Shore, John Linton 112

Sinn Féin 21, 51–52, 185;
    commemorating Kevin and Stagg
    148–149; as mistaken idealists 108
Skinnider, Margaret 200
Smith, Geoffrey Compton (Major) 108
Smyllie, R.M. 189
Smyth, T.J. 52
Solano, E.J. 39
The Soldier (poem) 3–4
The Soldier's Song 111, 162
Soloheadbeg ambush (1919) 5
Somerville (Admiral) 169
songs/stories, about Kevin Barry
    136–139
'S-Plan' British bombing campaign 140,
    149, 195
Stack, Austin 169; and Kitby Barry 170
Stagg, Frank 149
Stamfordham (Lord) 119
Stapleton, Bill 63
Stephenson, Frances 118
Stewart, Rod 138
St Mary's College CSSp, Rathmines 24
Stuart, Francis 144
students, as part-time soldiers 47–51
Sturgis, Mark 81, 94, 95, 109
Sunday Independent 158
Sweetman, Roger 76, 163

Tegart, Charles 199–200
Telefís Éireann 193
Thatcher, Margaret 84
Thomas, J.H. 119
Tierney, Michael 147
The Times: 'Alleged Torture in
    Ireland' 66
The Times of India 102
Tobin, Liam 62
Tormey, James 44
Traynor, Elizabeth 161
Traynor, Oscar 99, 204
Traynor, Thomas 156, 161; exhumation
    refusal of 157
Treacy, Seán 205

Treanor, Arthur 129–130
Treanor, Mary 129–130
Treaty split 154
Trinity College Dublin 92, 151
Tudor, Sir Hugh 53–54
Twomey, Moss 173, 185
Tyson, Mike 132

UCD 35, 47–49, 93; memorial for Kevin 146–148
UCD Commerce Society 148
Ulster Unionists 20
Ulster Volunteer Force 57
Ulvaeus, Bjorn 137
University of Dublin (Trinity College) 151

Volunteers 58; Barry brothers as 19; conscription crisis 21; fundraising for war-stricken 130; Kevin Barry as 43; killings of unarmed British officers 5; at King's Inn operation 8; for training purposes in Dublin 47

Walsh (archbishop of Dublin) 94, 95
Ward, Con 49
Ward, John 89–90
War of Independence: beginning of 21; in Carlow 45–47; Jesuits and 152–153

War of Independence (film) 5, 144–145
Washington, Harold 64
Waters, Canon 109–110, 117, 126
Watts, S.J. 84
Welch, F.J. 128
West Cavan Brigade ASU 46
Whelan, Leo 197
Whelan, Thomas 156
Whitehead, Marshall 64, 71, 87, 124
Whitehead, Phillip 149–150
White, Mary 163
Who Do You Think You Are? (BBC) 138
Williams, Kevin Barry 135
Williams, Thomas (Volunteer) 108, 162
Williams, Thomas (ex-RIC constable) 51
Wills, P.G.B. 123
Wilson, Henry 52, 53–54, 55, 72, 117, 206; assassination of 155
Wimborne, V. 20
Winchester College 2
Winder, Frank 189
Winter, Jay 35, 147
Winter, Ormonde 49, 82, 109, 149
Women's International League 92
Woods, Seamus 180
Wylie, W.F. 86

Yates, H.P. 84
Yeats, W.B. 3